Doomed to Fail

DOOMED TO FAIL

The Built-in Defects of American Education

PAUL A. ZOCH

IVAN R. DEE

Chicago 2004

Library of Congress Cataloging-in-Publication Data:
Zoch, Paul A. (Paul Allen), 1962–
    Doomed to fail : the built-in defects of American education / Paul A. Zoch.
        p. cm
    Includes bibliographical references and index.
    ISBN 1-56663-567-5 (alk. paper)
        1. Education—United States—Philosophy—History. 2. Student-centered learning—United States. I. Title.

LB14.7.I63 2004
370'.1'0973—dc22   2003066529

ACKNOWLEDGMENTS

Chester Natunewicz, who read an early draft of this book, offered invaluable advice for improving it and encouraged me to address a topic that often seems ignored by scholars of education; I have benefited from his experience in the classroom as well as from his scholarly abilities. At the very beginning of this project, Diane Ravitch answered my initial questions and through the years has given me the benefit of her expertise; the book is much the better for her reading of it. Steven Lagerfeld of *The Wilson Quarterly* steered me to Ivan R. Dee; without that suggestion, I might still be looking. For years my sister Julie has given me advice on computers and word-processing, saving me many hours of frustration. Any errors in the scholarship or writing are mine and mine alone. I thank my wife, Denise, for tolerating so many Saturday evenings at home while I read and wrote.

P. A. Z.

Missouri City, Texas
January 2004

CONTENTS

PREFACE:
MAYBE IF YOU'D
SING AND DANCE,
WE'D LEARN THIS STUFF

As the national frustration mounts over American schools' continuing failure to meet even respectable academic standards, so do increasingly strident calls from all sides of the political and social spectrum for the strict accountability of teachers: "The students aren't learning, the teachers aren't doing their jobs," critics howl. "Fire them and find some teachers who will get the job done," they mutter, often with faintly disguised contempt. William F. Buckley, Jr., voices an opinion shared by many Americans: "The primary responsibility [for student delinquency] is that of the teachers," he writes—though he grudgingly admits that the family and society play some part. A few professors express an opinion long and commonly held by experts in the colleges of education: "Are schools *responsible* for the failures of at least 10–20 percent of students? A synthesis of the research on learning styles has begun to suggest that they *are*." If presidential candidates would read Diane Ravitch's *Left Back: A Century of Failed School Reforms*, claims Gerald Grant, a professor of education and sociology, "they might be convinced that the best slogan

for the genuine reform of American education would be, 'It's the teachers, stupid!'"[1]

There is no shortage of comment from intelligent and not so intelligent people arguing that better, smarter teachers will produce better,
smarter students, and that culpability for the low levels of academic
achievement among our students undoubtedly lies with the teachers.
The very title of a collection of articles by the Fordham Foundation
shows with simple clarity the source to which people look for the academic success of our students: *Better Teachers, Better Schools*. Among
the many excellent and sober judgments in the articles one finds occasional statements like this: "Teachers should be evaluated based on the
only measure that really matters: whether their pupils are learning."[2]
The assumption is that there is a simple, direct, cause-and-effect relationship between a teacher's actions and the students' learning. Students
and their actions, apparently, play only subordinate or inconsequential
roles in their learning; only the actions of the all-powerful teacher matter. If the teacher does his job competently, the students learn; if the students do not learn, the teacher is at fault.

This emphasis on achieving educational excellence through the
teacher's actions (the student's role and responsibility in his learning
being largely ignored) is similar to the findings in another famous report,
What Matters Most: Teaching for America's Future: "What teachers
know and can do is the most important influence on what students
learn," Linda Darling-Hammond and her associates declare. "Policymakers are just beginning to grasp what parents have always known: that
teaching is the most important element of successful learning." (Ironically, in a companion volume the authors cite a study which found that
teacher qualifications account for 43 percent of the influence on students' academic achievement while the home and family account for 49
percent and class size for 8 percent. Such a finding is hardly new:
decades ago, in what is now called the Coleman Report, the sociologist
James S. Coleman and his research team found that the student's family
and social group are the greatest influence on a student's achievement.)
The authors of *The Essential Profession*, a report by Recruiting New
Teachers, Inc., cite a poll which found that "an overwhelming majority

of the public considers improving the quality of teaching as the most important way to improve public education," and later the report confirms that teachers "are the heart of school reform."

The superintendent of a school district for which I once taught twice announced that "the strength of a district lies in the quality of its employees," with the parents and the students themselves appearing to have less influence in determining a school's quality. At one faculty meeting, attempting to inspire the teachers, a principal at my school read to her captive audience a poem she had written about teaching: we, the teachers, she said, determine whether our students succeed or fail; students, again, seem to be powerless over their learning and behavior. It seems so self-evident, so commonsensical, so unquestionably logical: to improve our students' academic performance at school, we must improve the quality of teaching. Better teachers, better trained in the best and latest findings of educational science, will produce better, smarter students.[3]

This grossly simplistic and mechanistic view of learning—that teachers determine whether or not students learn—is, quite simply, wrong. A good point for starting the discussion that will be pursued in this book is a brief remark in the Fordham Foundation's *Better Teachers, Better Schools*. There the author, an educational psychologist and professor of education, refers to learning as "the product of teaching."[4] Learning, it must be said, is a change in behavior, an individual's adaptation to conditions in the environment. It results from an individual's *thinking* and exercising his nervous system toward the attainment of a goal; all teaching can do is make the learning quicker and more efficient. In fact, for learning in the broadest, most general sense, only two things are absolutely necessary: the learner, and the thing to be learned. Teachers are helpful but by no means absolutely necessary. People learn far more nonacademic knowledge in life without a teacher's help than they ever learn with such help. This is because surviving, adapting to a constantly changing world, fulfilling desires, and enhancing one's existence prompt individuals to try to understand their surroundings and the events of their lives. What people learn in this informal and sometimes haphazard way may not always be as challenging, formal, or intricate as calculus or ancient Greek, yet no one teaches us most of what we learn in life, because we create knowledge through our own experience. Consequently the driving force behind learning is not the teacher but the individual student, or learner, and the will to understand. No one plants understanding in our heads; we as individuals create our own private knowledge and understanding from the raw material of our experience and our interactions with, and adaptations to, our environment.

Examples abound of this process. A former student of mine was so interested in the space shuttle that he read many books about it and dazzled me and others with the range of technical knowledge he had acquired—how many pounds of thrust each rocket produces, how many miles of wiring make up the electrical system, what kinds of computers are on board, and so on. Who taught him that information? No one gave him lessons; he read books and aviation magazines. Another person I know, who did not graduate from high school, has acquired a great fund of knowledge about World War II—its battles, their locations and circumstances, the generals and the strategies they employed, and the armaments used by the combatants. Only the books he read taught him that. Students teach themselves the computer languages HTML and Java, using only books as a reference. Despite the absence of a teacher offering carefully planned lessons tailored to their individual needs and psychological profiles, teenagers learn the detailed and technical specifications of fast cars and motorcycles, the detailed history of the gang they belong to, the sometimes intimate life stories of their favorite pop star, or statistics about sports heroes. People teach themselves to play a musical instrument—the rock/blues legend Eric Clapton is said to have locked himself in a room for a year with only his guitar, and during that time he developed his own style.[5] How many twelve-year-old boys have learned to throw a curve ball just from reading a one-page entry in a book with a small diagram showing how to turn the wrist? The summer after eighth grade I taught myself to type, using only a typing book I had found; and when I got my first computer, I never took a lesson on WordPerfect 5.1 for MS-DOS, yet, with little more than a book to help me, I became proficient at it. Malcolm X taught himself to read while in jail.

The fact is that people have minds, and in order to survive and meet their needs in life, they learn to use their minds and to solve problems, in relative independence of others. The brain and nervous system that students use to solve problems in life are the same ones they use, or are supposed to use, in school. *Teachers are not the primary determinant in our learning and intellectual lives.* The individual has much more power in determining the direction his thoughts will take than the teacher does, and that fact holds true for the students in our classrooms and their learning of academic subjects.

I do not make this argument to defend incompetent or lazy teachers, nor do I aim to castigate students for low achievement. Rather, in this book I try to show how our educational thinking has gotten sidetracked. Philosophical, psychological, and social influences as varied as behaviorism, John Dewey's idealism, the Romantic conception of the child, and modern cognitive theory have converged into the widespread idea that the teacher and his teaching methods create (or fail to create) success for the students. The greater, more important, and more difficult role that the student plays in his creation of knowledge is largely overlooked.

Learning is a demanding task. It is a mental and physical change, an adjustment of the learner's mind, brain, and body to the demands of the environment. In order to learn, a person must seek answers and not infrequently struggle to understand the unknown and unfamiliar. A person must summon forth all his knowledge and experience to understand and comprehend new information; he must relate the new information to what he already knows and reconcile new knowledge with old knowledge; and he must make the knowledge a part of his personality and being, weaving the new knowledge into the fabric of his mental existence. Each individual is, after all, the sum of his experiences and knowledge. Each person is therefore unique, the result of stimuli and happenings that no one else has experienced.

The teacher does not know each student's peculiar and unique construct of reality and myriad private experiences; the teacher cannot know, cannot see what the student sees — just as a person cannot know what it is like to be someone else. Only I know what it is like to be me; only I know how I view reality, and every individual is similarly unique and, to some extent, alienated from the lives and experiences of other individuals. The psychologist and philosopher William James called the gulf that separates our private existences "perhaps the widest breach in Nature." Since the student alone knows how he understands reality, he has the most control over his mind, his thoughts, and his learning; he alone must struggle and direct his thoughts to make, from nonsense, what is sense to him; he alone must construct his own knowledge in place of ignorance, and adapt knowledge he already has to accord with new information that leads to new understanding. Consequently the focus in education should not be on teachers and their teaching techniques but on *students* and their mental processing of the information presented by the teacher. The student's job, learning, is far more difficult and important than the teacher's, and is the reason for the existence of schools. Yet many people in the United States, including parents, education scholars, social critics, and many professionals in the colleges of education and administrative offices of the schools, expect students to become educated primarily or even entirely through the teachers' efforts.

Of course teachers are important, but they do not determine what we learn and whether we learn. The role of the teacher is to help students by providing them with crucial information which they might otherwise find only with the greatest difficulty; the teacher's duty is to reduce the waste of trial-and-error learning. Then it becomes the student's duty and responsibility to work the new information or habits into his understanding of reality, to change his behavior and ways of thinking, even though doing so may be difficult—such is the learning process. After a certain point, an individual's own actions and thoughts determine his success or failure. For example, if a decent teacher had taught me word-processing and basic computer maintenance, I would have learned how crucial it is to defrag the hard-drive on occasion, and to make timed backups; when the hard-drive crashed, because it was too fragmented, I lost three hours of work. Thereafter it became my responsibility to remember to defrag the hard-drive occasionally and to type the commands correctly. The teenagers learning to play rock guitar without formal instruction could, with a competent teacher, learn music theory and superior technique that would enable them to play smarter and better; then it would be up to them to practice the scales and fingerings shown by the teacher, even though doing so is sometimes tedious. Ultimately all education is self-education. One learns by doing and by adjusting his actions and thoughts to the exigencies of life; the secret of success in our schools is the same regardless of the endeavor—music, athletics, drama, carpentry, cooking, and so on—the will to succeed as manifest in practice, practice, and, when one fails, more practice.

The claims that "Teachers create learning in students" and "Teachers determine whether students succeed or fail" seem to be anxious hopes rather than statements of fact. When one looks at the actual lives and conduct of students, both at school and at home, he sees that most students do not show the will and attitudes conducive to meeting high standards. Symptomatic of their indolence is the fact that every day in classrooms across the United States a surprisingly large number of students neglect to do something as basic as bring their book, paper, and pen to class, and then shrug their shoulders when given the punishment of detention and asked how they expect to get anything done that day without their materials. The teacher in the typical class will regard it as an outstanding day if more than half the students have done their homework and if just a few have done it with diligence and accuracy. Although the teacher uses an interesting fact or object pertaining to the day's topic to arouse a mild interest in some students at the beginning of the lesson, nothing will secure the curiosity of them all and for very long, as their minds, interests, and abilities are far too varied for a one-size-fits-all attempt to "reach" them all. Yet attempts to individualize lessons will also fail, because the teacher simply has not the time or resources to make a separate lesson for each student. When the new information loses its immediate appeal or demands complex thought, many students allow their minds to wander, and instead they talk, write letters to friends, or stare out the window. Not until the teacher is forced to use the last-resort warning—"This will be on the test"—do many students perk up and pay attention again. Even then, quite a few are not impressed by the admonition, as they know that when too many students fail a class, the teacher's competence, methods, and standards will be called into question—if the teacher were good, students wouldn't fail or be bored.

Statistics bear out this dismal portrait of student conduct. (The top 15 to 20 percent of students succeed admirably.) "Student apathy" was cited by 38 percent of high school teachers in one poll as a major problem, and lack of parental involvement by 35 percent. Student apathy shows itself in other ways: absenteeism, with 26 percent of seniors nationally missing seven or more days in just the first half of the school year, and 35 percent missing three to six days; almost one in four seniors admitted to cutting classes "at least sometimes." American students do not study—that is, "practice"—as much as their foreign counterparts: the American average is less than four hours per week while the international average is four hours per *day*. In one study, 39 percent of seventeen-year-olds and 29 percent of thirteen-year-olds did no homework (some had not received assignments, one probable reason being that many teachers have given up assigning homework); 26 percent of seventeen-year-olds and 37 percent of thirteen-year-olds did less than one hour per day.[6]

Various other activities prevent their studying: 13 percent of eighth graders watch more than six hours of television a day, while 46 percent of thirteen-year-olds and 34 percent of seventeen-year-olds watch it more than three hours a day, leaving very little time for serious study. Student employment shows the lack of commitment to schoolwork: 23 percent of seniors work more than twenty hours a week, and 16 percent work 16 to 20 hours a week. Only 32 percent did not work at all during the school year. Student involvement in extracurricular activities is mostly positive, but the activities that most students belong to—athletics, band, and drama—consume huge amounts of their after-school time and far too often place academics in a subordinate position. As another survey indicates, knowing a lot about intellectual matters ranked last among students in conveying high status on campus; what matters most for popularity is being a good athlete.[7]

The belief that the teacher determines whether or not the student succeeds handicaps the efficacy of our schools and thus harms both teachers and students. It misleads students into thinking that the true source and fount of their success, both in academics and in more mundane affairs, lies outside their own actions and character: someone else must "achieve excellence" for them, as the web page of the Texas Education Agency has proudly proclaimed.[8] Since they are thought to have little responsibility or only a subordinate role in their becoming educated, many, if not most, students in our public schools never engage themselves in the intellectual activity and effort necessary for learning, and thus expend very little effort at school. Freed from the necessity of working hard to meet high standards, and having few negative consequences for failure, they need not sacrifice their energy and free time for success in academics. One can't blame students for being so cavalier about studying and achievement. Our society overwhelmingly believes it is the teachers' responsibility to "achieve excellence" for them. Students have the right to enjoy a carefree, stress-free youth.

Predictably enough, they learn very little and neither succeed nor meet their potential. They never learn the truth of the means of accomplishment and become passive spectators during their education, which forms the basis of their adult lives. Many never learn the habit of doing what is necessary to succeed, much less the concept of overcoming their shortcomings or achieving excellence. Our debilitating and destructive thinking about education does not compel students to strive so that they may discover the full range of their talents and abilities; so their lives become limited by their learned helplessness and impotence and the exceedingly narrow parameters of things they understand readily and easily. Tragically, some even become convinced they are stupid—"I'm no good at this," they said, whenever the subject doesn't come easily and naturally, and shut themselves off from many ways of understanding the world and enriching their lives.

Not only do most students in our public schools fail to learn academics in any depth, they also learn the invaluable lesson that *someone else is responsible for their success or failure in life.* Thus it happens in the public schools of the United States that *the teachers want the students to succeed more than the students do,* and for the most part—there are, of course, many exceptions—*the teachers work harder for the students' success than the students themselves do.* Since American students, generally, are not expected to work as hard as they can in order to succeed, many sit back in their desks at school, arms crossed, waiting for the teacher to do what *will make them smart.* The words of one former student, who was failing my class, reveal pointedly where he placed the focus of his success: "Maybe if you'd sing and dance," he said to me, "we'd learn this stuff."

In the chapters that follow I aim to show why it is that our education system, despite its incessant devotion to being "child-centered," has evolved into a system in which the students seem nearly irrelevant in the process of learning. For more than a hundred years, the development of American thinking about learning, teaching, and the nature of young people has created a teacher that is theoretically all-powerful, able to instill knowledge or create the circumstances that instill knowledge in the passive, helpless, student. The notion that students may be failing to learn simply because they are not working hard enough is drowned out by an unceasing barrage of accusations of teachers' incompetence and the never-ending hope that teachers, if only they would care enough and really teach, would make students learn and love learning.

This philosophy does not benefit students. Its benefits accrue only to the bloated educational bureaucracy and the colleges of education—the "interlocking directorate" of educational administrators and the colleges of education, as Arthur Bestor called it in *Educational Wastelands*—for when students fail to learn, educationists are entrusted with finding the causes and creating the solutions. When learning is so basic, mostly a matter between a student and the subject matter, there is little need for educationists. However noble the educationists' intentions may be— they want students to learn easily, joyfully, and naturally—the fact is that colleges of education profit from the failure of students to learn, and the educationists continue to promote an educational philosophy that ensures continuing failure.

DOOMED TO FAIL

1

WILLIAM JAMES AND PRE-PROGRESSIVE EDUCATIONAL THINKING

The public education system in the United States experienced its great period of formation and expansion in the late nineteenth and early twentieth centuries, evolving into what we today think of as public primary and secondary education. Many of society's fundamental beliefs about the worth of knowledge and academic studies, the acquisition of knowledge, the nature of young people, and the function of schools in American society were formed during that time and are still with us today as largely unquestioned assumptions. Our nation's thinking about education is governed and constrained by these basic assumptions, because it has never been any other way in the modern United States.

Of course we should not impose high academic standards on all students, for few of them have the ability or inclination for serious academic study, and youth is supposed to be a time of joy and fun. Intellectual endeavors and bookishness are unimportant unless they lead to profit. *Of course* learning should be fun, and students should learn through games and social activities with plentiful opportunities for self-expression and creativity. *Of course* the teacher should create lessons that meet students' individual needs and capitalize on students' interests and abilities. *Of course* the teacher is the most important figure in a student's learning and bears the blame when students fail to learn.

All these various assumptions about education in the United States go largely unquestioned in the larger society. For a different perspective, one can look at foreign school systems (which I do in Chapter Seven) and at some private schools in the United States. Or one can look at the thought of William James, for he represents an enlightened and well-rounded perspective on teaching, learning, and the growing mind that prevailed before the crystallization of our educational thinking along Progressive lines.

William James (1842–1910) is widely regarded as the father of American psychology, the first American representative of the "new psychology" that arose in the aftermath of Darwin. (The new psychology sought to distance itself from philosophy and the unscientific faculty psychology—which held that the mind is divided into separate powers—and strove instead to understand mentality on the basis of physiology and the organism's struggle to survive.) Over the course of his career at Harvard University, James taught anatomy and physiology, philosophy, and psychology before late in life moving completely to philosophy. At Harvard in 1878 he established the first psychological laboratory in the United States. That same year he was commissioned by the publisher Henry Holt to write a textbook on psychology; twelve years later his two-volume *Principles of Psychology* was published and immediately established his reputation as the preeminent American psychologist of his day. He applied and popularized a psychology which, to its German pioneers Hermann Helmholtz and Wilhelm Wundt, had been strictly a theoretical endeavor, confined to the laboratory. "Probably the best-known book in all psychology," comments Ian M. L. Hunter, "it is a treasure-house of ideas and finely turned phrases which psychologists continue to plunder with profit." James later published an abridged version of his magnum opus (*Psychology: The Briefer Course*, called "Jimmy" in contrast to the massive *Principles*), which "became and remained for some years the most widely used English text in the subject." He also published a splendid and charming book on psychology for teachers, *Talks to Teachers*, compiled from lectures he had begun in 1894 and derived largely from the *Principles*. James was immensely popular as a professor and lecturer, and his books were translated into German, Russian, French, and even Japanese. His psychology dominated American education until 1910, the year he died; the historian Merle Curti estimated that nine of ten teachers who learned psychology between 1890 and 1910 learned it from James's books, and the educationist Arthur I. Gates credits James for inspiring people to use science to solve the problems of education.[1]

It was a long and meandering road that led James to psychology. Because of his family's wealth and his father's restless search for his own fame as an intellectual, William and his siblings traveled extensively and lived much of their youth in Europe and in various homes in the United States. His father, Henry, who never achieved the stature he craved as a writer in theology, encouraged his children in their intellectual pursuits and eclectic philosophies. William and his siblings became sometimes brilliant, often neurotic adults: his brother Henry became "the novelist who wrote like a psychologist," James himself being "the psychologist that wrote like a novelist"; their sister, Alice, like her father and brother William, had a nervous breakdown and was briefly institutionalized; another brother, Bob, died of alcoholism.

Like the perpetual students who nowadays are such a fixture at many public universities in the United States, William James studied many different subjects—for a while art, then chemistry, then biology under Louis Agassiz (the rigors of field work in Brazil deterred the tender, if not hypochondriacal, James), then medicine; he earned his M.D. yet chose not to practice. He was a polymath, fluent in French and German and competent in Italian; one finds him quoting French and German authors indifferently—Pierre Janet and Charles Renouvier, Helmholtz and Wundt. James took his first job at age thirty, being hired by Charles W. Eliot, then president of Harvard (and James's former chemistry instructor), to teach one class of anatomy. Over the next decade he secured his position at Harvard and published papers on psychology and philosophy, which established his intellectual reputation and led eventually to his contract with Henry Holt.

Not long after completing his great work on psychology, he retired from his position as chairman of Harvard's psychology department, having grown weary of the increasingly narrow scope of scientific psychology. He spent the rest of his life in the Department of Philosophy, writing on philosophical and religious issues. One of these was the peculiarly American philosophy of pragmatism, which he and John Dewey spearheaded. Today James's most widely read book is probably *The Varieties of Religious Experience*.

One episode about the youthful James explains his outlook on his own mind and mental life. While studying in Europe in 1870, he went through an existential crisis, during which he seriously contemplated suicide. What saved him was reading an essay by Renouvier on free will. In contrast to the determinists of his age, who believed that "those parts of the universe already laid down absolutely appoint and decree what the other parts shall be," James became convinced that man had some free will, and his first step to show his free will was to believe that he had it. "My first act of free will shall be to believe in free will," he wrote in his diary.[2] He then willed himself to be not unhappy: in other words, he chose to feel happy, or at least not unhappy.

His psychology is thus marked by his wide-ranging reading and catholic interests, his broad culture, his sympathy with humanity, and his knowledge of the mind in general and his own mind in particular. James was an intellectual of the highest order, learned in many different fields, interested in not only how the mind operates but also in helping people enrich their lives and experience. He believed that philosophy and psychology should help people live better lives, and if it did not do that, there was no purpose for it. James, according to Gordon Allport,[3] wrote in an era of intellectualism; he also wrote in an age when the individual was viewed as paramount, and the focus of his psychology is firmly on the individual and his perception of reality. His psychology largely ignores social psychology and social issues. He has been called Victorian in his morals and his emphasis on character and personal development, and is viewed as somewhat old-fashioned, both today and during the Progressive Era, which was seduced by a more scientific psychology.

THE USE OF INTELLIGENCE: FUNCTIONALISM

Early in his masterpiece on psychology, James offers an example of intelligence, or mental activity. A frog, trapped underwater in an inverted glass, will try various ways to escape and get to air. When one way does not work, it tries another; if that way does not work, it tries still another; if that way fails too, it tries another, until it either succeeds and gets to air, or dies. The frog, in other words, changes its behavior to meet its goal. When the environment poses an obstacle, the organism strives to overcome it and meet its demands—a very Darwinian outlook. James along with others in the new psychology showed, or tried to show, the functional aspect of emotions, intelligence, and consciousness, and how they help man survive. Thus James posits his theory of intelligence: *"The pursuance of future ends and the choice of means for their attainment are thus the mark and criterion of the presence of mentality* in a phenomenon." In other words, intelligence is achieving an end, a fixed and determinate end, by changing one's behavior. Later he defines reason as the ability to handle novel data, which is simply adapting one's thinking to changing conditions (information taken in through the senses) in the environment.[4]

The use of intelligence and the course of behavior are, of course, fluid and dynamic, for the organism must constantly change and adapt its behavior to meet goals and to respond to the demands of an ever-changing environment. The nervous system, which culminates in the brain, makes such rapid adaptation and learning possible by reacting to stimuli received through the senses. "The whole neural mechanism, it will be remembered, is, physiologically considered, but a machine for converting stimuli into reactions," he writes. By learning through experience, man—or any organism, for that matter—organizes his brain and nervous system in relation to his environment in order to increase his chances of survival. Although it had never been taught how to escape when trapped under a glass under water, the frog, by trial and error, learned how to escape (it swam lower until it came to the lip of the glass). And in finding the solution to the problem, it internalized the change in its tissues, chemical composition, and neural network and brain. These physiological changes in the neural network open the way for future performances of the action, making them easier and smoother, even automatic and habitual. Hence, as James writes, "The great thing, then, in all education, is to *make our nervous system our ally instead of our enemy*. It is to fund and capitalize our acquisitions, and live at ease upon the interest of the fund. *For this we must make automatic and habitual, as early as possible, as many useful actions as we can*, and guard against the growing into ways that are likely to be disadvantageous to us, as we should guard against the plague."[5]

Like the frog, the learner in Jamesian psychology is naturally active, making his way through life, striving to change himself and his behavior to meet the demands of the changing environment so he can survive in it. For man, changing and adapting demand that he gain an understanding of himself and the environmental forces that influence his life. The struggle to understand reality commences at birth; the baby has no understanding at all and must start the construction of his personality and understanding of reality from nothing. "To the infant, sounds, sights, touches, and pains, form probably one unanalyzed bloom of confusion," writes James, for everything is new to the infant and he has no experience to use as a reference point in understanding his world. His coming to understand his environment and himself is instinctual and a terribly unique affair since a person, as an individual, learns and understands in reference to what he already knows from his past experiences. That unique conglomeration of experiences and the understanding a person creates from them make him who he is as an individual and separate his experiences from those of other people. We are the results of our past: "Each present brain-state is a record," writes James, "in which the eye of Omniscience might read all the foregone history of its owner." A person cannot know what it is like to be someone else; he can know things only from his own individual perspective and experiences. The responsibility for success or failure to learn therefore lies primarily with the individual, because no one else has access to the individual's thoughts, and no one can adapt another's thoughts and behavior to changes in the environment.[6]

JAMES'S LEARNING THEORY

According to James, a person learns—that is, changes his behavior in accordance with the demands of the environment—by discriminating among the many stimuli that the senses receive from the environment, and by relating them to what he knows from past experiences. Consequently the most important components of our ability to learn are our senses, which bring stimuli from the environment into the brain; our ability to pay attention, that is, to concentrate on a problem, break it up into its elements, and reorganize them in different ways; and memory, for it is only in terms of what we already know that we can learn new things and create new knowledge.

Learning, says James, is a very active affair. "By the ancients, and by unreflecting people perhaps today," he writes, "knowledge is explained as the *passage* of something from without into the mind—the latter, so far, at least, as its sensible affections go, being passive and receptive." But a person actively constructs an understanding of his world by attending to stimuli in the environment and relating the stimuli to what he remembers from his past; "The mind, in short, works on the data it receives [through the senses] very much as a sculptor works on his block of stone."[7]

To "work on the data," one must pay attention. James defines attention as "the taking possession by the mind, in clear and vivid form, of one out of what seem several simultaneously possible objects or trains of thought. Focalization, concentration, of consciousness are of its essence." While thinking, the individual is highly active, and determines what he will and will not pay attention to. Attention is a wave or a pulse—sometimes it is on, then it is off, and when it turns off, we must switch it back on to the problem at hand. *"There is no such thing as voluntary attention sustained for more than a few seconds at a time,"* he writes. "What is called sustained voluntary attention is a repetition of successive efforts which bring back the topic to the mind." As a consequence of the individual's efforts, James concludes, *the mind chooses what it will and will not pay attention to,* consciousness being, as James writes, "at all times primarily *a selecting agency*." In other words, one thinks what he directs his mind to think, and he does not think what he chooses to ignore.[8]

This sustained, voluntary attention to a given topic is quite important because, as James writes, the longer and harder one thinks about a problem—that is, attends to it—the more likely he is to solve it. When describing the process of association in someone doing scientific research, James explains, "The inquirer starts with a fact of which he seeks the reason, or with an hypothesis of which he seeks the proof. In either case he keeps turning the matter incessantly in his mind until, by the arousal of associate upon associate, some habitual, some similar, one arises which he recognizes to suit his need." Particularly important is the view that the learner—whether a mature scientist or a student in school—creates his success or failure by his own actions and the management of his thoughts; he is the source and fount of his own success. The learner succeeds by attending, recalling, and "turning the matter incessantly in his mind" to create a solution and establish neural pathways, just as the frog did when escaping from under the glass. Today we call that "turning the matter incessantly in his mind" the learning process.[9]

In Jamesian psychology, the student is thus in charge of controlling, or learning to control, his mind and thoughts toward some end. That is for James the essence of education: to help students develop their minds in order that they may solve whatever problems life presents. One succeeds in learning therefore by attending to the details of a problem at hand and adapting to it the knowledge constructed from past experiences and new available information. "But, whether the attention come by grace of genius or by dint of will, the longer one does attend to a topic the more mastery of it one has. And the faculty of voluntarily bringing back a wandering attention, over and over again, is the very root of judgment, character, and will. No one is *compos sui* [in control of himself] if he have it not."[10] "Attending to" a topic means studying it—paying attention to it, breaking it down and putting it back together again, seeking to understand it and its relation to the world and one's past experiences, working it and the new knowledge into one's schema of reality. Doing so requires effort; the most important determinant of success is the will to understand, for it drives one to keep "turning the matter incessantly in his mind" and summoning up past knowledge to use in solving the problem. One notes automatically the difference between the Jamesian way of thinking and that of modern education, in which the *teacher*, not the student who manages his thoughts, bears the primary responsibility for the student's learning.

A key part of one's perception of the world—if not the very bedrock of an individual's perceptions and understanding of reality—is memory, for one always and inevitably seeks to understand what happens by relating it to what he already knows. The process of remembering and relating has a physiological basis in the neural pathways of our brain and nervous system. Memory, according to James, is little more than a habit, for when one repeats an action or thought, the neural pathways responsible for that action or thought are deepened. Thus they are more likely to discharge the thought or act under similar situations in the future. Memory aids man in his survival; without it, he would never learn, for everything would always be frighteningly new; he would never have a background of knowledge to use in interpreting new information. These habits make people "conscious automata," yet free their minds so they may solve more complicated problems. "The more of the details of our daily life we can hand over to the effortless custody of automatism, the more our higher powers of mind will be set free for their own proper work," James writes. His views are sound educational thinking; E. D. Hirsch, Jr., studied findings from modern psychology and arrived at the same conclusion: "Basic processes need to be made unconscious and automatic as early as possible in order to free the mind for critical thinking and problem solving."[11]

Since the young solve problems by using their knowledge and past experiences, James believed that students must simply memorize some information in order that they may learn more and solve more complicated problems later. "The excesses of old-fashioned verbal memorizing . . . have perhaps led those who philosophize about teaching to an unduly strong reaction; and learning things by heart is now probably somewhat too much despised," he comments to his audience of teachers, decades before the worst anti-intellectual and sentimental excesses of Progressive education. Memory is a habit, and students must drill some basic facts and information into their heads. James here attests to the importance of prior knowledge, for the more one has learned, the more capable he is of learning and solving problems in the future. For example, he notes, recitation and reproduction are very effective in making a mental impression, and that impression is a habit used for association. He also believed that verbal memorization was necessary: since "abstract conceptions are far and away the most economical instruments of thought, and abstract conceptions are fixed and incarnated in words," "constant exercise in verbal memorizing must still be an indispensable feature in all sound education."[12]

The emphasis on the development of the intellect and of a person's human potential through his intellect via a basic liberal arts curriculum was common in American education during James's day. In 1893 the National Education Association completed and published the report of the Committee of Ten, which advocated a rigorous academic curriculum for all students, regardless of their career aspirations or socio-economic class—doctor, lawyer, mechanic, policeman, farmer—*all* students needed an education rich in English language and literature, history (ancient and modern), a foreign language (Latin and Greek being well represented), the sciences, and mathematics. W. T. Harris, U.S. commissioner of education at the time and a member of the Committee of Ten, saw the five core academic subjects—mathematics, English, foreign languages, history, and the sciences—as the "windows" by which "the pupil gets a better insight" into the five "cardinal provinces" of nature and man. By mastering the fundamentals of these subjects, wrote Harris, the student increased his individuality and power, for he "can now by his own effort master for himself the wisdom of the race." The emphasis was on substantial knowledge, and on the student's doing what was necessary for success, the goal being "the self-active individual, the reasoning person who can exercise true freedom in the terms of his own civilization."[13]

Yet James knew well that intelligence is not determined solely by a large store of factual knowledge. It is the use of factual knowledge, or how that knowledge is adapted to conditions, that marks intelligent behavior. James had great sympathy for what educators today call learning styles and individual differences. He knew that each individual is unique, and learns and understands in different ways. So he advised his audience of teachers to be sympathetic to the student "that cuts a poor figure in examinations" while also admitting that it would be impossible for the teacher to create different lessons for students' different needs. "What tells in life is the whole mind working together, and the deficiencies of any one faculty can be compensated by the efforts of the rest," he wrote. Still, the fount of success was to be found in the individual student's actions: "If any one of them do have the casting vote," he told his audience of teachers in a discussion of mental traits, "it is more likely to be the strength of [the individual's] desire and passion, the strength of the interest he takes in what is proposed."[14]

THE WILL: "YES, I WILL EVEN HAVE IT SO!"

James's Victorian morality is best seen in his pages on will. Despite his awareness of the limitations imposed on the individual by his genetics and his experiences (indeed, he advised the teachers in his audience to look upon their students as being "partly fated and partly free"[15]), James believed that the individual has a measure of free will, and his pages on the subject constitute an inspiring paean to the human spirit and human potential.

> Of course we measure ourselves by many standards. Our strength and our intelligence, our wealth and even our good luck, are things which warm our heart and make us feel ourselves a match for life. But deeper than all such things, and able to suffice unto itself without them, is the sense of the amount of effort which we can put forth. Those are, after all, but effects, products, and reflections of the outer world within. But the effort seems to belong to an altogether different realm, as if it were the substantive thing which we *are*, and those were but externals which we *carry*. If the "searching of our heart and reins" be the purpose of this human drama, then what is sought seems to be what effort we can

make. He who can make none is but a shadow; he who can make much is a hero. The huge world that girdles us about puts all sorts of questions to us, and tests us in all sorts of ways. Some of the tests we meet by actions that are easy, and some of the questions we answer in articulately formulated words. But the deepest question that is ever asked admits of no reply but the dumb turning of the will and tightening of our heartstrings as we say, "*Yes, I will even have it so!*" When a dreadful object is presented, or when life as a whole turns up its dark abysses to our view, then the worthless ones among us lose their hold on the situation altogether, and either escape from its difficulties by averting their attention, or if they cannot do that, collapse into yielding masses of plaintiveness and fear. The effort required for facing and consenting to such objects is beyond their power to make. But the heroic mind does differently. To it, too, the objects are sinister and dreadful, unwelcome, incompatible with wished-for things. But it can face them if necessary, without for that losing its hold upon the rest of life. The world thus finds in the heroic man its worthy match and mate; and the effort which he is able to put forth to hold himself erect and keep his heart unshaken is the direct measure of his worth and function in the game of human life. He can *stand* this Universe. He can meet it and keep up his faith in it in the presence of those same features which lay his weaker brethren low. He can still find a zest in it, not by "ostrich-like forgetfulness," but by pure inward willingness to face the world with those deterrent objects there. And hereby he becomes one of the masters and the lords of life. He must be counted with henceforth; he forms a part of human destiny.[16]

One looks in vain for such ennobling, inspiring words about the individual in the writings of the Progressives and the behaviorists who followed James and whose theories constitute the bedrock of American educational thinking today. James's "heroic" thinking about living life vigorously and to the fullest, meeting its challenges with vim and vigor is, for all intents and purposes, now completely absent in public education. The will becomes of crucial importance in James's thinking because it keeps one striving to survive, succeed, and fulfill his human potential. Note that he wrote this decades before the excesses of Progressive education.

> *Soft* pedagogics have taken the place of the old steep and rocky path to learning. But from this lukewarm air the bracing oxygen of effort is left out. It is nonsense to suppose that every step in education *can* be interesting. The fighting impulse must often be appealed to. Make the pupil feel ashamed of being scared at fractions, of being "downed" by the law of falling bodies; rouse his pugnacity and pride, and he will rush at the difficult places with a sort of inner wrath at himself that is one of his best moral faculties. A victory scored under such conditions becomes a turning-point and crisis of his character.[17]

This attitude today is not foreign to our society; it simply isn't associated with modern American thinking about education. One principal conveyed to me his beliefs on such matters when we were discussing what to do with a student who was failing after only six weeks of class. The principal's advice was "Get that kid out of that class!"—presumably so that the student's self-esteem would not be damaged. No mention was made of the student's need to face a great difficulty and conquer it. "Just do it" is a popular expression among high school athletes, but that pragmatic, courageous, and inspiring message is confined to the locker room and athletic fields, rarely entering the classroom where most students are told to depend upon the teachers to "achieve success for them" in shallow, watered-down courses. Self-esteem is something given away with abandon instead of being earned by substantial accomplishments. Yet after slouching through twelve years of an anemic curriculum, during which few students learn what they are truly capable of accomplishing through sustained effort and hard work, many graduates and failures in our schools are drawn to the army because it respects them and their abilities enough to challenge them to "be all you can be."

One cannot always change reality, James well knew; but his experience in dealing with his own emotional problems convinced him that even so, one can at least influence, if not determine, what he thinks

about reality, what he will turn over in his mind: "The practical and theoretical life of whole species, as well as of individual beings, results from
the selection which the habitual direction of their attention involves. . . .
Each of us literally *chooses*, by his way of attending to things, what sort of
universe he shall appear to himself to inhabit."[18] With James it becomes
an issue of morals as well as of courage, a view sadly lacking in more scientific psychology, in which one becomes merely a product of his environment, his conduct beyond his control, determined by his past history
and his genes.

James's old-fashioned view supports education in the broadest, most
humane sense, for it entails the maximizing of one's human abilities, living life to the fullest, each person doing his all to meet his individual
human potential. It means being engaged with life, fully appreciating its
problems, doing everything possible to solve them, being active and
doing rather than passively submitting to life's events and the vicissitudes
of the environment. Concerning difficulties in life, James argues, "It is,
indeed, a remarkable fact that sufferings and hardships do not, as a rule,
abate the love of life; they seem, on the contrary, usually to give it a
keener zest. The sovereign source of melancholy is repletion. Need and
struggle are what excite and inspire us; our hour of triumph is what
brings the void."[19] Facing and overcoming difficulties in life give it more
meaning, make it more a product of one's will than of happenstance and
the vagaries of the environment and fickle fortune. This full engagement with living and the conduct of life is in strong contrast to the passive behaviorist view—again, the bedrock of American educational
psychology—in which one is seen merely as a product of his environment and genes, unable to work his will because, lacking a mind (as behaviorists believe), he doesn't *have* will. Many students in our schools
today expect success immediately, after no work or little effort, and thus
their failure or difficulty in meeting a problem disillusions them. They
are not fully engaged with living and doing but content (or so it seems)
with mere *being*. For their school experience to be worthwhile, students
must not only learn facts and how to think logically, analytically, and
creatively. They must also acquire confidence and self-respect by overcoming difficulties and meeting challenges.

To the word "is" and to the words "let it be" there correspond peculiar attitudes of consciousness which it is vain to seek to explain. The indicative and the imperative moods [the indicative denotes statements of fact, the imperative statements of command] are as much ultimate categories of thinking as they are of grammar. The "quality of reality" which these moods attach to things is not like other qualities. It is a relation to our life. It means *our* adoption of the things, *our* caring for them, *our* standing by them.[20]

Since habit is so important to our lives, James devotes a long chapter to it in *Principles of Psychology* and *Talks to Teachers*, calling it "the flywheel of society." To develop a good habit, he says, we must never neglect an opportunity to perform it: "*Never suffer an exception to occur till the new habit is securely rooted in your life*," he urges his readers, otherwise the neural grooves supporting the habit will not be deepened. We become calcified in our habits because the more we perform an action, the deeper its grooves grow in our neural systems, and the harder it is to break out of the habit. In typical Jamesian style, he calls that condition of being dominated by habit and unable to change as "old-fogyism." If, however, you wish to ward off old-fogyism and remain vibrant, active, and continually growing, he advised his audience of teachers, do something demanding every day, just for the sake of doing something different: "*Keep the faculty of effort alive in you by a little gratuitous exercise every day.* That is, be systematically heroic in little unnecessary points, do every day or two something for no other reason than its difficulty, so that, when the hour of dire need draws nigh, it may find you not unnerved and untrained to stand the test." We may buy books that we know are good for us but fail to read them because we don't feel like it; or, in today's terms, join a gym yet never find the time to work out, or buy the healthy food we need yet succumb instead to Burger King and McDonald's. "We forget that every good that is worth possessing must be paid for in strokes of daily effort. We postpone and postpone until those smiling possibilities are dead. . . . By neglecting the necessary concrete labor, by sparing ourselves the little daily tax, we are positively digging the graves of our higher possibilities," James warns.[21]

Note how utterly alien the following statement is to our modern, scientific educational thinking.

> Let no youth have any anxiety about the upshot of his education, whatever the line of it may be. If he keep faithfully busy each hour of the working day, he may safely leave the final result to itself. He can with perfect certainty count on waking up some fine morning to find himself one of the competent ones of his generation, in whatever pursuit he may have singled out. Silently, between all the details of his business, the *power of judging* in all that class of matter will have built itself up within him as a possession that will never pass away. Young people should know this truth in advance. The ignorance of it has probably engendered more discouragement and faint-heartedness in youths embarking on arduous careers than all other causes put together.[22]

Today students who have such attitudes succeed at school. But, lamentably, they learn such attitudes at home and from their families, *not at the public school*, for Progressive education explicitly rejects not only formal academic studies but also the mentality of the Protestant work ethic, personal responsibility, self-control, and delayed gratification. And the cultural revolution of the 1960s has made it less likely that they will learn them at home. The crucial factor in determining student achievement is not the school itself but the student's family and social environment. When education researchers began analyzing school quality in terms of student achievement instead of by dollars spent, noted James S. Coleman and his research team, "the most striking result was that variations in schools made considerably less difference in a child's achievement than did variations in that child's family background." Variation in school characteristics could account "for only 10 to 25 percent" of the variance in student achievement. Similarly, students whose parents inculcated in their children values commonly described as the Protestant work ethic were more likely to attain higher grades than other students without those values.[23] While we should expect teachers to do all they can to help students learn both academics and productive habits and attitudes, we should understand that the teacher's power is limited, even small when compared with the power of the family and the social environment. To assign to teachers the responsibility for overcoming the problems of families; the larger culture with its anti-intellectual tendencies; adolescent culture with its youthful rebellion; and the school culture itself, is absurd and unproductive. Instead we should urge, expect, and train students to acquire habits and attitudes that lead to success: hard work, diligence, sustained effort and concentration, and accuracy.

THE ROLE OF THE TEACHER

James is realistic about the limited powers of psychology to help teachers instruct the young. "Psychology is a science, and teaching is an art," he writes, and the qualities or actions that make a good teacher "are things to which psychology cannot help us in the least." True, he informs his audience of teachers, "The teachers of this country, one may say, have its future in their hands." Yet his other observations on the power of teachers belie his words that students are so plastic and malleable.[24]

Still, James urges his audience of teachers to know about the needs and nature of children and their learning, in order to enhance their success. "The first thing . . . for the teacher to understand is the native reactive tendencies,—the impulses and instincts of childhood,—so as to be able to substitute one for another, and turn them on to artificial objects." He then lists the various instincts and impulses one can use in teaching students. One, for example, is love, "the instinctive desire to please those whom we love. The teacher who succeeds in getting herself loved by the pupils will obtain results which one of a more forbidding temperament finds it impossible to secure." Sometimes, he admits, you might have to yell at students and command them to pay attention, but do those things rarely, as "the more you have to do them, the less skillful you will show yourself to be." Instead he advises, "Elicit interest from within, by the warmth with which you care for the topic yourself. . . ." He also discusses what a bad practice it is to "break" a child's will, in contrast to a commonly held belief of the day. Don't preach too much, he also advises the teachers, as the words soon come to mean nothing to the students; actions speak louder.[25]

James does not discuss curriculum explicitly. From other remarks he makes about education (for example, his approval of using marks and grades, and of recitation; his encouraging of competition and a student's pugnacity toward the subject matter; and his occasional denunciations of "soft" pedagogy), one may conclude that he believed in a traditional academic education. "It was surely not his intention," remarks the educationist Paul Woodring, "that the new emphasis on the processes of teaching and of learning should in any way lessen the attention given in formal education to knowledge, intellectual development, discipline and values." He did praise the inclusion of courses such as carpentry, however, because such courses helped students become more accurate thinkers and doers and compelled them to work with precision.[26]

James knew about the learning processes of young people, and he was sympathetic to their needs and natures. "Your pupils," he tells his audience of teachers, "whatever else they are, are at any rate little pieces of associating machinery. Their education consists in the organizing within them of determinate tendencies to associate one thing with another, — impressions with consequences, these with reactions, those with results, and so on indefinitely. The more copious the associative systems, the completer the individual's adaptations to the world." The phrase "associative systems" doubtless refers to basic facts and information learned through lessons on formal subject matter and inculcated through drill and recitation and application. The more one knows, in other words, the better one's chances of surviving and thriving in the world. Therefore the teacher—in contrast to the new education emerging as James wrote, and which exerts great power today—should teach students basic facts and information, as his job is mainly *"building up useful systems of association in the pupil's mind."*[27]

Another trait of children is their intense curiosity, and teachers can and should capitalize on it. Children have great curiosity for material things, living things, human actions, and accounts of human action, James writes, while adolescents become curious about more abstract and theoretical matters. "The teacher's earliest appeals, therefore, must be through objects shown or acts performed or described." The teacher's job is to use instincts such as curiosity to teach formal subject matter, so that students will more likely associate things in their experience with formal knowledge and therefore learn the abstract through the concrete: *"Begin with the line of* [the child's] *native interests, and offer him objects that have some immediate connection with these. . . . Associate the new with the old in some natural and telling way, so that the interest, being shed along from point to point, finally suffuses the entire system of objects of thought."* Thus students will learn the new on the basis of what they already know and understand, and the good teacher's mind "will fairly coruscate with points of connection between the new lesson and the circumstances of the children's other experience."[28]

James also advises teachers to respect the students and their abilities; children should be expected to work and to strive. Here James clearly chastises what would become Progressive education with its narrow emphasis on the child's immediate experience:

> To hear some authorities on teaching . . . you would suppose that geography not only began, but ended with the school-yard and neighboring hill, that physics was one endless round of repeating the same sort of tedious weighing and measuring operation: whereas a very few examples are usually sufficient to set the imagination free on genuine lines, and then what the mind craves is more rapid, general, and abstract treatment. . . . Too many children "see" as immediately "through" the nambypamby attempts of the softer pedagogy to lubricate things for them, and make them interesting. Even they can enjoy abstractions, provided they be of the proper order; and it is a poor compliment to their rational appetite to think that anecdotes about little Tommies and little Jennies are the only kind of things their minds can digest.[29]

Clearly James believed that children must be challenged if they are to grow intellectually, yet he knew that success issues predominantly from the student's actions rather than from the teacher's actions. He is realistic about what students must expect of school, and how they will succeed: "It is certain that most schoolroom work, till it has become habitual and automatic, is repulsive, and cannot be done without voluntarily jerking back the attention to it every now and then." The teacher must teach the lesson and help the students learn by explaining the new information in relation to what they already know, but he cannot cross the widest breach in nature into the student's experience and create understanding. "When all is said and done, and your best efforts are made, it will probably remain true that the result [of your teaching] will depend more on a certain native tone or temper in the pupil's psychological constitution than on anything else." James was not simply attempting to ingratiate himself with his audience of teachers; when his own son Aleck was faring poorly in school, James commented in a letter, "Can school *impart* anything? It seems to me that they can only furnish [opportunities], and the boy's own spontaneity has to do the work." The student must learn, by the training of habits, to control and direct his mind to useful and productive ends. "The exercise of voluntary attention in the schoolroom must therefore be counted one of the most important points of training that take place there; and the first-rate teacher, by the keenness of the remoter interests which he is able to awaken, will provide abundant opportunities for its occurrence."[30]

THE ECLIPSE OF JAMES'S PSYCHOLOGY

James was an individualist; in his psychology he did not address the troubling social conditions of his era. With the rise of Progressive education, individualism became anathema in one strain of the new ideology. James's belief in set subject matter and traditional schooling also alienated him from the psychologists and educators who followed. His sometimes Victorian morality and somewhat introspective psychology fell out of favor, replaced by behaviorism and social psychology. These focused less on individual mental development and perception and enjoyed superior scientific status. "To those who read the 'Talks' in the nineteen-twenties and thirties, much that James had to say sounded a little old-fashioned," Paul Woodring notes. "His concept of mind and of will seemed dated to psychologists, and educators were prone to reject the values he placed on competition and effort, for this was the day of a softer pedagogy which failed to perceive its own softness."[31]

The sad irony of the demise of James's ideas is twofold. First, the stu-

dents in today's schools who live in accordance with old-fashioned principles of effort and will to succeed are the stars of our public schools, the
usually unsung heroes who in the future will provide the great brain-
power of our country. Such students are actively working to create their
own reality and destiny. If they live by the old-fashioned values of applying themselves unflinchingly to a task without expecting an immediate
reward, they have almost certainly learned such values at home, from
their families, and *not at school*, for the ideology of the public schools—
founded upon Progressive ideas that rejected James's thinking—does
not inculcate those attitudes, and even disparages them. Second, many
private schools across the United States and most public schools
throughout the world, who adhere to Jamesian Victorian morality and
unscientific approaches, are much more successful than our schools
with their superior scientific psychology.[32]

2

THE PROGRESSIVE PARADIGM, PART ONE: BEHAVIORISM AND THE INDIVIDUALIZED STIMULUS

The modern American educational system is the product of three distinct influences that developed concurrently during the Progressive era. These three influences have coalesced into our nation's attitudes toward teachers and their role in education; students and the nature of young people; knowledge and the intellect in general; and the place of the school in American society. Although the Progressive era has long passed, many of its educational tenets survive today and provide the often unexamined bases and unquestioned assumptions of our thinking about education. This chapter explores the influence of science on the nascent educational psychology, and how it transformed the roles and expectations of the student and teacher.

Our educational system began its great expansion and institutionalization in an age of science, at the onset of the flowering of scientific thought that had originated in the Enlightenment, when reformers hoped to apply science and the use of reason to the improvement of society and mankind. The faith that science could solve mankind's problems had received impetus particularly from industrialism and the writings of Henri de Saint-Simon and Auguste Comte. In the chaos of France after the French Revolution, the two men made a cult of science and its application to the improvement of human society.[1] In the United States, intellectuals such as Herbert Croly (in *The Promise of American Life*), Walter Lippmann (in *Drift and Mastery*), and John Dewey (particularly in *Human Nature and Conduct* and *The Public and Its Problems*) delineated the need for scientific management of American society, economy, and culture, for the greater good of the country and its civilization. In the United States during the 1920s, Frederick Lewis Allen writes,

> The prestige of science was colossal. The man in the street and the woman in the kitchen, confronted on every hand with new machines and devices which they owed to the laboratory, were ready to believe that science could accomplish almost anything; and they were being deluged with scientific information and theory.[2]

Allen's observation is equally true of the twenty to thirty years that preceded and followed the 1920s. So dominant did science seem that in his *Principles of Psychology*, published in 1890, James called the desire to appear scientific an "idol of the tribe"; and, following the epochal achievements of the detonation of the hydrogen bomb and the creation of a vaccine for polio, U.S. scientists were voted "Men of the Year" by *Time* magazine for the year 1960.[3] The veneration for science has been strengthened by its fantastic success in solving many formerly intractable human problems. In the infancy of science's growing domination, the United States, among all nations the most optimistic, modern, technologically friendly, and least encumbered by tradition, was creating a modern educational system based on scientific principles, to help establish the new, ideal society.

The growing educational system needed scientific certainty to meet the country's expectations for its schools, and the new psychology supplied it. With the science of human behavior and learning, educators and laypeople as well hoped that education would achieve scientific status and meet the many expectations that society had of its schools. Later educational psychologists would testify to the contribution made by

William James, for he was credited with applying scientific psychology to the problems of education. At the end of the nineteenth century, writes Geraldine Joncich, "listening to James has convinced more than one educator that, if there be a 'science of education,' it must be psychology," even though James himself had stated emphatically that psychology was merely the hope of a science, and that teaching was an art, not a science.[4]

Increasingly, however, James's brand of psychology fell out of favor. Despite its physiological basis, it simply was not scientific enough, since it relied chiefly upon introspection, or the psychologist's study of his own thoughts and consciousness. Psychology could hardly be rated as one of the sciences when its findings were so subjective and unquantifiable; what was true of one person's thoughts and cognitive processes might easily be untrue of another's. Psychology seemed little more than a pseudoscience. Indeed, a group of biologists polled in 1910 did not consider psychology a real science and classified it as merely a subdiscipline of philosophy or physiology. And the educational practices based upon so unscientific a psychology could hardly solve the problems embroiling American society: the vast hordes of immigrants from southern and eastern Europe, with their foreign ways and different languages; the ghettos, slums, labor unrest, anarchism, communism, alcoholism, atheism, political corruption, and growing gaps between obscenely wealthy plutocrats and the dirt-poor laboring masses. Education needed more than mythological or metaphysical psychology in order to help solve the country's problems and shape a stable, unified culture and society.[5]

THE RISE OF BEHAVIORISM

In response to these problems and in opposition to Jamesian introspective psychology arose behaviorism — "objective" or "scientific" psychology. John B. Watson, one of the early behaviorists in the United States and one of its great champions (he is even regarded by some as its founder), declared its philosophy in 1924: "Behaviorism . . . holds that the subject matter of human psychology *is the behavior of the human being*. Behaviorism claims that consciousness is neither a definite nor a usable concept." James had asserted that the proper study of psychology is consciousness, yet he had sought to explain it and human behavior by analyzing the physiological basis of neurons and their pathways. Watson claimed that the belief in the existence of consciousness went back to the days "of superstition and magic." In short, the behaviorist believes that the mind does not exist; what we call thoughts, thinking, or stream of consciousness is simply internal verbalization or, in the words of B. F. Skinner, the most famous behaviorist, "covert behavior" — an odd choice of words, since behaviorism sought to reduce behavior to phenomena both observable and quantifiable (if it is covert, how can it be proven to exist?). Skinner scoffed at the thought that the mind exists: only observable behavior matters. Whereas Jamesian psychology had aimed chiefly to help us understand how our minds work and cause our behavior, so that we can improve ourselves, behaviorism had another goal entirely. The theoretical goal of behaviorism, wrote Watson in his 1913 behaviorist manifesto, "is the prediction and control of behavior."[6]

According to behaviorism, people act the way they do in response to a problem in the environment. "We can throw all of our psychological problems and their solutions into terms of stimulus and response," writes Watson.[7] A problem in the environment serves as a stimulus: it causes dissatisfaction and thus calls for resolution. We solve — or at least address — the problem with our response, and responses that bring success are more likely to be repeated. Behavior that does not solve the problem tends to disappear, because it is not rewarded.

In a way, behaviorism became the perfect psychology for education, for it explained how educators could teach students and shape their behavior (its inadequacies will become evident). For a long time, "behaviorism *was* learning theory."[8] Its scientific nature also enhanced the reputation of education in academia and society at large, thus increasing the grandiose expectations many had of the schools. The promise that education bolstered by science could deliver is best seen in a famous quote by Watson. Arguing against the dominance of inherited traits and for the power of scientific psychology — behaviorism, in other words — he boasted,

... Give me a dozen healthy infants, well-formed, and my own speci-
fied world to bring them up in and I'll guarantee to take any one at random and train him to become any type of specialist I might
select—doctor, lawyer, artist, merchant-chief and, yes, even beggar-man
and thief, regardless of his talents, penchants, tendencies, abilities, voca-
tions, and race of his ancestors.[9]

Certainly, educators armed with this scientific psychology could
mold the young into effective citizens and stave off the chaos that threatened the nation's stability in the early twentieth century. Watson even
prophesied (as Skinner did thirty years later) a near utopian society of
equality and obedience to the law *if* individuals were trained by social
scientists using behaviorist methods. Watson would certainly be enthusi-
astically applauded by today's proponents of teacher accountability: "It is
our own fault, then," he said, "that individuals (other than defectives and
psychopaths) go 'wrong,' that is, deviate from set standards of behavior—
and by 'our own fault' I mean the fault of the parent, the teacher and
every other member of the group; we have neglected and are neglecting
our opportunities." Educators in the United States, eager to solve society's problems, usher in that utopia, and enhance the professional status
of education, embraced scientific psychology. But behaviorism was only
part of a larger scientific movement in education during the Progressive
Era that promised to solve society's problems and meet society's expectations of the schools. Lawrence Cremin, a historian of American education, observes, "Little wonder that professors of education, ever under
attack for having no real content to teach, saw in science the great
panacea for their field." Behaviorism continues to form the foundation
for today's educational psychology and supplies the rationale behind the
expectations for teachers.[10]

EDWARD L. THORNDIKE AND CONNECTIONISM

The foremost scientific psychologist in American education is Edward
L. Thorndike (1874–1947) of Teachers College of Columbia University.

One might recognize his name from the dictionary he compiled using statistics of the most commonly used and misused words. To classicists, Thorndike is something of a villain, for he "proved" that the study of Latin does not increase one's intellectual discipline, and thereby he contributed to the demise of Latin in American schools. When his *Educational Psychology* (later abridged into *Educational Psychology: Briefer Course*) was published in three volumes in 1913–1914, Geraldine Joncich observed, it represented "in form and substance a marked departure from the genre of texts and treatises in both general and educational psychology; it promises to become more—the bible of a still young field." In his long and prolific career Thorndike published dozens of books and scores of articles, virtually creating the field of educational psychology, and was instrumental both in designing psychological tests and in applying statistical methods to educational problems. During a ceremony held to honor him late in his life, the educational psychologist C. H. Judd reported that "no school in America is uninfluenced, no humanistic science unaffected, by Thorndike's labors." After the publication of *Educational Psychology*, Thorndike's stimulus-response learning theory dominated the field and "is thought to be bringing pedagogy nearer to being a science than ever before."[11]

Although Ivan Pavlov, the great Russian physiologist (he had been studying the gastric reflexes of dogs when he inadvertently discovered what is now known as Pavlovian conditioning, and in 1904 won the Nobel Prize for his work in physiology), called Thorndike the founder of behaviorism,[12] Thorndike was not a strict behaviorist. He had in fact studied under James at Harvard. (When Thorndike's landlady objected to his housing experimental chickens in his apartment, the kindly James lent him the use of his basement.) He retained great respect for the elder statesman of physiological psychology, sending James copies of his books and corresponding with him. Upon James's death in 1910, Thorndike wrote a laudatory notice on his influence on education for the inaugural edition of the journal *Educational Psychology*.

Thorndike preferred to see learning as "connectionism," that is, drawing connections between a stimulus ("situation" in his words) and a response. A cat trapped in a problem box, for example, will want to get out, and will try various actions to escape; when by chance it finally hits the release lever, it connects "escape" with "hitting the lever." After more times of being trapped and hitting the release lever for escape, the cat knows the means of escape, and the resultant "learning curve" shows how a procedure that once took the cat ten minutes to perform now, after many successful solutions, is executed almost immediately. (This may be James's frog dressed up in fancier clothes, but whereas James studied the mind, Thorndike ignored it.) Thus one of the cardinal rules of education, writes Thorndike, is to get the learner to associate desired behavior with reward, and undesired behavior with annoyance or the lack of a reward. He called this the Law of Effect.

The teacher's task is therefore to provide the stimulus that will lead the student to respond in the way desired by the teacher and society, and to give or withhold rewards as appropriate. That stimulus might be presented in the form of a problem on, say, the concept of the square root, or the ablative absolute in Latin, or typing "The quick brown fox jumps over the lazy dog," or writing cursive script in a way that meets established criteria. "Learning is connecting; and teaching is the arrangement of situations which lead to desirable bonds [of responding in certain ways to stimuli] and make them satisfying." The stimulus is the problem to be solved, and the response is the student's attempt to solve it; the reward stamps in the desired behavior and ensures that the student or organism will repeat the desired behavior when the proper stimulus is applied. "Education makes changes chiefly by rewarding them," Thorndike writes. "The prime law in all human control is to get the man to make the desired response and to be satisfied thereby."[13]

To prompt the desired response, the teacher must use his scientific knowledge of human learning and of the individual student. "The competent teacher expects variety in human beings and examines each pupil to learn what he really is and needs. From the variety of individual human wants education selects its aims, and to the variety of individual interests and capacities it fits its means and methods." Teachers' training in scientific psychology endows them with great power, Thorndike argues; he calls the teacher "the architect of human lives" and classifies education among the branches of "human engineering." Because of its theoretical power to shape behavior, education empowered by science is increasingly seen as something *we*, the teachers and adults with the knowledge and power, do to *them*, the helpless and passive students being molded for good or ill by the stimuli we apply and the responses they incur. "Education," writes Thorndike, "makes changes in a child's intellect and character by making the changes in this [neural] mechanism. . . ." It is a metaphor appropriate for the age of factories, when inanimate, passive, raw materials were molded, shaped, beaten, and otherwise transformed through the magic of science into Model-Ts and other consumer goods.[14]

The thousands of teachers, administrators, education professors, psychologists, and educated laypeople reading Thorndike's books and articles on educational psychology learned that all the wonderful things desired of our educational system would be realized through scientific psychology. "At the bottom of the endless variety of human nature and circumstance," he states, "there are laws which act invariably and make possible the control of human education and progress by reason. So the general rule of reason applies to education: *To produce a desired effect, find its cause and put that in action*."[15] All that one needs to do, in order for students to learn, is to supply the stimulus appropriate for each student. Scientific psychology will help the teacher find the appropriate stimulus that results in the desired behavior.

"To an understanding of the material of education, psychology is the chief contributor," Thorndike writes—words that presage the growing dominance of psychology over academics in American education. "Just as the science and art of agriculture depend upon chemistry and botany, so the art of education depends upon physiology and psychology," he writes, using a simile which implies that students are as simple, passive, manipulable, and quantifiable as dirt.[16] Yet dirt has no will; if it lacks certain chemicals that are essential for the growth of plants, it cannot create those chemicals or compensate by emphasizing chemicals it has in abundance. Soil does not—it cannot—care whether or not plants grow, and it has no behavior to change in accordance with meeting its goals. People, however, can and *do* change their behavior in pursuit of consciously formed goals; people have will. The implied comparison between students and soil is erroneous, and the power to know and control students as one farms the soil is chimerical. Unfortunately for both teachers and students in our classrooms today, however, teachers are thought to possess an absolute, all-encompassing knowledge of students' psyches, and with it the absolute power to mold their behavior and create learning.

Behaviorism and connectionism, with their theoretical scientific certainty, mark a profound shift in American attitudes toward education. This shift results in two elements of what I call the Progressive Paradigm, that is, certain unquestioned assumptions that govern and inform our educational thinking. The first element is that it is no longer incumbent upon the student to do what is necessary to succeed, for it becomes the responsibility of the *teacher* to find the right stimulus that will cause a student to respond as desired. The student appears to have a relatively passive, or minor, role in his learning, since he only reacts to stimuli created by the teacher. If the student fails to learn, the fault lies with the teacher for failing to supply the appropriate stimulus. The student is thereby relieved of the responsibility of striving for success and of doing what is necessary to succeed.

The second element is the expectation that the teacher will *individualize lessons* (that is, stimuli) according to the characteristics and needs of each student in the classroom. "The teacher of the future," predicts Thorndike, "will think out from scientific principles the best way to teach a given child to subtract or divide, as the engineer thinks out the best way to bridge a given river or tunnel a given hill." Note his confidence in the power of psychology and science to solve educational and intellectual problems, an optimism that no doubt spread to the high-minded thousands reading his scientifically based books at the height of progressivism and attending his courses in educational psychology before embarking on their crusade to improve society along rational, scientific lines.[17]

That the teacher simply does not have sufficient time during the day to gain such in-depth, scientific knowledge of each student's psychological makeup and to create individualized lessons for each of his hundred or so students was taken into account as little then as it is now. Teachers are routinely expected to modify their lessons for students' differing learning styles and to be sensitive to students' idiosyncratic needs. The public was (and still is) overawed by the promise of scientific education and psychology: "Freud, Adler, Jung, and Watson had their tens of thousands of votaries," Frederick Lewis Allen writes; "intelligence-testers invaded the schools in quest of I.Q.s; psychiatrists were installed in business houses to hire and fire employees and determine advertising policies; and one had only to read the newspapers to be told with complete assurance that psychology held the key to the problems of waywardness, divorce, and crime." Thorndike, writes Joncich, had read Karl Pearson's *The Grammar of Science* "and accepted fully its proposition that science, rightly understood, is competent to solve all problems." E. G. Boring, historian of psychology, writes that by the 1920s "it seemed as if all America had gone behaviorist." So enchanted was the public by behaviorism that Dr. Louis Berman, a fan of Gestalt psychology, showed his hostility to behaviorism by giving his anti-behaviorist polemic the title *The Religion Called Behaviorism*.[18]

B. F. SKINNER AND OPERANT CONDITIONING

The theoretical power of behaviorism to mold behavior reaches its apogee in the work of B. F. Skinner (1904–1990). Skinner's influence on educational psychology is small, especially when compared with Thorndike's; when Skinner was at the height of his career, in the 1950s and 1960s, the cognitive revolution was well under way in psychology, and behaviorism was on the wane. Yet Skinner is arguably the most famous American psychologist among the American public, and his ideas were, and still are, widely current in American culture, having been somewhat repudiated only since the conservative reaction of the 1980s. *Walden Two*, his novel of a utopian community founded on behaviorist principles, has sold millions of copies since its publication in 1948; *Beyond Freedom and Dignity* went through ten printings in the first two years after it was published in 1971. Skinner was honored in 1971 with an appearance on the cover of *Time* magazine and appeared on numerous television talk shows, including William F. Buckley's *Firing Line*. In 1970 the *American Psychologist* listed Skinner second (after Freud) in his influence on twentieth-century psychology. The TV show *The Simpsons* shows his influence on American thought and culture: the principal of Springfield Elementary is Seymour Skinner.[19]

Skinner was an inventor and general provocateur in American society. He believed there is nothing called the mind, which he considered "an explanatory fiction." He compared the search for causes of behavior in inner sources (that is, the "mind") to astrology, mythology, and the occult. The emotions, he said, "are excellent examples of the fictional causes to which we commonly attribute behavior." He argues that there is no "spirit" or "ghost in the machine" driving our actions and thoughts. "A self or personality is at best a repertoire of behaviors imparted by an organized set of contingencies." Elsewhere he denies that a person is an originating agent and defines a human as "a locus, a point at which many genetic and environmental conditions come together in a joint effect."[20]

Skinner is best known for his theory of operant conditioning. Since the mind is unobservable, uncontrollable, and hence insignificant, the environment, an organism's responses to it, and the reinforcements the organism receives for its responses assume crucial importance. The environment shapes our behavior by stimulating us in certain ways, and the reinforcements, whether negative or positive, make it more probable that we will or will not act in a particular way. The environment dominates us and determines our behavior by rewarding certain actions and punishing others. A person and his actions appear to be ruled by the environment or forces beyond his control: "A scientific analysis of behavior must . . . assume that a person's behavior is controlled by his genetic and environmental histories rather than by the person himself as an initiating, creative agent; but no part of the behavioristic position has raised more violent objections." James had similar thoughts—"minds inhabit environments which act on them and on which they in turn react"—but he nonetheless allowed for the existence of the mind and purposive behavior. James, it must be remembered, advised the teachers in his audience to see their students as being partly fated (by genetics and their past) and partly free (by what they *decided* to pay attention to and think). Skinner would have none of that.[21]

In other words, Skinner believes, organisms do not initiate action; the environment prompts organisms to respond, and conditions in the environment determine the response an organism will make. "As we learn more about the effects of the environment, we have less reason to attribute any part of human behavior to an autonomous controlling agent," he declares. The independent human being who seeks to understand his environment is passé, unscientific, an antiquated view of man. We are controlled by our environment, our behavior determined by our past history of responses to the environment and the reinforcements for our responses. Hence, in Skinner's mechanistic view, we have no free will.

> In the traditional picture a person perceives the world around him, selects features to be perceived, discriminates among them, judges them good or bad, changes them to make them better (or, if he is careless, worse), and may be held responsible for his action and justly rewarded or punished for its consequences. In the scientific picture a person is a member of a species shaped by evolutionary contingencies of survival, displaying behavioral processes which bring him under the control of the environment in which he lives, and largely under the control of a social environment which he and millions of others like him have constructed and maintained during the evolution of a culture. The direction of the controlling relation is reversed: a person does not act upon the world, the world acts upon him.[22]

With this view in mind, students can scarcely be held responsible for their actions, since they lack a mind, and the environment and their own pasts determine their behavior. Skinner repeats time and again that individuals cannot be held responsible for their actions. For example, he discusses how, traditionally, we would blame someone for whispering in church but not for coughing; we would be wrong, he maintains, for doing so: "there are variables which are responsible for whispering as well as for coughing, and these may be just as inexorable. When we recognize this, we are likely to drop the notion of responsibility altogether and with it the doctrine of free will as an inner casual agent." "Those who suffer [from their inability to control their behavior] are the first to speak out for the inevitability of their behavior," he continues. "The alcoholic insists that he can't help drinking and the 'victim of a bad temper' that he can't help kicking the cat or speaking his mind. *We have every reason to agree.*" Society, he writes elsewhere, "is responsible for the larger part of the behavior of self-control. If this is correct, little ultimate control remains with the individual." Playboys everywhere are off the hook. Decades later, Skinner had not changed his position: "If we do not punish a person for a club foot, should we punish him for being quick to anger or highly susceptible to sexual reinforcement?" (The problem, the playboy would joke, lies in his genes.)[23]

Contrast this with what James had written:

> It is as easy physically to avoid a fight as to begin one, to pocket one's money as to squander it on one's cupidities, to walk away from as toward a coquette's door. The difference is mental: it is that of getting the idea of the wise action to stay before our mind at all.[24]

According to James, in other words, we choose to behave in certain ways by paying attention to one idea rather than another. In Skinner's behaviorism, the individual's choice gives way to the *environment* or factors outside his control, for they present conditions that dominate his attention: "Attention is a controlling *relation* — the relation between a response and a discriminative stimulus. When someone is paying attention he is under special control of a stimulus." Twenty years later Skinner writes, "We pay attention or fail to pay attention to a lecturer or a traffic sign depending upon what has happened in the past under similar circumstances. Discrimination is a behavioral process: the contingencies, not the mind, make discriminations."[25]

So when students fall asleep or allow their minds to wander in class, it is obviously the teacher's fault, for the lesson and the environment he created have failed to retain the students' attention. To combat students' inattention, teachers try to incorporate glitzy elements into their lessons. The unfortunate effect is that the students never learn to pay attention on their own or to develop intellectual discipline—their behavior is determined by the environment the teacher has created, not by their own conscious intentions. Hugo Muensterberg, who succeeded James as head of the psychological laboratory at Harvard (and, incidentally, thought psychology absolutely useless for education), discussed that very problem in terms as reasonable as the advice given to teachers by James:

> It is clear that a sensory attention which depends entirely on the external impressiveness and which appeals to the mere instincts is ultimately inefficient. It leaves the power of voluntary attention untrained and soon reaches the end of its possibilities. Constant alternation is necessary. The teacher may make the perceptions impressive by his loud voice for a little while, but if he were to shout all the time, an adjustment would set in by which the stimulus would become ineffective. Every appeal to curiosity, every mere amusement, or any external impressiveness, is therefore effective only when it is rarely used. On the other hand, the continuous appeal to the voluntary attention must overtax the psychophysical resources. Fatigue sets in, and the fatigue sensation in itself is a stimulus for antagonistic reaction. . . . The most satisfactory result can be expected when the attention is directed neither by the appealing qualities of the stimulus from without nor by the mere good will to attend, but *by the ideas which the pupil's own mind supplies* in connection with the attended objects of perception.[26]

Since in behaviorism the environment controls us so tyrannically, the way to change behavior is to change the environment and the contingencies of reinforcement—in other words, to provide different stimuli to elicit the desired responses, and to offer appropriate rewards. "One person changes the behavior of another by changing the world in which he lives," explains Skinner. "In doing so, he no doubt changes what the other person feels or introspectively observes." So strong is operant conditioning that it "shapes behavior as a sculptor shapes a lump of clay." Note, however, that Thorndike—despite his unshakable optimism and faith that science could solve every problem—stated emphatically that students are *not* lumps of clay to be molded at the teacher's will. While

James had reminded his readers that you can lead a horse to water but you cannot make him drink, Skinner believes otherwise: "It is decidedly not true that a horse may be led to water but cannot be made to drink. By arranging a history of severe deprivation we could be 'absolutely sure' that drinking would occur."[27] There is some truth to that statement, but it is irrelevant for today's classroom. Since—thanks to another current of our educational philosophy—students are not supposed to work hard at school but rather to experience absolute freedom and joy there, teachers have no power to deprive them of *anything*. Even their power over the assignment of grades is circumscribed both by legal issues and by the fact that many students simply do not care about their grades or whether or not they pass the class. (Students don't have to care, for it is the teacher's responsibility to inspire them to care.) Consequently we see how the teacher, in the strict behaviorist view, is expected to shape students like lumps of clay without, however, damaging their self-esteem or trampling on their rights.

Many conservative proponents of teacher accountability, who, ironically enough, usually subscribe to the philosophy of "rugged individualism" and reject Skinner's arguments that individuals cannot be held responsible for their actions, nonetheless embrace the behaviorist view, at least when it concerns teacher accountability. Yet they fail to apply the theory consistently: teachers too are merely part of the environment, and—in Skinner's view—lack control over their actions. They too are mere collections of behaviors, controlled by their environment and their past. Skinner at one point acknowledges the problem but fails to solve it: ". . . it is now commonly said that there are no dull students but only poor teachers, no bad children but only bad parents. . . . But of course we must ask in turn why teachers, parents, governors, and entrepreneurs are bad. The mistake . . . is to put the responsibility anywhere, to suppose that somewhere a causal sequence is initiated."[28] His refusal to seek a cause is especially hypocritical, because science must seek the causes of things being the way they are. Skinner seems to refuse to want to do that; it might lead him to questions to which science can offer no definitive answers.

THE BEHAVIORISTS' RESERVATIONS ABOUT THEIR SCIENCE

The confidence—even arrogance (eventually, Skinner prophesied, "We shall know the precise neurological conditions which immediately precede, say, the response, 'No, thank you.' ")—of the behaviorists in their power to mold human behavior is particularly puzzling, in as much as they recognized that there are limits to what a teacher or controller can do. The reason is the complexity of human behavior. Thorndike freely admits the complexity of the human mind and the existential insularity that we experience: "The average elementary-school child at graduation almost certainly has formed over a million such [stimulus-response] bonds in working order. A complete inventory of him would require at least twenty books the size of this!" Elsewhere he observes, ". . . the result [of connection forming, learning, etc.—in other words, a person's personality] is a mixture of organized and unorganized tendencies that, even in an average three-year-old child, baffles description and prophecy." To create such a detailed, truly scientific study of an individual, a team of psychologists would need to have studied the individual in his every moment from birth, noting every stimulus, every response, every reward or punishment received, and every word spoken. Even this could scarcely constitute a totally accurate study of the child since his "covert behavior" could not be analyzed. Because of the unique nature of each person, Thorndike himself noted, a stimulus that works for one may well fail to work for another: "the environmental stimulus adequate to arouse a certain power or ideal or habit in one man may be hopelessly inadequate to do so in another." That whole complex of connections and attitudes is mostly hidden from the surface, too; the outward manifestations of the students' behavior are merely the tip of the iceberg. After Freud's lecture series at Clark University in 1909, Thorndike was no doubt aware of his theories and the fantastic permutations of stimuli that the human mind can make when coming to understand experience. James wrote that "the eye of Omniscience" could read our past in each one of our acts; teachers, of course, lack such divine omniscience, and trained psychologists cannot achieve such pinnacles of knowledge either. Perhaps a physicist said it best: "To tell the truth about an experiment in physics [is] child's play, compared with telling the truth about a man."[29]

Yet to have the scientific knowledge necessary for programming each student and creating a stimulus appropriate for him, the teacher would need the "twenty books" of knowledge of each child's every response to past stimuli, plus absolute control over the child's life and environment. Science cannot allow for so many crucial unknowns and variables. Hence teaching can never be a science, for each individual student is sui generis in how he learns and understands reality. Teaching must forever remain only an art, as it can never proceed beyond basic principles, so many hard facts of others' ways of understanding of reality being forever a mystery.

Skinner too was no naif about the individuality and unique nature of each person. He readily acknowledges that each repertoire of behaviors, with its history of contingencies of reinforcement, is unique. He also acknowledges the enormous complexity of human behavior and how it might be impossible to understand all the influences that have created any given individual, and thus to control him. That human behavior is unpredictable does not mean it is free, argues Skinner, "but only that it may be beyond the range of a predictive or controlling science." In a statement that sounds much like a description of a teacher's situation, Skinner confesses, "When human behavior is observed under conditions which cannot be exactly described and where histories are out of reach, very little prediction or control is possible. . . ."—such conditions being a student's detailed psychological history, home life, social life, engagement with popular media, time spent surfing the Internet and sites visited, and so forth.[30]

Skinner also fails to resolve the sensitive issue of control. He admits that attempts to control humans easily cause active and passive reactions and attempts to escape control, even attempts at countercontrol. The controlled organism can in fact end up controlling the controller. After all, it is the responses from the controlled that determine or influence the subsequent stimuli given by the controller—Skinner even joked that his pigeons controlled him with their responses. (When Skinner was training rats as part of his graduate research at Harvard, the student paper ran a cartoon poking fun at him. In the cartoon a rat says, "Gee, have I got this fellow conditioned. Every time I press the bar he drops in a piece of food.")[31]

Despite the uncertainty of his science and the unknowable mysteries of others' histories of stimuli and reinforcements, Skinner readily sacrifices human freedom and dignity in his belief that a better "human product" will emerge from a scientifically managed society: "the control of the population as a whole must be delegated to specialists—to police, priests, owners, teachers, therapists, and so on, with their specialized reinforcers and their codified contingencies." Another early behaviorist, Edward C. Tolman, had a more realistic attitude: behaviorism could scarcely be expected to guide human behavior when it could not predict which way a rat would turn in a maze.[32]

Teachers do not have the kind of power to shape behavior that Skinner and many people today imagine (and it is right to wonder if it would be safe for anyone to exercise such power). The misunderstanding of behaviorism has thus created enormous problems for today's teachers. Through their theoretical power to manipulate the environment, stimuli, and the conditions of reinforcement, teachers are thought to wield great, if not absolute, control over their students' behavior, *greater than the control the students themselves have over their own actions and thoughts*, and greater than the power held by parents and guardians.

Skinner and Thorndike could so easily control their animals' behavior because its range was so limited. Pigeons and cats can do only so many things: a pigeon may be trained to play a simple tune on a four-key piano, but will it ever compose a new song, know that it is composing a new song, and get delight either from the process of composition or from the music itself? Will a Ludwig van Pigeon ever arise to shatter all our conceptions in his revolution of pigeon music? The reason the chicken crossed the road was probably to seek food or sex, or to escape a predator; why humans do things is much more complicated. One need not look too hard and long at human behavior to note its wide range, with enormous variations in religion, clothing, customs, language, and patterns of thought. Since the students' environment today includes the Internet and popular culture (brought to students through the various media), to say that teachers control students' behavior through the manipulation of the environment is patently absurd.

THE WILL AND PURPOSIVE BEHAVIOR

Skinner's pigeons and Thorndike's cats were so trainable because their relatively simple and stereotyped behavior allows for very little creativity and little individual differentiation, instinct and appetites being so dominant in their simple brains. They do not have will, and the reasons for their behavior are much more comprehensible. Humans, however, formulate abstract goals and pursue them relentlessly. They often behave in ways that defy logic and sense, that even jeopardize their very survival. Yet the behaviorists have little, if anything, to say about will and purposive behavior. Thorndike at least admits that it is a powerful force: "Purposive behavior is the most important case of the influence of the attitude or set or adjustment of an organism in determining (1) which bonds shall act, and (2) which results shall satisfy."[33] Otherwise Thorndike tends to see students' minds as being constructed by the teacher's actions and limited by their genes.

Since the will is a mental phenomenon, Skinner does not believe that it or purposive behavior, such as planning, exists. When, for example, a person loses his glasses, we say that he looks for them. But according to Skinner,

> There is no *current* goal, incentive, purpose, or meaning to be taken into account. This is so even if we ask him what he is doing and he says, "I am looking for my glasses." This is not a further description of his behavior but of the variables of which his behavior is a function; it is equivalent to "I have lost my glasses," "I shall stop what I am doing when I find my glasses," or "When I have done this in the past, I have

found my glasses." These translations may seem unnecessarily round-about, but only because expressions involving goals and purposes are abbreviations.[34]

Skinner even takes pains in his three volumes of autobiography to dissociate his success from any personal causes or characteristics: he wanted his autobiography to be that of a "non-person."[35] He attributes his outstanding success to his history of stimuli and reinforcements and some plain good luck, and he calls himself merely a repertoire of behaviors created by his past history of responses and contingencies of reinforcement. (For someone who claimed to take no personal credit or glory for his accomplishments, he certainly wrote a great deal of autobiographical material.)

The truth has to be more complicated. Skinner's biographer Daniel Bjork devotes a full chapter to the details of how Skinner created an environment that would mold his behavior for greatest efficiency and productivity. "A major emphasis of his adult life had been on managing his work schedule so as to ensure intellectual production. He not only started and stopped writing by the buzz of a timer; he counted the number of words he had written in a given period, kept records of how many hours he spent on each book, and made a graph charting the sales of *Walden Two*—a very reinforcing activity, as sales approached two million in the late 1980s."[36] Are we to believe that Skinner's will and mind had nothing to do with it, that only his past and contingencies of reinforcement were responsible, there being no goal, incentive, or purpose? The behaviorist doth protest too much: he designed the environment so that it would encourage him to be more productive; in other words, he *planned* that such an environment would result in the greater efficiency of his work, and he *planned* that the reward would prompt him to continue doing such work. Such planning is, of course, the result of thinking and foreseeing, or imagining, the future.

Still more, Skinner allowed himself to be manipulated by the environment that he himself had created. He just as easily could have gone back to bed after the alarm clock rang, but he *chose* to get up and write.

When he heard the alarm clock ring, he got up because he wanted to write, meet his goals for the day, and get the reward, as well as reinforce his faith in his psychological theories. Did he not have a plan, an end result in mind, when he trained the pigeon to play the piano? While this argument does not prove the existence of a metaphysical soul, it nonetheless shows thinking and volition, and the making of choices in conscious pursuit of a goal, as Skinner created an environment for molding his own behavior. To some extent he controls his behavior after all: "Man himself may be controlled by his environment," Skinner admits, "but it is an environment which is almost wholly of his own making."[37] Ergo a person can control himself and plan; to some extent (admittedly, there are factors in life over which one has little or no control) a person is his own controlling agent. James's words about the students in the classroom apply to us all: we too are partly fated and partly free.

THE LEGACY OF BEHAVIORISM

American education, because of behaviorist psychology, is far from child-centered. First and foremost, it states clearly and emphatically that the source of the student's success lies outside his conscious actions and intentions. The student is seen as relatively passive, since his success depends upon the teacher's ability to mold lessons in accordance with the student's psychological constitution. The helpless student can only wait for the teacher to do what will bring him success. The student is viewed not as a person coming to understand reality in order to develop himself and his abilities, but rather as something being programmed to behave in certain ways. The student in the behaviorist/connectionist philosophy appears to lack control over his actions, thoughts, and destiny; this control passes to the scientifically trained teacher and the environment and stimuli he creates for his students. The students, lacking minds and purpose, merely *exist*, reacting to what the teacher programs them to do. The students are not expected to strive for success and are free *to let someone else determine their success or failure in life*. When a student has failed to learn, the teacher is obviously at fault for not providing a stimulus appropriate to the student's abilities, wants, nature, and needs, and for not creating an environment that elicits the desired behavior. The teacher has failed in any number of ways approaching infinity, since the student's failure to learn may lie in millions of unknown connections in the student's experience, or in the individual's twisted perceptions resulting from millions of unique and private experiences.

The sage advice given by James, that one solves problems by "turning the matter incessantly in his head," with his emphasis on the student's doing what is necessary to succeed, reveals the great contrast between educational thinking before and after behaviorism. The Jamesian way of thinking is also the hallmark of the highly successful Japanese system and characteristic of successful students in the United States, who shoulder the responsibility for their success.*

The connectionist-behaviorist view is the polar opposite of what a democratic education should be. A citizen in our country needs to understand, as much as possible, the forces that influence his life. By doing so, he can survive, if not thrive, in our world as an independent human being controlling his own actions and thoughts directed toward useful goals. In no other country does the individual create his own destiny as he does in this one, and in no other country does a citizen bear the responsibilities and enjoy the freedom that an American does, with so little interference from social norms and provincial attitudes. The goals of education, as formulated by W. T. Harris before the advent of behaviorism, bear repeating: "the self-active individual, the reasoning person who can exercise true freedom in the terms of his own civilization."[38] Behaviorist-connectionist education downplays the individual's responsibility, autonomy, potential, and worth. Control over the student's life and thoughts passes from the student to someone else who supposedly determines whether or not the student succeeds. Since the teacher does not in fact have that control, no one really controls the student.

Education embraced behaviorist psychology because its superior scientific standing promised greater certainty and control over students' behavior and development. After nearly a century of behaviorism, how-

---

*This topic is discussed in greater detail in Chapter Seven.

ever, it seems a graver threat to our civilization and freedom that individuals are thought to have so little control over their minds, thoughts, and behavior. The quest for certainty through the implementation of scientific education has resulted in the most uncertain methods, and our students' success is largely a matter of chance.

3

THE PROGRESSIVE PARADIGM, PART TWO: THE QUEST FOR SOCIAL AND INDIVIDUAL INTEGRATION

> Never before have we had to rely so completely upon ourselves. No guardian to think for us, no precedent to follow without question, no lawmaker above, only ordinary men set to deal with heartbreaking perplexity. All weakness comes to the surface. We are homeless in a jungle of machines and untamed powers that haunt and lure the imagination. Of course, our culture is confused, our thinking spasmodic, and our emotion out of kilter. No mariner ever enters upon a more uncharted sea than does the average human being born into the twentieth century. Our ancestors thought they knew their way from birth through all eternity: we are puzzled about the day after to-morrow.
>
> —Walter Lippmann, *Drift and Mastery*, 1917

The late nineteenth and early twentieth centuries brought massive social change, if not chaos, to the United States: industrialism, urbaniza-

tion, immigration, competitive individualism, and unregulated capitalism caused great ruptures in the national culture and social fabric. The
movement to solve those problems became known as progressivism, and
it marks the beginning of the modern American nation. Progressivism
strove to control, direct, and temper some of the forces that were tearing
the traditional fabric of American life, and to order society along scientific, rational lines. It expressed itself as "a desire for the political, social,
and economic perfection of American society"—and such perfection
seemed eminently feasible on the basis of science. In the simpler, predominantly agricultural society of former days, active government had
been unnecessary and even intrusive; in a modern industrial state with
complex needs, the best government was not necessarily the one that
governed least. The nation needed intelligent direction. The ideal society that Americans want, wrote Herbert Croly, a leading theorist of progressivism, "will have to be planned and constructed rather than
fulfilled of its own momentum. . . ."[1]

In education, intelligent direction and social planning took the form
of behaviorism. But Progressives in education also viewed schools as the
means toward constructing a new American society and individual.
Then, as now, it fell to ordinary classroom teachers to fulfill the pedagogical experts' visions of education and the ideal society. Thus teachers
became vulnerable to the contempt of the experts and the larger society
for failing to create that ideal society as well as for attempting to do so.

The spiritual leader and sometimes guru—whom Progressive educators viewed "as a Moses who would eventually lead them toward the
pedagogic promised land"—of the new education was John Dewey
(1859–1952), America's most famous philosopher, the philosopher and
educator of democracy. While growing up in Vermont, Dewey saw the
changes wrought in Burlington because of industrialism; he is said also
to have noticed with dismay the growing class differences between
Burlington's genteel middle class and the rough, laboring class living
along the shores of Lake Champlain. Reading Edward Bellamy's popular utopian novel *Looking Backward* was another formative moment for
him—he cited the book as being one of the most important of his life

(indeed, the book's ideas about social harmony reflected a longing felt by many others of the time: it sold 300,000 copies in two years).[2]

After receiving his bachelor's degree at the University of Vermont in 1879, Dewey taught high school for two years in Oil City, Pennsylvania, and then, less successfully, the winter term in Charlotte, Vermont. In Charlotte he submitted a paper to the *Journal of Speculative Philosophy* which the editor, W. T. Harris, accepted for publication while encouraging Dewey to pursue further studies in philosophy. Dewey soon quit teaching school in order to enroll in the recently formed Johns Hopkins University, where he earned his Ph.D. in philosophy in 1884, concentrating on the German idealist philosopher Hegel. Next he joined the faculty of the University of Michigan; ten years later he left to join the University of Chicago, where he became head of the Department of Pedagogy. While there, Dewey established the Laboratory School, where teachers, under the leadership of Dewey's wife Alice, implemented many of his ideas about education, ideas that were ultimately influenced by Jean-Jacques Rousseau and his naturalistic educational philosophy.

After various disputes with William Rainey Harper, the president of the University of Chicago, over the Laboratory School, Dewey resigned in 1904 and accepted a position in the philosophy department at Columbia University, where he remained for the rest of his long and productive career. Once Dewey left Chicago and the Laboratory School, his days of direct experimentation with education came to an end; at Columbia he was professor of philosophy and only occasionally wrote books and articles directly pertaining to education. According to William Heard Kilpatrick, Dewey's great admirer and colleague in Progressive education, Dewey ranks with Plato and Aristotle, and "more than any other one person is responsible for changing the tone and temper of American education" from 1910 to 1940.[3]

On the other side of 120th Street (which has been called "the widest street in the world," as it separates the rigorously academic and intellectual Columbia University from the university's Teachers College), was William Heard Kilpatrick (1871–1965). At Teachers College, Kilpatrick expounded upon Dewey's educational theories and ideas and taught prospective teachers and administrators how to implement them in the classroom. Unlike Dewey, Kilpatrick had considerable teaching experience: four years teaching high school mathematics, one year as a principal and seventh-grade teacher, nine years as a professor of mathematics at Mercer College, his alma mater in Macon, Georgia, and another at the University of Georgia. In 1907 he had gone to Teachers College for graduate school, and in 1913 had joined the faculty, being appointed assistant professor in 1915 and full professor two years later.

Apparently Kilpatrick was a good teacher. Testimonies show the high regard in which many former students held him, and he was immensely popular at Teachers College. He was called "the million-dollar professor" since his dynamic teaching style drew the tuition payments of thousands of students to his packed classes.[4] Kilpatrick is estimated to have taught more than 35,000 students, from all over the world, during his career at Teachers College. He was heavily influenced by Dewey's ideas; in fact, one can often detect verbal echoes of Dewey's work—especially from *How We Think*—in Kilpatrick's writings. But Kilpatrick also uses the terminology and ideas of Thorndike's connectionism to give his writings a scientific and objective veneer. As it happens, Kilpatrick took Dewey's ideas further probably than Dewey himself had intended.

Together Dewey and Kilpatrick exercised a profound influence on the educational philosophy of Teachers College and, through the school's leadership position, on public education in the United States. As graduates of Teachers College assumed positions not only in the classrooms of the expanding public school system but in the administrative offices of the public schools, the education and pedagogy departments in universities and state colleges, and in national think tanks, they spread the doctrine of Progressive education and established the public school system on the foundation of Dewey's and Kilpatrick's beliefs. (Lawrence Cremin found that in 1930 Teachers College was staffing 20 percent of instructional and administrative positions in the country's teacher education institutions, and that almost every national education committee counted a Teachers College professor among its members.) Our school system today is largely a product of Progressive education, and many of our assumptions and unquestioned beliefs about schools, knowledge, and education were created during the Progressive Era. Its peculiar cant, vocabulary, and dogma survive with vigor in today's colleges of education, in the administrative offices of American public schools, and in national thinking about education.[5]

THE QUEST FOR MENTAL AND SOCIAL
UNITY AND INTEGRITY

Dewey, the Progressives, and other intellectuals of the age, fearing the seeming chaos of American society and its centrifugal forces ("Society," writes Henry Steele Commager of the 1890s, "always fluid in America, seemed in process of disintegration . . ."[6]), believed that society and the individual needed to be reconstructed and reformed. The chief problem, as Dewey saw it, was fragmentation at all levels. The individual was fragmented: the faculty psychology that prevailed before the scientific era fragmented man into artificial divisions of will, memory, intellect, and so forth, and philosophical dualism (mind versus body) drew an unnecessary and harmful division in a person's experience. The result was an overemphasis on the intellect, with a corresponding denigration of action and work, and, in the schools, complete neglect of a child's social, physical, and emotional nature. Furthermore, the old psychology and philosophical dualism separated man from his environment and society; it assumed that man lives and operates in a sort of existential vacuum, regardless of his surroundings, peers, and society. Because of these erroneous beliefs about the nature of man, society itself was rent by artificial divisions created by capitalism and competitive individualism; the system pitted rich against poor and oppressed the many for the benefit of the few. According to the Progressives, this fragmentation—of the individual, between his mind and body, and in relations with his fellows in society—and of society, through the fragmented individuals comprising and constituting it—had brought on the social chaos they deplored.

Dewey and his associates in Progressive education aimed to design schools that would perfect American society by creating a new individual and a new concept of individualism, built upon the scientific basis of psychology. That the school is, first and foremost, an instrument of social reform, is a constant through Dewey's long and prolific career: "I believe that education is the fundamental method of social progress and reform," he states in an 1897 publication. And years later: ". . . The chief means of continuous, graded, economical improvement and social rectification lies in utilizing the opportunities of educating the young to modify prevailing types of thought and desire." The idea of improving American society through the schools was by no means new; the schools had long been seen as a means of social amelioration, a view going all the way back to Jefferson's letter to George Wythe and Horace Mann's drive to establish common schools. Yet to many prominent intellectuals the perfection of American society now seemed entirely possible through schools constructed along scientific lines. This was a pretty tall order for ordinary teachers—to change society and human nature—and incidentally established an antagonistic relationship between teachers and the public, who might have thought that schools should concentrate on educating children in the three Rs and traditional academic subjects, rather than try to reform society and change human nature.[7]

In order to create the wholly new individual needed to reform the dysfunctional, burgeoning industrial democracy, Dewey had to create an entirely new educational philosophy. What he produced contained much more social psychology than academic content—indeed, he calls education "primarily a social affair" and educational science "first of all a social science." His approach sought *unity* and *integrity* for both the individual and society. For Dewey and the Progressive educators, the individual had to be "integrated"—a kind of buzzword in the psychology of Progressive education. As elaborated by Dewey, the concept of personal "integration" has its roots in Dewey's Hegelian background. "Hegel's synthesis of subject and object, matter and spirit, the divine and the human was . . . no mere intellectual formula; it operated as an immense release, a liberation," recalls Dewey in a memoir of his earlier days, when he found relief from the various divisions he had experienced while growing up in New England ("isolation of self from the world, of soul from body, of nature from God"). Thus Dewey and Kilpatrick (and other Progressives as well) posit the students' "integration" as a goal for the schools. "A paramount school objective should be that a child shall not simply grow, but shall grow more and more unified," writes Kilpatrick—and that could be accomplished only under his and Dewey's brand of education.

Apparently the concept of "integration" was as nebulous then as it is now. After it had been used for decades in educational writings, L. Thomas Hopkins, a professor of education at Teachers College, wrote a book on "integration" in 1937 and argued, "The term *integration* bids fair to become increasingly helpful as a point of orientation in educational thinking. In the first place, it refuses to lend itself easily to mere definition." Considering that the Progressives constantly touted their brand of education as scientific, one must be troubled by Hopkins's— and Dewey's as well as other Progressive educators'—eagerness to devote a young person's time and efforts in school to so nebulous a concept.[8]

An integrated personality, the goal of Progressive education, seems to have denoted a Perfect Citizen, a well-adapted individual who, in service to society and his fellows, does what he wants and wants to do what he does. He is integrated when all aspects of his existence—his emotional, intellectual, physical, and social beings—are equally and harmoniously developed, when there is no artificial distinction between mind and body. Not only does the individual live for the improvement of society by applying reason and the experimental method in the minutiae of his vigorous and confident day-to-day life, but society exists for the perfection of each individual by allowing each an equal opportunity for self-expression and self-realization. Only in that way could society be reformed: its main purpose was to fulfill the individual's capabilities, and the focus of the individual's life was to meet his highest potential in service to his democratic community and society. When the individual is restored to his natural place in society, and society is composed of integrated individuals who are free to express themselves, but for the good of society, the individual will be integrated. "Our aim," writes Kilpatrick, "is such an integration and organization of all the habits in char-

acter that the full character shines out in each act, speaks through each
act." Dewey himself compared his new program to a Copernican revolution in educational thought.[9]

THE ASSAULT ON RUGGED INDIVIDUALISM

One key to achieving a society perfected with integrated individuals was
to socialize the young by emphasizing traits other than individual intellect. Progressive educators believed that America's laissez-faire economy
and tradition of rugged, competitive individualism were relics from a by-
gone era. Now they had become a menace. New conditions demanded
a new social philosophy that stressed cooperative action rather than
rugged individualism ("or is it ragged?" individualism, as Dewey once
commented). Showing the influence of George H. Mead, with whom
he had become good friends while at Michigan—Dewey is said even to
have given up his own research into social psychology after meeting
Mead—Dewey explains, "Society is a society of individuals and the individual is always a social individual. He has no existence by himself. He
lives in, for, and by society, just as society has no existence excepting in
and through the individuals who constitute it." Only through interactions with the environment and society does the individual assume and
develop individuality, identity, and mind. Mind is "a consequence of
the manifestation of instincts under the conditions supplied by associated life in the family, the school, the market place and the forum. . . ."
Our social environment and our biological instincts therefore combine
to make us who and what we are and how we act and think. We assume
all knowledge and powers through a social medium, for knowledge is itself a social construct which we acquire only by participating in society.
". . . In fact, knowledge is a function of association and communication;
it depends upon tradition, upon tools and methods socially transmitted,
developed and sanctioned. Faculties of effectual observation, reflection
and desire are habits acquired under the influence of the culture and institutions of society, not ready-made inherent powers," Dewey explains.

There is no such thing as private knowledge. Only through active participation in society can the human being operate and meet his highest potential.[10]

To change the individual, Dewey advised, we must therefore change the conditions in which he lives and works, his physical and social environment; this will bring about change in a person's psychic life and behavior. Contrasting the old individualistic psychology with the new social psychology, Dewey writes, "The new point of view treats social facts as the material of an experimental science, where the problem is that of modifying belief and desire—that is to say mind—by enacting specific changes in the social environment."[11]

Consequently, in Dewey's educational philosophy, socialization of the young—*not* intellectual development—receives priority because it is the key to reforming society:

> The introduction [into elementary school] of active occupations, of nature-study, of elementary science, of art, of history; the relegation of the merely symbolic and formal to a secondary position; the change in the moral school atmosphere, in the relation of pupils and teachers—of discipline; the introduction of more active, expressive, and self-directing factors—all these are not mere accidents, they are necessities of the larger social evolution. It remains but to organize all these factors, to appreciate them in their fullness of meaning, and to put the ideas and ideals involved into complete, uncompromising possession of our school system. To do this means to make each one of our schools an embryonic community life, active with types of occupations that reflect the life of the larger society and permeated throughout with the spirit of art, history, and science. When the school introduces and trains each child of society into membership within such a little community, saturating him with the spirit of service, and providing him with the instruments of effective self-direction, we shall have the deepest and best guaranty of a larger society which is worthy, lovely, and harmonious.[12]

The mastery of academic subjects is much less important, possibly even detrimental to progressive education's social goals. The reason behind this view is not difficult to find. Seeing that a laissez-faire economy and rugged individualism (sustained by a dysfunctional and unscientific educational system and social philosophy) had been responsible for the social hemorrhages of their day, Dewey and the Progressives thought it imperative that the people discover themselves as a unified political force and make the United States a true democracy, in which the wealth and benefits of the nation would be more evenly distributed among the people for the benefit of all, not the few. Kilpatrick put it in his own peculiar way: the common people, he writes, "are in danger of being mentally and morally overwhelmed by the growing bigness." To meet that challenge, he says, "The school must somehow help people to assert themselves, somehow help them to overcome the threats of overpowering bigness."[13]

Rugged individualism pitted the people against one another and divided their energies and power. The schools of the past had embraced the traditional beliefs of the individual and had to be changed to address the conditions of the new age, in which the group and collective action were more important than an individual's efforts, beliefs, and desires. "The outworn and irrelevant ideas of competitive private individualism, of *laissez faire*, of isolated competitive nationalism are all strenuously inculcated [in our present schools]," Dewey and other Progressive educators write during the darkest days of the Great Depression. "We are demanding the abolition of all such indoctrination, on the ground that it is injurious equally to the health and growth of genuine individuality and to that of a collective public order." The vehemence with which some embraced collective action and disparaged the individual can be seen in something Herbert Croly had written decades earlier: the nonunion laborer was a species of industrial derelict that should be rejected "as emphatically, if not as ruthlessly, as the gardener rejects the weeds in his garden for the benefit of fruit- and flower-bearing plants." The purpose of education, Croly declared, "consists chiefly in experimental collective action aimed at the realization of the collective purpose." While in the old schools, students—under duress, quiet, and isolated from one another—learned formal academic subjects for selfish reasons, the new schools would focus on the reform of society and socialization of the young. The only knowledge worth being called knowledge, writes Dewey, "is obtained only by participating intimately and actively in activities of social life."[14]

Dewey claims further that an individual's attention to traditional academic subjects is selfish: "The mere absorption of facts and truths is so exclusively individual an affair that it tends very naturally to pass into selfishness. There is no obvious social motive for the acquirement of mere learning, there is no clear social gain in success thereat." This anti-individualistic and even anti-intellectual stance is exemplified in comments about the Francis Parker School in Chicago, the philosophy of which Dewey and his daughter Evelyn described in 1915: "Studying alone out of a book is an isolated and unsocial performance; the pupil may be learning the words before him, but he is not learning to act with other people, to control and arrange his actions and thoughts so that other persons have an equal opportunity to express themselves in a shared experience."[15]

The triumph of socialization over the development of the intellect came in 1918 with the completion and promulgation of the "Cardinal Principles of Secondary Education" by the National Education Association's Commission on the Reorganization of Secondary Education. This document repudiated the rigorous academic curriculum of the Report of the Committee of Ten of 1893 and recommended instead that American students take courses to meet the following goals: "1. Health. 2. Command of fundamental processes. 3. Worthy home membership. 4. Vocation. 5. Citizenship. 6. Worthy use of leisure. 7. Ethical character." Academics is given some attention in the "command of fundamental processes," a phrase omitted from the first draft of the document. Kilpatrick, a member of the commission, proposed that algebra be required only of college-bound students, since knowledge of mathematics was used as a badge of superiority. The nonacademic and social lessons of school, Kilpatrick writes, "are not only no less important [than the academic], but in certain respects even more important, because they underlie the discharge of one's duty to himself and to society. Without

them a merely bookish education may be a menace."[16] (He does not en-
tertain the possibility that an ignorant citizen may be menace to himself
and his society.)

Since academic education, with its emphasis on individual learning,
dominated the school day, leaving little time for socialization and indoctrination, Kilpatrick advised, "Rid the schools of dead stuff. . . . For most
pupils Latin can and should follow Greek into the discard. Likewise
with most of mathematics for most pupils. Much of present history study
should give way to study of social problems. . . . Modern foreign languages can hardly be defended for most who now study them."[17] The
irony of these recommendations is that Kilpatrick wanted the schools to
produce students who commanded breadth of knowledge and could
also further scientific research in order to solve the problems of society
in a modern, industrial world.

The anti-individualistic stance of this strain of Progressive education
is terribly destructive of learning. While there can be no doubt that a
young person needs to learn how to live in society and cooperate with
others in pursuit of his own and society's goals, it is also true that each
student's focus in life remains the satisfaction of his own desires and the
development of his unique abilities and powers. Even altruism is ultimately selfish, as acting for others produces feelings of pleasure. Self-
interest is a remarkably powerful motivator; "the public good" or "the
collective good" is far too abstract, too distant, too intangible to motivate
a student for long. A proper middle course between the ugly extremes of
rugged individualism and Dewey's disappearing individual would have
students learning to see that their survival and welfare are wrapped up in
the survival and welfare of society. The individual always remains to
some extent an island in the social sea; he naturally views all events in
life from his own perspective. But he must learn to see that his survival
and his desires are best achieved within the bounds of society and its
laws.

In Dewey's social/educational philosophy, with its behaviorist foundation, the individual is subsumed within the group. His actions and
thoughts pass under the control of the nameless and amorphous group
and the physical environment, with the result that no one (except, of

course, the teacher, whose training in scientific pedagogy is thought to endow him with divine powers of discerning and meeting students' real needs and wants) is responsible for anything. The dominant factor in the student's learning is therefore not the student and his struggle to understand reality and maximize his potential; rather it is the *teacher* and his ability to manipulate the physical and social environment. The way adults control the education of the young, Dewey writes, "is by controlling the environment in which they act, and hence think and feel." As the students change, as the community changes, the teacher determines what the students learn and do not learn, and whether or not they learn. Academic and intellectual content are to be taught, Dewey writes, using the theories of behaviorism, "by means of the action of the environment in calling out certain responses." The student as an independent individual, able to stand out from the environment and apart from it or in opposition to it when necessary, seems scarcely to exist—the demands of the tyrannical group and environment (whose characteristics have been created by the teacher) determine all.[18]

Yet the acquisition of knowledge demands an assertion of the self, an independence of view, an ability to be both in and outside the environment, both physical and social. When I learn, I make understanding *mine* and peculiarly *mine*. Others may know the same facts, but when I learn them they become *my* knowledge, an enriching clarification and illumination of *my* experience. Of course it is selfish; I am making the knowledge my own, for my own individual purposes, so that I can better understand *my* existence and enhance it, and even improve the society of which I am a part. In learning, I am creating something that no one else can experience (my understanding), because learning is an enrichment and enlargement of my experience, an improvement of my understanding of the world.

Dewey's definition of education shows very clearly that he understood this. Education, he wrote, "is that reconstruction or reorganization of experience which adds to the meaning of experience, and which increases ability to direct the course of subsequent experience." In other words, when a person learns something new, he must revise his ways of thinking to accommodate the new information, and reconcile his old thoughts and past knowledge to fit with the new. The new knowledge has meaning for him, for it helps him understand the complexities of the world and society he lives in. This reorganizing or reconstructing is an active affair: no one creates knowledge for us; we create understanding from experience, something Dewey knew well. One good thing that came from Progressive education is recognition of the fact that one learns by doing, through one's own experience, and that what students learn should have real, vital connections to their experience instead of being words merely recited and poorly understood. Yet note how deceptive is Dewey's language when he describes the groundwork for a proposed secondary school: "If the elementary period has been adequately lived through, so that the child has secured positive experience in all these directions, has had intellectual hunger kept alive and quickened, and has acquired working use of the main lines of investigation, there is no doubt that a very large amount of technical generalization and of special detail can easily be acquired in a comparatively short time." No individual struggle to understand seems necessary—the child must only "adequately live through" his time at school and enjoy positive experiences in order to learn a very large amount "easily" in little time. As greater detail will show, Dewey and the other Progressives did not expect students to struggle and strain at school.[19]

In all this social psychology and behaviorism, the individual and his struggle to understand his world are lost. Learning seems more of something that merely happens to him by virtue of larger social or environmental forces outside his control.

DEWEY'S ANTI-FORMALISM

Another key element in creating the integrated individual within an integrated society was to restore knowledge and its formation and function to its proper place in human affairs. Dewey and Progressive educators were unrelentingly hostile to the teaching of formal knowledge, that is, to the idea of a teacher coming into a classroom and setting forth a lesson on, say, the concept of the square root, the use of the subjunctive in conditional sentences, or the causes of the American Civil War, which the students would then dutifully learn. The reasons were partly psychological and partly social. All knowledge, Dewey believed, is a social construct: it is created by society, for social purposes, to meet social needs; there is no such thing as private knowledge. Before there were schools, Dewey and the Progressives believed, children learned naturally as they grew up in society, for there was no separation between learning and living. Before industrialization, growing up on a farm or in communal life provided natural learning through one's everyday life. Learning was life, and life was learning, there being no boundary where one stopped and the other started.

Yet as civilization became more complex, Dewey theorized, this natural living-and-learning relationship ended. The schools took responsibility for teaching what students needed to learn. But the schools soon separated the knowledge they taught from the society and reality in which the knowledge functioned and served a vital role, so eventually the knowledge became artificial, distant from dynamic society, something used even to separate people by classes. Students were expected to learn knowledge divorced from its social context and social purposes; consequently what teachers taught and what students learned at school came to be arbitrary, something to learn in and for itself, not for social purposes or the improvement of society. The education of his day, Dewey writes, "is an education dominated almost entirely by the medieval conception of learning. It is something which appeals for the most part simply to the intellectual aspect of our natures, our desire to learn, to accumulate information, and to get control of the symbols of learning; not to our impulses and tendencies to make, to do, to create, to produce, whether in the form of utility or of art." Formal knowledge even leads to division among classes: "The academic education turns out future citizens with no sympathy for work done with the hands, and with absolutely no training for understanding the most serious of present-day social and political difficulties." Eighteen years later, during the depression, Dewey has essentially the same view: "In spite of all educational endeavors, there are many subjects in our schools which remain academic and aloof and which are pursued in a pedantic spirit, or from the traditional identification of culture with a polish belonging to the few in distinction from the mass." Academic education produces "factory fodder" as the separation of knowledge from conduct "leads to permanent division in one's psychic makeup."[20] Dewey ignores the fact that if the masses gain academic knowledge, it can no longer be used to separate the few from the hoi polloi—if everyone learns math, it cannot be used as a badge of superiority.

Dewey objected to the teaching of formal academic subjects also on psychological grounds. When the lesson is presented by the teacher in the traditional manner, the students learn the thoughts and findings of others, not through their own experience. Dewey objected to what he called the *logical* approach of teaching: academic subjects were presented in a manner that was logical to the teacher and to scholars, but not to the students, who needed a more basic experience in order to construct their knowledge. In fact, he claims, students might be harmed by having to learn formal knowledge: "experience has proved that formalization is hostile to genuine mental activity and to sincere emotional expression and growth."[21] Unfortunately he provides no proof for such an assertion. The music of Mozart, Beethoven, and Brahms provides examples of formal composition with genuine emotional expression, and in Latin the poetry of Catullus and Virgil are highly formal yet express sincere emotion. Yet educators today continue to crusade against the teaching of "mere knowledge" under the highly questionable argument that the development of the intellect is hostile to emotional growth and sincere expression. (Were that so, our ignorant students would be well adjusted; yet the United States leads the industrialized world in teenage pregnancy, drug and alcohol use, and juvenile crime.) A more judicious and sober view would hold that a certain amount of formalization in intellectual and artistic endeavors in fact provides structure and context for easier and more fluent expression of emotions and thoughts. Of course there is a point at which slavery to established norms produces stale and desiccated art and literature.

Hence Dewey's emphasis on students' learning by doing, and his hostility to what Progressives derisively referred to as "subject-matter-set-out-to-be-learned." The new approach became the infamous *child-centered* education. Instead of lessons presented by the teacher in a logical, intellectual fashion, the students would follow their interests, learning only what they had to in order to solve problems arising from their own experience and needs in social situations. They would thus become integrated personalities as their instincts, intellects, emotional lives, social natures, and bodies worked harmoniously to broaden and reorganize their experience. In theory they would learn the same academic material that students in traditional schools did, but more effectively because they would create their own knowledge through activities they chose for themselves, rather than learning from fear of a teacher's ruler or of angry parents. Being naturally and instinctively interested in the world and society around them, the Progressives believed, students would learn best by studying the things that interested them in their environment and surrounding society. In the process not only would they learn the various arts and sciences but how that knowledge was used in modern industrial society. Life becomes education, and education becomes life: ". . . If the school is related as a whole to life as a whole, its various aims and ideals—culture, discipline, information, utility—cease to be variants, for one of which we must select one study and for another another. The growth of the child in the direction of social capacity and service, his larger and more vital union with life, becomes the unifying aim; and discipline, culture, and information fall into place as phases of this growth." The students must only live their normal lives (which certainly doesn't include formal academics) and they will learn what they need to. Dewey summed it up in what became a mantra of sorts for Progressive education: "I believe that education . . . is a process of living and not a preparation for future living."[22]

The student thus learns all he needs to, and all we want him to, just by pursuing his own interests and by living a full, free life interacting with his peers, teachers, and society. Children, for example, will wonder where bread comes from; the teacher can then arrange for them to grow grain, which they will grind into flour and bake into loaves. This experience can serve as an introduction to the history of civilization. (The children in Dewey's Laboratory School at the University of Chicago did in fact grow their own grain, grind it, and bake it into bread.) Or by learning to cook, children may be introduced to the rudiments of chemistry. Dewey notes that children playing house are conducting research into life (more likely, children playing house are merely rehearsing what they perceive to be reality).[23] Perhaps students will wonder where clothing comes from; a new lesson on clothing and its place in human society will offer them countless opportunities to learn in a genuine, natural way, free of compulsion.

Dewey's faith in this type of learning is almost comical: "You can concentrate the history of all mankind into the evolution of the flax, cotton, and wool fibers into clothing," he declares with unbounded optimism. Later he reiterates, "If we seek the kingdom of heaven, educationally, all other things shall be added unto us—which, being interpreted, is that if we identify ourselves with the real instincts and needs of childhood, and ask only after its fullest assertion and growth, the discipline and information and culture of adult life shall come in their due season." One can see the absurd lengths to which this notion was taken in the results of an informal poll of more than six hundred graduate students in education, reported in 1951: they voted that Latin, Greek, and mathematics offered little potential for educational growth in contrast to the great potential offered by playing with dolls. Perhaps they were inspired by something Dewey had written: ". . . Any subject, from Greek to cooking, and from drawing to mathematics, is intellectual, if intellectual at all, not in its fixed inner structure, but in its function—in its power to start and direct significant inquiry and reflection." ". . . As long as any topic makes an immediate appeal, it is not necessary to ask what it is good for."[24] In the hands of someone with Dewey's acumen, doll-playing may indeed lead to intellectual growth. Most people, however, do not have Dewey's intellectual power. He possessed a powerful intellect because of his rigorous study of the classics, the sciences, mathematics, foreign languages, history, and philosophy. To make the study of dolls a truly intellectual adventure, one would need a great deal of background knowledge and habits of analysis, both of which are acquired through rigorous and formal study of basic subjects.

THE DOCTRINE OF INTEREST

Since Dewey did not believe in teaching subject matter per se (he even discusses the question of whether or not students should be aware that they are learning), the teachers take on a new and different role. Teachers are crucial in Dewey's educational philosophy because, being trained in scientific psychology (that is, social psychology and behaviorism), they alone are competent to control and manipulate the environment in accordance with the students' needs and interests. "We are born organic beings associated with others," Dewey writes, "but we are not born members of a community. The young have to be brought within the traditions, outlook and interests which characterize a community by means of education: by unremitting instruction and by learning in connection with the phenomena of overt association." Without teachers to mold the young into citizens with desirable traits, the schools would be resigned to the old competitive individualism and its attendant chaos and brutal competition.[25]

Dewey was dead set against teaching subject matter as subject matter, but he was not hostile to the intellect and organized knowledge. He simply did not like the idea of students learning academic subjects because they were told to, without a genuine inner need compelling them. Other educators had sought to make students active, engaged learners by making lessons and subject matter interesting; Dewey argued against that idea. He felt it was inefficient and spoiled the child with attempts to "sugar-coat" the subject. Instead, Dewey writes, the teacher must run the class in accordance with the students' interests and felt needs. He can do that by posing problems, the solutions to which are so imperative and vital to the students that they feel compelled to solve the problems and thereby learn subject matter. The teacher's job is to "psychologize" the subject:

> When the subject-matter has been psychologized, that is, viewed as an outgrowth of present tendencies and activities, *it is easy* to locate in the present some obstacle, intellectual, practical, or ethical, which can be

handled more adequately if the truth in question be mastered. This need supplies motive for the learning. An end which is the child's own carries him on to possess the means of its accomplishment.[26]

In other words, the teacher must find a problem that so urgently calls for a solution by the students that they solve it and, in the process, naturally, willingly, and wholeheartedly learn subject matter and become integrated personalities. Dewey repeats the theme many times in a variety of ways during his prolific career:

> The problem [of education] is to find what conditions must be fulfilled in order that study and learning will naturally and necessarily take place, what conditions must be presented so that pupils will make the responses which cannot help having learning as their consequence. The pupil's mind is no longer to be on study or learning. It is given to doing the things that the situation calls for, while learning is the result. The method of the teacher, on the other hand, becomes a matter of finding the conditions which will call out self-educative activity, or learning, and of coöperating with the activities of the pupils so that they have learning as their consequence.[27]

> The problem of instruction is thus that of finding material which will engage a person in specific activities having an aim or purpose of moment or interest to him, and dealing with things not as gymnastic appliances but as conditions for the attainment of ends.[28]

> The educator's part in the enterprise of education is to furnish the environment which stimulates responses and directs the learner's course.[29]

> It is [the educator's] business to arrange for the kind of experiences which, while they do not repel the student, but rather engage his activities are, nevertheless, more than immediately enjoyable since they promote having desirable future experiences.[30]

> [The teacher's job is] to provide the materials and the conditions by which organic curiosity will be directed into investigations that have an aim and that produce results in the way of increase of knowledge, and by which social inquisitiveness will be converted into ability to find out

things known to the others, an ability to ask questions of books as well as of persons.[31]

The starting point [of education] is always the impulse to self expression; the educational process is to supply the material and provide (positively and negatively) the conditions so that the expression shall occur in its normal social direction, both as to content and form or mode.[32]

If we can discover a child's urgent needs and powers, and if we can supply an environment of materials, appliances, and resources — physical, social, and intellectual — to direct their adequate operation, we shall not have to think about interest. It will take care of itself. The problem of educators, teachers, parents, the state is to provide the environment that induces educative or developing activities, and where these are found the one thing needful in education is found.[33]

It is crucial, according to Dewey, that the students learn in this manner if they are to become integrated. If students are forced to learn without an inner compelling need, they will suffer psychological damage or mental disintegration and consequently perpetuate a disintegrated society. The goal of mental and social integration thus produces — in the third element of the Progressive Paradigm — an attitude that persists in American educational thinking today: students must be free to follow their own interests, to learn only what they want and feel a need to learn. They must never be forced to learn formal knowledge presented by teachers in lessons that do not satisfy a preexisting need (a belief held even today by many in the colleges of education). Somehow the teacher must teach the subject in such a way that by learning, students meet their needs and become integrated socially and psychologically. Teachers must devise lessons in accordance with what students want to learn, not what teachers want them to learn. It is immoral to have students feel strain while working at problems not of their own choosing and creation.[34]

From this complex of ideas — socialization, anti-formalism, and learning through natural, normal living — William Heard Kilpatrick created the "Project Method," or as he also called it, the "purposeful act."

As the student feels a need arising within his own experience and sets out to solve the problem, he learns what he needs to and becomes integrated. "As the purposeful act is thus the typical unit of the worthy life in a democratic society, so also should it be made the typical unit of school procedure," he claims.[35] Kilpatrick's description of the educational and moral benefits gained when two boys build a castle shows how the Progressive method aimed to educate students intellectually, morally, socially, and physically. (Today's educationists would praise the cross-curricular nature of the assignment, as would Dewey, who felt it unnecessary to have academic subjects taught separately—that is, English taught as English, biology as biology, and so forth.)

> Some older boys were making a castle of concrete. Was it art they were studying? Yes, the "project" began with a broad-minded teacher of "art." But was it not also history—and warfare? And was it not also chemistry or physics or whatever be the science or technology that tells us about making concrete? And was it not oral English, since the boys must explain on exhibition day all that they had done? And why not social-morals, since they had to learn how to compose their differences and stick to the job as one failure after another made increasing demands on moral strength? And was it not also a larger social-morals as they studied the significance of the castle in that long warfare when private greed had at length to yield to law and order?[36]

If left to pursue their own interests, students would naturally desire to learn what they needed to, "because children are interested in the things they need to learn" (a belief not uncommonly held today), just as, we must suppose, they are naturally interested in the foods and behaviors most conducive to health and growth.[37]

Under the Progressive method the teacher's job is, Dewey much to the contrary, less than easy: to create a structureless environment, liberated of the strictures of formalism, in which students will learn naturally, through pursuing their own interests, knowledge that is highly structured, formal, and abstract. Moreover the student must never be compelled or forced to learn what he has no interest in, otherwise he will suffer "a virtual division of attention and the corresponding disintegration of character, intellectually and morally." If the educative process does not coincide with the child's activity, Dewey claims, "it will result in friction, or disintegration, or arrest of the child nature." When a child's activities in school are not real and definite to him (that is, if the classroom activities don't stem from his instincts and drives, which, apparently, fresh and untainted from the bosom of Nature, are always right), Dewey tells us, "the inevitable result is artificiality, nervous strain, and either physical and emotional excitement or else deadening of powers." A student forced to learn something he really has no interest in, like multiplication tables, explains Kilpatrick, "therefore conforms, but principally on the outside. Inside he still finds the tables uninteresting and gives himself but partially to them. Thus follows what Dewey calls the danger of a 'divided self.' If he works long enough under a regime of outward conformity but inward rejection, he will grow warped. Thus did Dewey anticipate what we now call 'personality maladjustment.'" The division of self—caused by being compelled to learn things one feels no need for—makes for "weakness of character, for inefficiency of moral outlook and response. . . ." Kilpatrick chastises teachers for keeping students after school and keeping them from their normal, desired activities (such as football) after they have failed to learn during class. The concomitant learnings in such a situation are disastrous, as the student builds up destructive negative attitudes.[38]

Yet if the teacher manipulates the environment in accordance with the students' natural interests and instincts (whatever they may be), the students will be so captivated they will learn naturally and without nervous strain or the feeling of compulsion, and will even grow into integrated personalities. Learning may not come easy to them, but the problems the students wish to solve will have so much meaning for them that they won't notice how intently they are working. The teacher can accomplish this by relating all subject matter to the student's interests and to community and social life. The problem in teaching history, for example, is "giving material which takes vital hold upon the child," and the science teacher's job "is that of inducing a vital and personal experiencing." How absurdly idealistic this conception is can be seen in Dewey's *Interest and Effort in Education,* a book that Kilpatrick describes as "epoch-making." When we solve problems in real-world situations, Dewey writes, "The existing experience holds us for its own sake," and we needn't struggle to maintain our attention on the task—the nature of the problem and its importance to our lives command our attention. When we are that absorbed in solving a real-world problem vital to our interests, "The emotional accompaniment of the progressive growth of a course of action, a continual improvement of expansion and of achievement, is happiness—mental content or peace, which when emphatic, is called joy, delight."[39] (Perhaps Dewey never had to fix a leaking toilet or rid the yard of crabgrass. Resolving such real-world problems is scarcely emotionally fulfilling, but it depends chiefly upon one's attitude—that is, which thought we decide to pay attention to, as James put it.)

Dewey and his daughter also suggest that students should look forward to school as a pleasure—an ironic goal for one who wanted schooling to be like living. Can we reasonably expect to look forward to life's travails as a pleasure? Do we not mislead the young when we imply that life is supposed to be pleasure? Does that not prepare them for a lifetime of disappointment, disillusionment, and cynicism when life turns out to be less than fun? Do we always get to do in life only what we want to do? Does society never make just demands on us that we would prefer not to meet but which we must do in order to fulfill our duties? But then, Dewey does say that if people don't like their jobs, we should consider "what the social condition is which makes productive work uninteresting and toilsome."[40]

Dewey's thinking, later seconded by Kilpatrick, is not uncommon in public education today. Many parents, administrators, students, and teachers will, without hesitation, declare it of paramount importance that the student enjoy learning, not simply that he succeed at learning, in order that he may be a lifelong learner. The assumption is that a student cannot and will not learn unless the learning is fun or natural, not to mention the morally questionable assumption that the supreme good in life is individual pleasure.

THOSE INCOMPETENT TEACHERS

If the teacher is incompetent and cannot teach in accordance with the demands of Dewey and Kilpatrick, the student will not learn. In Progressive education, the student is not expected to overcome conditions not to his liking; the teacher must adapt conditions to the student's interests and felt needs. Learning in Progressive education—and in American public education today—is thus unnecessarily conditional. Students are not expected to pursue success outside the possibility that the teacher can create an environment suited to the whims of each individual child; outside the possibility that the student can learn formal and abstract knowledge via an informal discovery approach in a structureless environment; outside the unlikely possibility that the teacher can create a situation so enthralling for all his students that in their passion to learn they will forget themselves. Students are expected to achieve only if they have the Perfect Teacher, and teachers are expected to do it all.[41] "From the beginning," comments Lawrence Cremin, "progressivism cast the teacher in an almost impossible role: he was to be an artist of consummate skill, properly knowledgeable in his field, meticulously trained in the science of pedagogy, and thoroughly imbued with a burning zeal for social improvement." Such being the expectations (which are not uncommon today), teachers cannot but fail in their jobs.[42]

That the schools and the teachers in them were failing to create ideal environments for students Dewey repeats on occasion. And Kilpatrick felt it obvious that many, if not most, of the teachers of the day were incompetent. They no doubt persisted in teaching subject-matter-set-out-to-be-learned, regardless of the students' immediate interests and felt needs, and were probably not terribly concerned about developing integrated, more adequate personalities for producing a new society. Discussing the demands put upon the teacher in Progressive education and the unlikelihood of those demands being satisfied, Kilpatrick laments, "Remember how many inferior teachers we have." In Kilpatrick's way of thinking, it is easy to understand why teachers fail. Consider this job description he offers:

... There must be teachers who, on the one hand, sympathize with childhood, knowing thus that growing can take place only through progressive pupil activity, and who, on the other hand, see and know that growing is growing only as it leads to ever widening effectual control— who know that growing, judged thus by control, is effected only as better and more adequate ways of behavior are in fact progressively acquired, and that for this the race experience and accumulation is an invaluable treasury and source of supply, neither finished nor perfect, but yet available for fullest use.[43]

Kilpatrick again borrows from Dewey in addressing the responsibility of teachers and their accountability for their students' learning. Showing his disdain for teachers who believe that teaching involves merely delivering a lesson on subject-matter-set-out-to-be-learned, the education guru insists, "We don't teach unless children learn. . . . So teaching children must mean they learn something." Dewey had said something similar: "Teaching may be compared to selling commodities. No one sells unless someone buys. We should ridicule a merchant who said that he had sold a great many goods although no one had bought any."[44]

Dewey and Kilpatrick see only the social side of knowledge and experience, ignoring the private and individual experiences that one has during his lifetime. It is undoubtedly true that the sciences, the arts, the humanities—all our knowledge—could not exist without society and individuals communicating it. Yet at some point what one learns depends upon his own management of his thoughts, something Dewey recognized.

Ironically, Dewey's educational philosophy seeks to make students independent learners, yet they end up passive, heavily dependent upon others. The following quote from the psychologist Gordon Allport, echoing Dewey's words, shows how minuscule are the expectations that students will create their own solutions in the face of difficulties not to their liking: "Psychology provides the teacher with tools for discrimination and analysis. She cannot deal with a total, unanalyzed personality. She needs instruments of discernment to confront a personality in the forming. Specifically, psychology must tell the teacher what stimuli shall be presented to the sense-organs to obtain a desired result; what stable complexes of associations may be created; what coördinations and adaptations can be evoked and what their effect will be." Clearly, without the perfect teacher, the student is helpless.[45] For all of Dewey's rhetoric about empowering students to become effective, confident citizens actively creating an ideal democracy, they end up helpless and dependent, passive, waiting for others—psychologists and educators trained in educational and social psychology—to do what only they can do for themselves.

THE LEGACY OF PROGRESSIVE EDUCATION:
EDUCATIONAL PARALYSIS

To such extremes was the naturalistic philosophy of Progressive education carried that it led to chaos in the classroom, for any authority exercised by the teacher was seen as wrong. Teachers were not to give lessons, direct students, or manage their classrooms except to keep students from hurting themselves and one another. After occasional mild criticism of the excesses of Progressive education, Dewey, its very architect, in 1938 wrote a small book (*Experience and Education*) to oppose its extremes.[46] He argued that authority and school subjects were not inherently bad; that teachers had to exercise a measure of authority in the classroom; and that the activities of students demanded a purpose, otherwise students were running wild and acting out every impulse, yet learning little in the process. Teachers, in their defense, were merely implementing Dewey's and Kilpatrick's vision of a democratic education. Dewey continued to bash the old education, yet he faulted the excesses of the new education as well. Unfortunately there was no middle ground. The type of education Dewey envisioned—teachers presenting lessons, students following their own interests—was impossible, for one premise contradicted the other.

Dewey's failure to solve the problem in *Experience and Education* reveals the kind of educational paralysis that prevails today in most

American classrooms. Although one still finds in the colleges of education the Kilpatrickian diehards who insist that we should allow students to learn only what they feel a need to, almost everyone else understands that students cannot run wild in a classroom and be expected to learn something, that they need intelligent direction in the form of lessons on subject matter. To that extent, Progressive education has been repudiated.

Yet Progressive ideas have left a substantial residue in our national thinking about education. One can see this influence in many of the attitudes and practices in our public schools today that make widespread high achievement among our students highly unlikely, if not impossible. Since by Dewey's principles the lessons are supposed to emanate from students' interests, needs, and abilities, there has been almost a taboo against teacher-centered, whole-class instruction on formal academic topics. In a 2002 survey conducted by the Center for Survey Research and Analysis at the University of Connecticut, 56 percent of fourth- and eighth-grade teachers described their teaching philosophy as more characteristic of student-directed than of teacher-directed. If students in classes run according to Deweyan ideals met high standards, there would be no argument against the Progressive Paradigm; yet studies show that students in classes where the teacher simply teaches a formal, straightforward, in-depth lesson to the whole class learn more. The greater effectiveness of teacher-directed instruction over child-centered approaches for economically disadvantaged children has been proven conclusively by Project Follow Through, a longitudinal study of more than 70,000 students taught by 20 different approaches in more than 180 schools. The children whose teachers gave carefully structured lessons far outstripped the children in the child-centered classes; some of the latter even performed more poorly than the control group.[47]

In their studies of elementary schools in Taipei, Sendai, and Minneapolis, Harold W. Stevenson and James W. Stigler found that the teacher was the leader of the class 90 percent of the time in Taiwan, 74 percent in Japan, and only 46 percent in the United States. No one was leading the class 9 percent of the time in Taiwan, 26 percent in Japan, and 51 percent of the time in the United States. Consequently American children receive much less instruction, and their low levels of achievement are the inevitable result. That something so simple as a teacher giving the class a straightforward, in-depth lesson on an academic topic has not been the rule under the Progressive Paradigm in recent decades is shown also by the fact that such basic, no-nonsense teaching has been given its own name: Direct Instruction (it was "invented" in the 1960s by Siegfried Engelmann, then a professor of education at the University of Illinois), and a model for teaching a lesson in such a way was created in the 1980s by Madeline Hunter.[48]

Today's classrooms reveal the Progressive Paradigm's hostility to formal academic studies and its preference for affective goals. The survey by the Center for Survey Research and Analysis revealed that fewer than 15 percent of teachers believed that it was very important to teach students "specific information and skills." In contrast, more than 70 percent favored the premise that "learning how to learn is most important" for students. Not surprisingly, only 25 percent of the fourth-grade teachers and 28 percent of the eighth-grade teachers reported that during their evaluation of students' work they put primary emphasis on whether or not the student got the answer right. Thirty-eight percent of the fourth-grade teachers and 49 percent of the eighth-grade teachers set a single, class-wide standard while the majority assigned students their grades according to individual abilities. The Schools and Staffing Survey of 1990–1991 records that only 40.1 percent of public school teachers rated "Academic Excellence" as their first, second, or third most important goal. A similar finding was reached in the survey by the Center for Survey Research and Analysis. These teachers merely reflect their training, for their education professors show a bias against substantive knowledge and stress affective goals more than the intellect.[49]

Pushing students to achieve high standards through painstaking diligence would probably result in negative attitudes, which is absolutely contrary to Deweyism. For an experience to be educational, wrote Dewey, it must create the desire for future educational experiences. Teachers are therefore expected to teach in such a way that students become "lifelong learners," the modern restatement of Dewey's criterion; it is now almost ubiquitous in schools' mission statements across the country. If students must struggle to learn and meet high standards, they aren't very likely to want to learn later.

Further proof of the continued influence of Deweyan principles on the expectations of our schools comes from an anecdotal report which asked high school students to record in journals their thoughts about school, their teachers, and their classes. The authors of the report, Lawrence A. Baines and Gregory Kent Stanley, then analyzed what the students had written. The students filled the journals with bitter and scathing critiques of school, their classes, and their teachers: "Sitting on your a— and doing nothing all day is a waste. I wouldn't come to school, even if someone paid me. Personally, I'd rather take out the trash than show up for first period," sneered one student. Yet worth noting is the fact that the standards by which the teachers and schools were judged, by both the students and Baines and Stanley, represent pure Deweyism. The report shows hostility to a set curriculum, textbook learning, and standardized tests, and recommends that lessons be created in accordance with students' interests and abilities. The authors go so far as to recommend that teachers be allowed to teach to their talents (the curriculum being, apparently, a trivial matter). "Signs of joy in journals," lament Baines and Stanley, "appeared most often in descriptions of extracurricular activities, lunch, or encounters in the hallways between bells."[50] One notes that the students are to some degree *expected* by youth culture and the tenets of the Progressive Paradigm to be alienated from school subjects and to hate being expected to learn academic subjects presented in a formal manner.

4

THE PROGRESSIVE PARADIGM, PART THREE: THE CULT OF THE CHILD

The social changes that prompted the expansion of the public education system in the late nineteenth century made many people long for simpler days when life was—or so they imagined—less complicated and stressful, more beautiful and fulfilling. The evils of industrialization, urbanization, and unbridled capitalism were stark; to many Americans, modern civilization was ugly, especially when compared with the idyllic, preindustrial Eden. Acting from a psychological need to find beauty and innocence in such an ugly and squalid world, some education reformers, strongly influenced by romanticism, and others, drawing upon the psychological theories of Freud and Jung, found solace in primitivism and the idealization of the child and child nature. And they idolized creativity and the expression of individuality to counteract the growing scientism and materialism of society and education. Despite their hostility to reason and the intellect, they did not hesitate to use what they perceived to be scientific truths in pursuit of their anti-intellectual goals. This strain of Progressive educators directed their efforts toward making school practices more in accordance with, if not dominated by, the needs and idealized nature of children. This was to be "The Century of the Child."

Admittedly there was a great deal wrong about the treatment of children both in schools and in society in the late nineteenth and early twentieth centuries. It appears that in elementary schools young children had little activity during their learning. The elementary curriculum was dry and uninviting, with discipline by the rod. In the cities, parks and playgrounds were lacking, and the schoolhouses themselves were not conducive to good health and hygiene. In society at large, the ugly specter of child labor was a scandal at the turn of the century; not until the New Deal was it ended.[1] Progressive education addressed these problems and did much to improve the treatment of children in schools and in the larger society. Studies in child psychology, for example, disseminated information about the nature of children, the most important being that they were not simply adults in miniature but had their own peculiar needs for growth and development. Psychologists also were right to emphasize the role of the environment in the formation of children's characters, which helped to bring about fairer treatment of young offenders in the courts.

Like everything good in education reform, however, the changes also brought in their train many habitual assumptions about young people and schooling that haunt our educational system and even today hinder its improvement. As reformers sought to make schools more attuned to the needs and nature of youth, they projected their primitivistic and romantic beliefs of childhood and mankind onto education, creating the fourth element of the Progressive Paradigm that survives in today's thinking. That element includes the sentimental tendency to see students (no matter what their age) as passive, helpless, and dependent; a rabid hostility to formal knowledge, the intellect, and the use of reason; and the idea that, hard work being destructive to the physical and psychological health of the young, students' experience in school should be emotionally fulfilling and joyous—in other words, as Dewey had suggested, learning should be natural, stress free, and fun.

COL. FRANCIS W. PARKER AND G. STANLEY HALL

Our educational system today, with its views of children and young people, bears the stamp of two highly influential education reformers of the late nineteenth century. Their beliefs, ultimately derived from German romanticism and the writings of Pestalozzi, Froebel, and Herbart, remain current in colleges of education and in American thinking about youth in general.[2]

The first of them is Col. Francis W. Parker (1837–1902), who, according to John Dewey, was the true father of Progressive education. In contrast to many of the erudite reformers of the time, Parker was not well educated. Upon the death of his parents, Parker was apprenticed as a child to work on an uncle's farm. However eager a pupil he was, his schooling was spotty. He earned no college degree, and his highest academic experience was two and a half years he spent in Berlin studying German philosophy. He was motivated by a great love of children, though he was a classroom teacher for only six years (1853–1859). After serving in the Union army (hence his rank), for the rest of his career he showed his love of children from the office of principal or superintendent, by telling teachers how to teach. In a way, Parker created the mold for the modern superintendent—highly paid (despite his less than stellar educational background) and imperious to his often better-educated subordinates in the classroom, all the while professing a great love of children—but from a safe distance.[3]

Parker gained fame for instituting naturalistic teaching methods and nature study in the schools of Quincy, Massachusetts, in the 1870s. So enchanted were educators by the "Quincy Method," it is said that more than six thousand of them came to observe the Quincy schools in 1878 alone. The Quincy Method is said even to have initiated Progressive education. Parker quickly moved on to the schools of Boston, yet there he felt unwelcome and out of place because of his own spotty educational background and the failure of his methods to improve test results. He left after two years.[4]

As Parker was pondering whether to move to a leadership position in
the schools of Philadelphia or in the Cook County Normal School outside Chicago, the chairman of the committee on teachers and salaries
of the Cook County Board of Education informed him, "Do not
frighten us by naming too high a salary"—words we can safely assume
no teacher has ever heard. Despite a generous offer from the Philadelphia schools—reported to have been $6,000 a year—Parker in 1883 took
the position at Cook County, for it would allow him greater scope in
promoting his plan for educational reform: "*In some sense,*" he wrote to
the chairman making the generous offer, "*I am or have been made responsible for the success of a reform in teaching.*" (Parker was not above
grandstanding: he allowed himself to be greeted at assemblies with a
chorus of "See, the Conquering Hero Comes; Sound the Trumpet, Beat
the Drum.")[5]

Parker saw the old schools, with their traditional teaching methods
and materials, as anti-democratic and oppressive of the common people.
He believed that progress in democratic living, through the common
schools in America, would bring "universal salvation," whereas if the
new education failed, "free government *will* fail." In a talk on teaching
he summed up his educational philosophy: "The motive [of education]
commonly held up is the acquisition of a certain degree of skill and an
amount of knowledge. The quantity of skill and knowledge is generally
fixed by courses of study and the conventional examinations. This is a
mistake. In contrast with this false motive of education, to wit, the gaining of skill and knowledge, I place what I firmly believe to be the true
motive of all education, which is the harmonious development of the
human being, body, mind, and soul." It was education for the whole
child.[6]

If the new education was to succeed, it needed hard scientific information about the physical and psychological characteristics of the
young—obviously one must know the needs of youth before one can
meet them. The scientific study of children and their needs and characteristics owes its genesis to G. Stanley Hall (1844–1924), the other education reformer who, early in the creation of the American public
education system, influenced national thinking about education and

youth. According to his biographer, Dorothy Ross, Hall became "one of the leading figures in American scientific and intellectual life" in the 1880s and a major power in American education in the next decade.[7]

Hall grew up as the son of devoutly religious parents in Ashfield, Massachusetts, his father being a stern authority figure, his mother gentle and loving. They loomed large in Hall's subconscious for the rest of his life in his concepts of masculine authority and feminine nature. After teaching school for two years (when he was sixteen to eighteen years old), he attended Williams College and was graduated in 1867. Despite his enthusiastic embrace of evolutionary theory, Hall then studied at Union Theological Seminary and earned his divinity degree. Eventually he found his way to Germany, where he studied German philosophy (including Hegel) and psychology, the latter under Wilhelm Wundt, the father of scientific psychology. Upon returning to the United States, Hall taught French, German, English literature, rhetoric, and Anglo-Saxon (though he knew nothing about the last subject) at Antioch College. Eventually he went to Harvard, where he studied under William James and was granted the first American Ph.D. in psychology in 1878. Next he became the first professor in the new psychology in the United States, at the newly established Johns Hopkins University (later he claimed that he had also founded there the first experimental laboratory in psychology in America, something the usually tranquil James hotly disputed), and in 1887 he founded the *American Journal of Psychology*, the first American journal devoted to the new psychology. One of his students at Johns Hopkins was the young John Dewey, but Hall, apparently intimidated by Dewey's brilliance, neglected to award him a much-deserved lectureship in psychology, prompting Dewey to seek employment elsewhere, which he found at Michigan. (Hall apparently drove young talent away from Johns Hopkins, leaving the department in poor shape upon his departure.) Hall left Johns Hopkins in 1888 to become the founding president of Clark University, where he stayed for the remainder of his career. He won attention in 1909 for inviting Sigmund Freud to the United States to lecture on his theories.[8]

Hall's psychology is a combination of his romantic nature and philosophy, Christian mysticism, and his desire to be strictly scientific.

While he condemned introspective psychology in others (jealous of James's magnum opus, he complained in his negative review that it was not scientific enough, and he called a psychology textbook by the young Dewey "pathetic"), his own psychology was itself a mixture of romanticism and hereditarian science. Eventually psychologists less patient with his philosophy and shoddy research methods found fault with his findings, and in the early 1890s "Hall was toppled from the crest of the rising scientific tide," though he continued to be popular among educationists.[9]

Hall exerted enormous influence on the American educational system through his enthusiastic leadership of the child-study movement. That effort aimed to supply the hard information that teachers in the expanding school system needed in order to understand and control the children in their classrooms. Although no longer a minister, Hall now preached the gospel of natural education and child study. His messianism about child study, writes Ross, "promised the anxious teacher a new professional basis for education in science." Needing also to heighten the mission of Clark University, which was suffering financially, Hall inaugurated not only the child-study movement but also summer pedagogy sessions for teachers, and in 1891 he started another journal, *Pedagogical Seminary*, devoted solely to pedagogical issues. Hall edited this new journal and contributed many of its articles, using it as a platform for his ideas. To obtain data for his studies, he sent questionnaires about children's behavior to teachers, nurses, and mothers across the country. He then analyzed the answers and published them in article form. The most famous of the articles, "The Contents of Children's Minds on Entering School" (which is said to have marked the beginning of child study in 1883), was mostly a list of common things children did and did not know about, despite their prominence in the children's environment. Hall cited a study which showed that many children living in Berlin, for example, did not know what the Brandenburg Gate or Unter den Linden was.[10]

Researchers of a more scientific bent blasted child study's shoddy methods and the conclusions drawn from them: "Many of the most cherished doctrines of the child study enthusiasts had little or no basis in scientific fact . . . ," writes Ross. James and Dewey too disparaged the child-study movement for its odds-and-ends contribution to pedagogy. Despite their unscientific basis, however, Hall's views and findings resonated with the public and teachers, with whom he was very popular: "Hall's message during [the] last thirty years of his life—his championship of health and self-expression for childhood, his idealization of adolescent experience, and his praise of the psychoanalytic point of view—found acceptance after his time in large segments of American education, psychology, and culture," his biographer writes. Many of our ideals about childhood, youth, and adolescence can therefore be traced to Hall. With science, Ross observes, "Hall was able to elevate the romantic doctrine from a submerged and sectarian strain in educational thinking and practice to a dominant ideology of pedagogical reform." To a large extent it remains with us today and, with the ideas of various other child-cult members, exerts considerable influence on educational policy and public attitudes.[11]

IDOLIZATION AND IDEALIZATION OF THE CHILD

Parker and Hall (and, indeed, others of the age) perceived in childhood and child nature an ideal existence of beauty, innocence, and purity, in contrast to the ugly, sordid, and materialistic world in which they lived. This view of child nature is illustrated in the hyperbole of a few of Hall's statements:

> The new education . . . holds that there is one thing in nature, and one alone, fit to inspire all true men and women with more awe and reverence than Kant's starry heavens, and that is the soul and the body of the healthy young child.[12]

> Childhood is thus our pillar of cloud by day and fire by night. Other oracles may grow dim, but this one will never fail.[13]

> Just as to command inanimate nature we must constantly study, love, obey her, so to control child nature we must first, and perhaps still more

piously, study, love, obey it. The best of us teachers have far more to learn from children than we can ever hope to teach them. . . .[14]

Similar feelings were held by Colonel Parker. Parker's gushing sentimentality reveals how deeply troubled and insecure the age was, that he and others were so repelled by adult behavior and the modern world they found childish behavior to be the ideal: "The child is the climax and culmination of all God's creations, and to answer the question, 'What is the child?' is to approach nearer the still greater question, 'What is the Creator and Giver of Life?'" Elsewhere Parker declares, "I think we can take it for granted that, as God made the child His highest creation, He put into that child His divinity, and that this divinity manifests itself in the seeking for truth through the visible and tangible." He also exclaims to an audience of teachers, "The spontaneous tendencies of the child are the records of inborn divinity; we are here, my fellow teachers, for one purpose, and that purpose is to understand these tendencies and continue them in all these directions, following nature."[15]

This worship and adulation of the child led to inherent contradictions. In the observations quoted above, for example, the child is seen as superior to the adult, whether teacher or parent; in fact, as Hall writes, the child is older than the adult, since the child existed first. If carried to its logical extreme, this would mean that the child should be teaching the adult, and that schools should exist for the purpose of educating adults to the superior ways of children. Hall says as much in this rhetorical outburst: "Alas for the teacher who does not learn more from his children than he can ever hope to teach them!"—a sentiment echoed by Agnes De Lima, an author writing later in the Progressive era, the title of whose book—*Our Enemy the Child*—shows the fervor behind the Progressives' drive to liberate the child from adult tyranny. She dedicated her book "To Sigrid Aged three and a half, from whom I have learned more about education than from any pedagogue or any book." The pinnacle of existence, says Hall, is adolescence, and everything after adolescence is decadence and degradation; if the world is to be saved, he writes, it will be saved by adolescents.[16]

The reason for this glorification is simple: children are closer to nature, and nature is necessarily right. Therefore children should *not* be expected to change in ways they do not want. They are closer to nature and as a consequence are more right than the adults who rule them, for adults have been corrupted by their experience in the sordid world— after all, Jesus himself called the child the greatest in the kingdom of heaven, and advised that to enter the kingdom of heaven, one must become like the child. To compel the young to do something unpleasant or contrary to their wishes or nature was therefore a violation of God's highest creation, even divinity itself. Teachers reading and hearing such sentiments from experts in scientific pedagogy must have been very wary about compelling children—who were superior, pure, and blameless, a model of Christian behavior—to do something they did not wish to do. "The moment a child can act from the dictates of his own reason, that tells him something is right," Parker informs his audience of teachers, "the super-imposed will of the parent should give way to the child's own volition." The belief remains strong today and puts teachers on the defensive, for many people automatically, almost instinctively, believe the best about children and the worst about their teachers and the demands they make upon children. No matter how reasonable the expectations of students in terms of academics and behavior, teachers are suspect for anything that causes the young inconvenience, discomfort, or stress. "The child, *until education intervenes*, is a unit of action and expression, and that unity is acquired and maintained because action is controlled by a motive with no overpowering consciousness of the means or forms of expression. Must that beautiful unity be broken or can it be perpetuated and strengthened?" Parker asks, showing very clearly the idea that schools, with their behavioral, intellectual, and academic demands on children, are harmful and contrary to nature and morality.[17]

THE PASSIVE, HELPLESS CHILD

Despite the many improvements Parker brought to the education of young children in Quincy and later in Chicago and even in the United States, his influence is particularly destructive in one respect. In a laudable effort to inspire teachers and parents to love children and understand their nature and needs, Parker too often portrays the child as helpless and passive, an organism to be molded at our will: "It is well for us as teachers to stand by the cradle of a little child who has drawn his first breath and is ready to be acted upon by the external energies which surround him," he intones.[18] Obviously an infant is helpless, and his control over his environment extends only as far as his cries are able to stir his caretakers to meet his needs. Yet that passive appearance is deceptive, for the infant is actually busily and actively struggling to make sense of his environment, which it finds (in James's words) "one unanalyzed bloom of confusion." How busy the infant must be is seen in the fact that it is constructing its view and understanding of reality from scratch as its nervous system grows and the stimuli flood in.

Parker's observation that the infant is "ready to be acted upon by the external energies which surround him" is especially significant, for he consistently portrays the environment as being the active force, producing knowledge in the helpless and passive young. According to Parker, a child's learning seems to result from the actions of the environment, rather than from conscious, willed cognitive processes: "Attention may be partially defined as a mental process immediately caused by the action of the attributes of external objects," he explains. While James, quoting Helmholtz, distinguished between two types of attention, one being the sensational type that grabs our attention for a second (as in a loud crash) and the other being our ability to find new information in old objects, Parker (as do a great many people today) sees attention as arising not from a person's willed, conscious processes but solely from qualities inherent in the object being attended to. Later he repeats himself, "Attention is the vital process of intellectual creation, *induced by the action of external attributes upon the brain and consciousness.*"[19]

Obviously a small child does not have the control over his attention and conscious processes that an adult has, nor should we expect a small child to have that control. But in our educational thinking we do not expect children, over the course of their years in school, to struggle to *gain* that control if doing so is not convenient, easy, and natural for them. The control over their attention and thoughts is thought to reside outside their powers. In the context of the classroom, this means that the teacher's lesson must hold students' attention, not that students are expected to jerk their attention back to the topic at hand, as James put it. Here is Parker's view of the child's cognitive processes:

> *The psychological fact that the unification of elementary ideas is automatic, not a conscious effort of the ego, is highly significant pedagogically, and many pedagogic errors have resulted from ignorance of this fact.* The "A, B, C" methods, the countless phonic and word-building methods, the systematic, prescribed, and predestined object-lessons, are all the bad results of ignorance in regard to this powerful, persistent, and spontaneous action of the mind.[20]

In other words, Parker seems to be saying, the child's thinking is beyond his control; intelligence and understanding just happen because, somehow, elementary ideas are "automatically" unified in the mind. "Not a conscious effort of the ego" states very clearly that the student's will and determination and drive to understand are irrelevant. Therefore, if the child fails to understand, it certainly cannot be his fault, for he has no control over the "spontaneous action of the mind." The student's role in his learning is merely to repress nonmental activities so that the energies in the environment can work their magic: "The power of the will in attention," Parker writes, "consists in holding the body and the mind in the most economical attitude for the most effective and complete action of external attributes through nerve tracts upon consciousness." Since Parker was a devout Christian and believed that the purpose of education was to learn the glory of God and truth, one has the impression that he believed the student needed only to suppress thoughts and impulses which obstructed God's workings. Many Americans today, in the classrooms and administrative offices of our public schools and in the colleges of education, and even on blue-ribbon commissions writing proposals for improving the schools, hold similar beliefs: learning just *happens* due to forces in the environment, not because a person actively seeks to make sense of stimuli. The sober, judicious, and scientifically more accurate words of James bear repeating, for his words seem to have been directed against the very thinking exemplified by Colonel Parker: "By the ancients, and by unreflecting people perhaps today, knowledge is explained as the *passage* of something from without into the mind—the latter, so far, at least, as its sensible affections go, being passive and receptive."[21]

Parker leaves us with no doubt that various aspects of a child's behavior are under the control of outside forces: "Observation is the continuous action of an object upon consciousness for the purpose of developing and intensifying its corresponding individual concept." The fundamental reason children do not behave, he says, is that they do not have the proper conditions for proper action. Again, the will and determination of the student are irrelevant, if not nonexistent; the student is supposedly passive, totally at the mercy of the teacher and the environment, and his behavior and learning result from all that the teacher or the environment does. Parker also argues, "The influence of the teacher's personality, moral and intellectual power, and skill, can never be overestimated; every act of the teacher is perpetuated in the conduct of his pupils." In other words, teachers have unlimited power to affect their students, who are passive entities, waiting to be molded. To achieve such power, the teacher must find the natural teaching methods—"the exact adaptation of the subject taught, to the learning mind"—so that the learning process will not cause the students discomfort and bring them only joy, pleasure, and truth. And the science of pedagogy invests the teacher with that awesome power: "The faculties of the mind are capable of infinite development; true, they await the teachers, as the mighty stored-up energies of steam, heat, electricity, and sound awaited their discoverers," he rhapsodizes. "When the teachers come, all the marvels of the nineteenth century will sink into insignificance before the full manhood and womanhood of realized possibilities." Such being the expectations—"The citizen should say in his heart, 'I await the regeneration of the world from the teaching of the common schools of America'"—teachers cannot but fail.[22]

Hall, despite his superior knowledge of psychology, enthusiastic embrace of Darwinism, and devotion to the Darwin-based new psychology, holds a similar belief about natural and easy learning. He writes, ". . . In every normal child at about every moment of its life there is some zest or curiosity just ripe for impregnation with information and suggestion, which will be *instantly and forever assimilated* with no need of explanation or review, which, indeed, these would positively injure, because they would interfere with the complete absorption of knowledge and keep it nearer the memory surfaces."[23] Particularly noteworthy is the belief that if the teacher merely waits for the right moment or opportunity to teach, the student will learn the subject easily and naturally, even joyfully—a belief not uncommon today. The very use of the word *impregnation* shows that the student is not expected to struggle to understand—does soil have to struggle for a plant to grow? If the seed is simply planted correctly—in the right type of soil, in the right climate, at the right season—learning will grow, and it is the teacher's responsibility to find the right time for sowing the seeds of knowledge. (It is tempting to speculate on the sexual imagery of the phrase: the one being impregnated is often regarded as *passive* and receptive, the one planting the seed *active*.) Needless to add, if the student fails to learn, the fault lies with the teacher for choosing the wrong seed for the given soil, or for planting at the wrong time. The teacher, as Hall admonished, is expected to know his students as a farmer knows his soils and his seeds, or an architect his ground plans, as if teachers "build" the knowledge in the helpless student's head.

Hall also believed in the recapitulation theory ("ontogeny recapitulates phylogeny"), that is, that the child, as it grows and develops, passes through all the stages of mankind's development. Thus the purpose of education is to make the child's passage more efficient—though this would appear to clash with the most cherished idea of child study and child-centered education, which was, in all aspects, to "follow nature."

LEARNING SHOULD BE FUN

From the complex of these various ideas—that the child is sacred, passive, and should not be hindered in his development—comes the thought that compelling the child to act against his wishes violates God's highest creation or forces him to develop in unnatural ways. That being the case, teachers and school officials must fit the school to the child and his characteristics, needs, and wishes, not expect the student to change in accordance with the demands of adults, who have been corrupted by their experience in the sordid world. Since one of the chief characteristics of children is play, Hall and others maintain that children should spend most of their time at play, not at books and academics. Teachers must follow nature: "play is always and everywhere the best synonym of youth," and play is "the great agent of unity and totalization of body and soul," he writes. Play is crucial to students' development, for it is part of their repeating the natural development of the human race. "Thus we see," he argues, "that play is not doing things to be useful later, but it is rehearsing racial history." Later in the same book he suggests, "Several have thought that a well-rounded, liberal education could be given by plays and games alone on the principle that there is no profit when there is no pleasure or true euphoria." Hall had come a long way indeed from his strict Calvinist upbringing and his conversion to Darwinism. Apparently the struggle to win salvation despite a sinful nature or survive in a world red in tooth and claw is supposed to be joyful.[24]

Hall gives an example of the playful, natural way of learning in "The Story of a Sand-Pile," another famous article in the annals of child study. He tells what a positive learning experience two neighborhood boys, ten and twelve years old, enjoyed when their mother bought a load of sand for them to play in. During the years they played in the sandpile, her sons and other neighborhood boys formed a little town with buildings, crafted small wooden dolls for people (who were much like the people of the town) and horses, made their own laws, and even worked out a little town economy, continually developing the town and the life stories of its characters. Hall saw the boys as mirroring the development of mankind through its various stages. The sandpile experience, he writes, "may perhaps be called one illustration of the education according to *nature* we so often hear and speak of. . . . On the whole, the 'sand pile' has, in the opinion of the parents, been of about as much yearly educational value to the boys as the eight months of school." The benefits from the sandpile? "Here is a perfect mental sanity and unity, but with more variety than in the most heterogenous and soul-disintegrating school curriculum. The unity of all the diverse interests and activities of the 'sand pile' is, as it always is, ideal."[25]

For Hall, another natural activity by which children might learn was dance, and it had great pedagogical possibilities: "The ideal purpose of instruction in this domain [dance] is to strengthen utterance, to make it more hearty and deep by restoring the motor elements that have degenerated, and to enable man once more to talk with his whole organism, and thereby to bring about a new and wholesome unity of action between the soul and the body. That this would make for moral efficiency, for transparency of life, and will reduce the element of deceit and distrust, there can be no doubt." Dance, he states elsewhere, "helps the young to orb out the soul and keeps that of the aged from shriveling and invagination." Elsewhere he says there must be something wrong with kids who don't like to dance, but then he also finds something wrong with the twelve-year-old boy who is a perfect gentleman. Dolls too are beneficial: "Certainly the doll, with all its immense educational power, should be carefully introduced."[26]

Hall is also inordinately fond of having students learn singing and music, but only under the right conditions: "The music teacher should have unusual range and strength of emotions, and should never require pupils to sing what or when they do not strongly feel." Music provides for mental stability, as it brings us back into contact with our primitive natures, away from the tawdry modern world. "And some feel, as a high-school girl expressed it, that they would like to 'shake off the dust of civilization and get back to nature and be at home'" by listening to barbaric music. "Music is thus a message to the ordinary and more superficial conscious and self-conscious life from the profounder regions of the unconscious and instinctive substrata of the human nature which constitutes nine tenths of life," Hall rhapsodizes, "a message which says 'all down here is beautiful, harmonious, and there is overflowing superfluity of vitality.'" One has the impression that Hall would prefer Muzak to Stravinsky or Bartok. He charged music teachers with the custody and responsibility of "the hygiene of the emotional life" of their students. Other child-cult members held similar beliefs. Harold Rugg, a professor at Teachers College, and his co-author Ann Shumaker, described the

Dalcroze scheme of rhythmic training: "When bodily, mental, and emotional control is achieved [through rhythmics], the way is made straight for the expansion of individuality, the realization of personality, of creative imagination, and the integrated life."[27]

Similar opinions were held by Margaret Naumberg, who founded the Walden School in New York City in 1914 (it was first called the Children's School) and established its educational philosophy upon the psychoanalytic theories of Carl Jung. She believed that schools should be about happiness and joy, and finding one's true self; modern society and overintellectualized education had caused Americans to lose contact with themselves, with the result that they did not know who and what they were. The philosophy of the Walden School therefore emphasized the arts and self-expression, so that children could learn about their true selves buried beneath all the detritus of corrupt, modern industrial life. There were no guidelines or standards for the children in their artistic productions, however; the only criterion for excellence was whether or not the student was satisfied with his work of art. An equally exacting standard was promoted by Rugg and Shumaker. (Still today, teachers and others involved in education argue that we should let students set their own standards.) Drama played a key role in the Walden School (and in the educational philosophy of Rugg and Shumaker); yet one apparently did not see performances of plays by Sophocles, Shakespeare, Ibsen, or other famous dramatists, for the students performed only plays they wrote themselves, improvising the script as the performance progressed. Yet Naumberg blasted the idea of using games to teach *academic* content, for she was snarlingly hostile to what she called "the pseudo-culture of the leisure class." That members of a labor union rejected her educational ideas, choosing instead a traditional education for their children, "doesn't make one too optimistic about the promise of our so-called democracy," she declared.[28]

So strongly did Junius L. Meriam, a professor of education at the University of Missouri and founder of its Laboratory School, believe in play that he thought it unethical of a teacher to use plays and games to teach academic content. Play existed for the sake of play, and schools should exist for students' play instincts: "The mere fact that play is recognized as one phase of the normal life of children justifies its place in the curriculum," he wrote. The whole problem of elementary education, Meriam felt, was *"to help boys and girls do better in all those wholesome activities in which they normally engage."* With that being the function of the school—to help children do what they already do—the country would not need professors of education, or teachers trained in the best scientific education, or even schools, for that matter.[29]

Colonel Parker holds similar beliefs about play and fun at school, though he is not quite as anti-intellectual. The purpose of the teacher, he writes, "should be to continue in the best possible way the spontaneous activities of the child in the directions which nature has so effectively begun." Since children love playing and having fun, Parker believes, as does Kilpatrick, that "Every subject of thought, every object of attention, truly studied and freely observed, must arouse in the mind emotions of pleasure. In a word, the test of whether you know a subject, whether you are really studying a subject, is your love for that subject. I think I can say positively that no one knows a subject unless he loves it." Thus teachers must somehow teach so that students love the class—if students merely *learn* the information without loving it, they're not really learning. It is more important that they love the subject first, for then they are more likely to learn. "All truly educative work is interesting; no one can ever study anything that is good without loving it," Parker argues. His thoughts on learning history are interesting: "Who can understand history without the love of all mankind in his soul? Love is an interpreter of history."[30]

Although Parker believes that students should work hard, it should be *only* work they love. He is quite clear about not pushing children too hard: "Overstepping the boundaries of self-effort results in weakness rather than strength; the overstraining in effort, the fearful consciousness of self, the mental entanglement in forms of thought–expression are all the outcome of mis-directed self-effort. Poise, equilibrium, *passive and receptive attention* [note how the student is portrayed when learning], mature reflection, ease in expression, and consciousness of power spring from wisely adjusted self-effort. 'Be still, and know that I am God.'"[31] Parker's idea of what children should be expected to endure is very, very low. For example, he claims that when children are learning to read, if they pay too much attention to the forms of the words (as in a phonics-based method), the result will be permanent mental weakness. Again, the clear conclusion, still prevalent in our educational thinking, is that students must not be expected to exert themselves in order to learn and succeed at school, unless it relates to something they want to do. Struggling and effort are bad for their health.

It is essential, Hall and others inform us, that the students be free to live out their childlike natures, instincts, and impulses, that is, play and have fun while at school. A student, they tell us, suffers grave harm if he is expected to work hard contrary to his wishes. The teacher must *never* force the student to learn: "Literature abounds in illustrations . . . of the superficial and even health-destroying effect of knowledge forced on minds deficient in interest," Hall writes. Elsewhere he even compares such forced learning to rape—"in many ways psychologically akin to a nameless crime that in some parts of the country meets summary vengeance." If a student is forced to learn something he has no interest in or use for, Hall admonishes, "his freshness, spontaneity, and the fountains of play slowly run dry in him, and his youth fades to early desiccation."[32]

On this point Margaret Naumberg totally agrees with Hall. She quotes Herbert S. Jennings, a professor of biology at Johns Hopkins University, who argues that it is positively dangerous to force children to learn something they have no interest in. Biologists and psychologists, she writes, "state in no uncertain words that the physiological effects of joy and happiness on the human organism are chemically positive and constructive, while the result of submitting our bodies to suffering and to pain is negative and deleterious." No doubt a certain kind of intense, continued stress is physically and mentally harmful; yet it is usually experienced in abusive homes or in tumultuous times. Naumberg, on the other hand, equates it with a child's having to learn reading, writing, and arithmetic. In her opinion, students must experience no discomfort during the learning process. She quotes Jennings again: "The condition of happiness, of 'joy,' is that in which development is unhindered, and flourishing; in which the functions are proceeding harmoniously; while worry, fear, unhappiness, are the marks of the reverse condition of affairs; something is blocked and is going wrong." The message to teachers, parents, and society is clear and unambiguous, and protected by the mantle of science: students must not be expected to struggle, strive, and experience stress when learning, because that is *dangerous* and threatens their health and happiness. If students are not enjoying their time at school, playing games and engaging in the normal, healthy activities of youth, we do them grave damage.[33]

ANTI-INTELLECTUALISM

According to the child-cult people, children do not naturally seek to know about reading, writing, numbers, or the causes of the Civil War, or wish to translate *Arma virumque cano.* In Hall's scheme, the development of academic subjects and formal knowledge came along very late in man's history (a stage that children have not reached in their recapitulation of man's development), and, besides, learning academic subjects is not one of their natural, instinctive drives. The intellect, according to practically all the Progressive educators, is just one of many aspects of the young that need to be educated, and schools stress intellectual functions too much. Like Dewey and Kilpatrick, the child-cult members sought to educate the whole child and produce integrated individuals for the new, reformed society. Citing data which show that students prefer vocational to academic education, Hall writes, "[These] facts show what it is very hard for pedagogues to realize, viz., that very few children have any real intellectual interests. Intellectual interests are very subordinate with most. Very few have taste or *ability* for learning." "Bookishness" he writes, "is probably a bad sign in a girl; it suggests artificiality, pedantry, the lugging of dead knowledge." Hall goes as far as to say that the good father is not a bookworm. Predictably enough, he vehemently opposed the passage of the academic curriculum promulgated by the Committee of Ten in 1893 (which produced rigorous academic guidelines for all students in American schools), blasting its emphasis on dead or formal subjects such as Latin and algebra.[34]

The child-cult members are unanimous in their hostility not only to formal knowledge but to the intellect itself. The public school "machine," writes Margaret Naumberg, with its overemphasis on the intellectual and mental, "kills the spirit of our best teachers and presses the life out of our keenest children." Naumberg proffers scientific evidence to show that the development of the intellect can be dangerous: "In our eagerness to develop [the organism's] mental powers, we are inclined to overdrive these, with the result that the vegetative life is interfered with; nutrition is weakened, resistance is lowered; growth slowed, and the very foundations of all life are undermined." Naumberg believes that the overemphasis on the intellect and the neglect of spiritual, physical, and artistic education have caused us to lose contact with our essential selves: "Our present education leaves us in a state of ignorance about ourselves and others that is simply colossal." It is a miracle we manage to function at all. ". . . Your body and all our physical organisms have lost, under the stress and strain of modern life, their right instinctive functioning." In her book, an observer recalls how tedious modern civilization seemed to him when he saw the movie *Chang*, which apparently chronicled the life of people in the jungles of Siam: "The bodily forms of these primitives, their pure and joyous movements, and the simple completeness of their lives, all held me bound in wonder." We note the obvious conclusion, one that students today would jokingly agree with: *It is detrimental to one's health to learn and develop the intellect and its rational capacities.*[35]

Meriam too (oddly enough, as he did his graduate work under Thorndike, who was hostile to child-centered education) blasts traditional schools and the traditional curriculum. Pupils do not withdraw from school, he writes, "They are *eliminated* from school by the conditions imposed upon them." He explains: "The traditional subjects, arithmetic, spelling, geography, etc., contribute but little to the present life of children," and argues further that a uniform curriculum is responsible for a large percentage of retarded pupils. "The curriculum must be made to suit the boy and girl, not the boy and girl shaped to the Procrustean curriculum," he argues, employing a classical reference that graduates of his school probably would not understand. Meriam claims that since working children will not use reading and writing, we might as well save money by not educating them, and he wonders whether or not it is feasible to educate all pupils "to the extent of the elementary school." Instead of academic subjects, Meriam suggests, the school should help boys and girls do better with the activities they are already engaged in, and subject matter should be found to enable the students to realize the motives they already have.[36]

Harold Rugg and Ann Shumaker called an 1890 group of college presidents and headmasters of private schools, which formulated a standardized college preparatory curriculum, "a reactionary group." Rugg and Shumaker claimed that some cultures bound the heads of babies in order to form their heads into a certain shape; modern peoples don't practice head-binding, they wrote, "but still they are given to the *less defensible* custom of forcing the minds of the young into prepared molds." In the new, child-growth schools, Rugg and Shumaker wrote, students should have the freedom to choose what they would learn, experience actual materials, and have opportunity for varied expression. Apparently the ideal school actively discouraged children from reading: "The bookish child, long the teacher's pet in the listening school, is looked on with concern in the new school. His evasions are analyzed and his interests directed to the active pursuits of *normal* child life." To the poor child unfortunate enough to enjoy reading at school, the message is clear: *Reading is bad, don't do it.*[37]

Hall's anti-intellectualism assumes an odd form as he takes aim particularly at Latin (and, to a lesser extent, algebra) in the schools, but not for the same reasons that other Progressive educators did. Then, as now, most students took two years of Latin or another foreign language and then stopped. Considering Hall's belief in the recapitulation theory, he should have wanted students to relive, as much as possible, the Golden Age of classical Rome; its myths, legends, epic poetry, and morality would fit well with his other romantic heroic beliefs. Yet starting to learn a subject and then stopping, Hall claimed, was harmful, because doing so left behind something that could atrophy: "Erudition and effort in lines later to be abandoned do not leave the faculties as a whole stronger but weaker. Primary ignorance in a subject is interesting; it often gives strong curiosity while secondary ignorance is both devolution and disenchantment."[38] Therefore students should not take Latin or any subject they might end up dropping and never using again in their adult lives, such as algebra. (How students are supposed to find out what subjects they like without experimenting a little or having introductory lessons, is a question Hall never answers.)

Another reason for Hall's hostility to foreign languages in general and Latin in particular seems to stem from his fear that the students, having learned a little Latin, German, French, or Greek, would then become pretentious:

> Very few [students] indeed, in this great country will make any real practical use of their modern languages in later life, and all others surely would have done better to devote their school days to other topics. For this old psychosis, the chief badge of scholarship is to be unintelligible. It is the same psychological impulse that prompts the use of technical terms when others would do as well, or to interlard speech and script with foreign phrases of which the vernacular has an equivalent. This gives to youth an exquisite sense of imposing superiority.[39]

His hatred of pretense is doubly ironic, because his own writings are in fact frequently interlarded with phrases in Latin, Greek, German, and French; the double irony is that with the Latin and Greek, at least, he often gets the quotes wrong. Elsewhere Hall rails against the idea of having students learn factual information on their own and then engage in discussions of their findings—they will think they have learned something: ". . . they are inclined to the delusion that their mental emptiness is filled and so grow complacent with their ignorance, are opinionated where experts differ, and, with more power to achieve than to receive, suffer like those who work hard on an empty stomach." True though those words may often be, we note that students are damned simply for trying, a situation strenuously to be avoided. One notes that if the students were working on a curriculum rich in factual content as well as as-

signments requiring application of those facts, they would not be working on an empty stomach.[40]

THE ROLE OF THE TEACHER

All the child-cult ideals place considerable pressure on the teacher, and
the child-cult people are unsparing and merciless in their criticism of
teachers, undoubtedly because teachers persisted in giving lessons on
subject-matter-set-out-to-be-learned and stressed intellectual development. Rugg and Shumaker call the traditional teacher "a blind, helpless
cog in the great machine of enforced mass education. She has no
chance to be a person in her own right. . . ." Naumberg believes that
teachers, like all adults, are not functioning adequately, having lost contact with their vital functions: "Until [the teachers'] own bodies are
given proper co-ordination [through psychoanalysis and kinesthetic con-
trol], they lack the actuality of such norms in dealing with children."
Meriam, for some reason, has this exceedingly harsh denunciation of
teachers: "Too many teachers display a pedantry repulsive to pupils.
These teachers have not the great amount of erudition of which they
would be pleased to boast." Teacher-bashing in the United States has a
long, inglorious history, not least from pedagogues, teachers' supposed
allies.[41]

Colonel Parker may have been loved by the children in his school,
but he was feared by many of the teachers on his faculty: ". . . One of his
teachers insisted that he was feared by the staff and 'practice' teachers,
that he struck real terror in their hearts. . . . Parker was accused of yelling
and bellowing at his teachers. One time when he found a teacher giving
report cards, in spite of strict orders to the contrary, he was said to have
actually 'roared' and to have torn up the cards *in front of the children*."
Parker shows the hostility that administrators not infrequently feel for the
teachers on their faculties: "Parker also blamed the teachers themselves
for their low wages," saying that if teachers wanted better wages, "they
should teach better and make themselves more indispensable to the people." Parker's thoughts on teachers' pay reveal his hypocrisy: when he

left the Cook County Normal School to establish a private school, he succeeded in getting a $3,000 raise beyond his $5,000 annual salary (which was augmented by his speaking fees). While he was making a minimum of $5,000 a year, the average member of the instructional staff in the United States was earning $252 a year. Merle Curti reports that the average annual pay for a female teacher in 1910 was $800. Parker might have opposed pensions for teachers because he thought that such security only encouraged bad teachers to stay at their jobs. When an economic downturn in 1887 forced the Cook County Normal School to consider reducing Parker's $5,000-a-year salary, he threatened to quit; yet he wasn't out for his own financial gain—"Parker had to hold his ground, not so much for his own aggrandizement as for the professional dignity of his position. Businessmen and politicians who controlled the schools, he said, would only be impressed by an educator who could command a good salary."[42]

Hall, in his many writings, also harshly criticizes American teachers. Unlike Meriam, Parker, and Naumberg, however, Hall had little experience with children or the schools to lend much credence to his criticism. He was headmaster of a school for two years in his teens, and he toured European schools during one of his trips; he admitted that his study of French, German, and English schools was superficial. Otherwise he had scant experience with children, the most detailed being his conversations with teenage girls that he conducted while writing his article "The Budding Girl."

> There can be no question that the [American] high school has drifted further from the real nature of the child than any other grade. Are some teachers living in a fool's paradise; or to change the figure, is their acquaintance with the child's soul limited to its front yard, hallway, or formal caller's parlor, while they know nothing of what takes place in any of the living rooms where the child moves and has its being?[43]

We note, first, that Hall refers to adolescents as children, even though they are capable of bearing children—a point he well knew, since one of his useful accomplishments was to plead the case for sex education for the young. Hall judges teachers in accordance with what he knows, or thinks he knows, about adolescents, as well as what he knows (or thinks he knows) about American schools. The problem with his knowledge is that it is filtered through his own neuroses and German romanticism. Nevertheless his categorical denunciation of American teachers has a curiously modern ring (*plus ça change!*) and would be applauded by many liberals and conservatives today, however much they might disagree with his views on child-rearing:

> The chief pedagogic disease to-day is artificial retardation and colossal underestimation of the child's real powers, insistence upon adult ways of doing things. But the chief handicap on our system is dull teaching that obstructs and makes hard the way of learning. The average teacher in my observation does his or her work in a wretched, stupid, and routine way without zest, insight, or ability. The nature of this occupation tends to make the incumbent a public functionary who goes through the daily task in the easiest way. Only very rarely do we see traces of pedagogic genius.[44]

Arguing that children do not owe bad parents their filial respect, he declares, "The same question may be addressed to mechanical hireling teachers."[45]

One wonders how much observation Hall actually performed in American classrooms. He was head of the psychology department at Clark University and therefore had to teach classes and oversee the dissertation work of many students who were earning doctorates in psychology (so many, in fact, that the poor quality of the doctorates was a scandal of sorts).[46] As president of Clark he also had to run the university, which was always experiencing problems in funding after Jonas Clark decided to limit his financial involvement with it. He wrote his many articles and books (two of which, *Adolescence* and *Educational Problems*, are two large volumes each), and he edited the two journals he established, the *American Journal of Psychology* and *Pedagogical Seminary*. It is fair to ask how much Hall really knew about the quality of teaching in American classrooms, and how deep his "expertise" really was. His peculiar ideas about education and his hostility to the development of the intellect hardly make him an impartial observer.

Hall gave his most detailed criticism of American teachers in a chapter in *Educational Problems* titled "The German Teacher Teaches," based on what he had observed in Germany "some years ago." To see how his criticism is filled with contradictions and inconsistencies (much like modern criticism of teachers), it is helpful to review his educational ideals. We have seen him admonish teachers to follow nature, allowing students to learn what they want to, when they want to, at their own, natural pace; to de-emphasize academics, since few students have the ability or interest; to have the students learn through games, song, dance, and play, with the school being a place of joy and exuberance; and to base schoolwork upon the interests of the students. Judged by those standards, the American teacher, then as now, fails miserably. The teacher is too much a hearer of recitations and a setter of lessons, too devoted to academics and to covering the material in the textbook; the teacher, it goes without saying, is out of touch with the needs and interests of youth.

Yet when Hall describes what he saw in a German Latin class, he praises the German teacher for many of the same qualities he condemns in American teachers. While the American teacher is faulted for expecting the students to memorize information and then recite it ("an educative process of but little value"), the German Latin teacher gets off scot-free when the students are expected to memorize what the teacher has translated for them. While the American Latin teacher is faulted for teaching grammar and other nuts-and-bolts information, Hall ignores such a fault in the German Latin teacher: "Each word [in a sentence in an elementary Latin class] is written; its stem, termination, gender, meaning, are gone over. Everything is parsed, for drill in grammar is incessant and thorough and reviews and re-reviews are unremitting."[47] For such dry and formal grammatical exegesis, the German Latin teacher is praised, the American Latin teacher condemned. While the American teacher is faulted for not basing his lessons in accordance with his students' interests and abilities, the German teacher is praised for his attention to depth in scholarship.

Here is Hall's ideal attitude for a school: "Knowledge of the child takes proper precedence over knowledge of the system and is coimportant with knowledge of the subject matter. The stress is placed where it belongs upon sympathy, tact, and analysis of the child's mental processes in coping with each topic." Now read his praise of the German teacher:

> The German teacher earns his bread by the sweat of his brow. He is generally animated, perhaps active, walking up and down, sometimes enforcing all he says with fire and gesture. He does not believe in soft or sessile pedagogy. Teaching is hard work, and the mind, not only of the master, but of the pupil, is tense throughout. The teacher is thorough, masterful, loves authority, and has it in full measure. He promotes by an act of sovereign will. There is almost no limit to the amount of scolding of which he is capable, and his tongue lashings and frequent bitter, biting sarcasm are well calculated to flay the slow or dullards into activity. If the authority of the teacher and parent conflict, it is the teacher generally who wins out.[48]

Why does Hall praise the authoritarian German way yet condemn the greater freedom of American classes, while urging American teachers to adopt still freer and more informal methods? It is nothing less than bizarre. "These are educational Dark Ages," he writes. "We have so lost touch with our children in home and school that we do not realize what vital contact with them means. We have no idea of our own decadence, no respect for our own craft as instructors, and do not know what teaching is, means or can do, so that we need a great, widespread, pedagogical revival and renaissance in industry as in moral training. . . ."[49] Here, for once, we can agree with G. Stanley Hall: he is confused.

Today the American public is also confused. Since child-cult attitudes have not been repudiated since the days of Hall, Parker, Rugg and Shumaker, and Naumberg—in fact, they have been strengthened somewhat by the countercultural revolution of the 1960s—the American public wants the teacher to be both the strict, authoritarian, Prussian officer type yet also sympathetic, friendly, spontaneous, loving, and gentle.

> When my daughter starts school [says a mother from Newark, New Jersey], I'm hoping for a teacher who is spontaneous, someone who can

follow a curriculum and yet meet the emotional and social needs of children as well. I hope for someone who has a vivid imagination and knows how to use ordinary objects to teach valuable lessons. I want my daughter to be exposed to as many cultures and ethnic groups as possible, and I want her to be academically motivated and challenged. That will take a teacher who is sensitive to the individual needs of each student. If my daughter is slow, I want a teacher who is immediately looking into that, and if she's surpassing the class, I want her to get what she needs and progress as far as she can. I want a teacher who has conflict resolution skills, who creates discipline, but not from his or her emotions. I want a teacher who uses different methods and different ways of reaching students—who can think in innovative ways and challenge the children while teaching them academically.[50]

American parents want teachers who maintain an orderly classroom, cover the material in detail in organized lessons, and do not accept excuses for students' failing to meet high standards—until, it all too often seems, it is their own child who is failing or being punished for misbehaving, at which point it is the fault of the incompetent teacher. The American public is right to want such teachers, for students with such teachers are more likely to learn the material. Yet the American public also wants students to feel free in their classrooms to experience joy and exuberance, to be creative, and so forth, under a teacher who is understanding and sensitive to their individual needs and abilities. The two teaching types can scarcely exist in the same teacher. While a teacher may incorporate many of the best aspects of both, a teacher cannot be all things to all students at all times and under all circumstances. Students must learn to create their own success and to succeed despite inimical circumstances, for the simple reason that the circumstances of life will never be optimal.

Today student success is seen as arising only when the teacher is perfect; only when the student has chanced upon The Compleat Teacher is he thought capable of meeting high standards and achieving excellence. The number of such perfect teachers will be small indeed; instead of gambling on our students' finding the perfect teacher, the one that can make learning fast, easy, fun, and emotionally satisfying, we should instead expect students to achieve and succeed regardless of the teacher. It would ultimately be better for the students to learn that their happiness and success depend upon what they do, not upon what others do to meet their desires and needs.

THE REACTION

Progressive education was not implemented without opposition. Thorndike, the most scientific of the Progressives, opposed the child-cult aspects of education, as did John B. Watson, both of whom thought the child-cult and child-centered education foolish. Both believed in students' learning formal subject matter; Thorndike sent his two sons to the conservative, college-preparatory Horace Mann school at Teachers College, not to the avant-garde Lincoln School. Both also knew that the student's formulation of a solution to the problem—the learning process, in other words—could be difficult and cause the student discomfort; Watson wrote a child-care book that sold poorly and was unpopular because it was too harsh on children. Thorndike also bashed the romantic trend in education, the thought that nature is always right. He dared to defend memorization and trashed the view that in order to be learning, students must necessarily be running around in the classroom, freely acting out their impulses. "It is of course true that many things must be done by a school pupil which produce no pleasure, but they may nevertheless be done with interest," he states reasonably. He even acknowledges that teachers harm students by doing too much for them. For his opposition to the child-cult and child-centered education, Thorndike was labeled a reactionary for his "consistent criticism of those who were entrapped by a teaching methodology which assumed that learning could be simply achieved, that schools operated on the reform principles of progressive education would make learning easy—indeed, almost automatic! There is no royal road to learning or teaching, Thorndike said."[51]

Still, Thorndike's realistic approach—that students could not always

be happy and joyful while learning—lost the argument with the Progressives. Many teachers, members of school boards, and administrators followed their sentimental yearnings and believed the experts, and trusted
that their scientific findings on education would create the ideal schools
and reconstruct American society. They incorporated Progressive education practices into their classrooms: freedom, self-expression, student-
directed activities, and democracy. The result was chaos, causing the
very experts who had written the theories to produce works that blamed
teachers for taking the experts at their word. John Dewey faulted the excesses of Progressive education in *Experience and Education* and sporad-
ically in other writings, declaring that one of the gravest dangers to
education was sentimentalism, and he took Progressive educators to task
for their hostility to knowledge and the symbols by which knowledge is
conveyed. Rugg and Shumaker faulted many child-centered classrooms
for having little order and for accomplishing little. Boyd Bode, another
Progressive, chastised the aimlessness of Progressive education in his little book *Progressive Education at the Crossroads*, which contains the
memorable anecdote of a child asking, "Do we have to do what we want
to do today?" Some graduates of the avant-garde Lincoln School are
recorded as criticizing the aimlessness of their school years there, for
they did not learn to study and apply themselves, and wandered aim-
lessly through loosely planned activities.[52] The teachers, in their defense, had simply done what the experts had recommended.

The legacy of the child-cult influence in education is, in many ways,
highly destructive. Students are not expected to work hard at school and
to struggle to achieve and excel. The belief that school should be a place
of fun, joy, and exuberance lives on. There is an unquestioned belief in
our society that "learning should be fun," and that if the lesson is not fun
and enjoyable, students have the right to turn off and disengage themselves from learning. Teachers who teach straightforward, no-nonsense
lessons are held in less esteem than those who play learning games and
use progressive practices. If the students are not happy and excited about
learning, the teacher is thought to be doing a poor job. In such an environment, and with those being the expectations, the mass of students
will not achieve the levels desired by society or reach their potential.

The best, least expensive way to improve our educational system is to let the students know that school is *not* about emotional fulfillment or happiness; they should know that they have a job to do at school—yes, a *job*—and that it requires hard work and dedication. Their success will come primarily from what *they* do, not from what their teachers do. If they work at their studies, they may even discover the joy of accomplishment and the pleasure of understanding more about their world and existence.

5

THE REVOLVING REVOLUTION: EDUCATION AFTER BEHAVIORISM

Behaviorism provided education with the scientific veneer and some of the respect it craved, but increasingly its shortcomings became apparent. Its insistence on studying only observable behavior glaringly neglected man's greatest characteristic, thinking, something that could be not casually ignored. After decades of dominance by behaviorism, scientists "shared an intuition . . . that the behaviorist answer to questions of the human mind was no answer at all," writes Howard Gardner in his history of cognitive science.[1] In the 1940s psychologists renewed their studies of the mind and how people learn and understand. These new studies, however, were not introspectionism or the faculty psychology redux; the Cognitive Revolution, as it came to be called, incorporated findings from biology, anthropology, linguistics, philosophy, comparative anatomy, even computer science, and used highly sophisticated techniques and experiments in an attempt to elucidate how the mind perceives and understands. The findings from the cognitive sciences have gone hand in glove with recent research on the workings of the brain and nervous system. New technologies such as EKG, PET, and MRI have led to such an explosion of knowledge that some called the

1990s the "decade of the brain." Education has sought to use the findings from the cognitive sciences to enhance, if not ensure, students' success at school.

Yet this greater understanding of the brain and of man's cognitive processes has not increased the certainty of students' success at school. By the teaching methods associated with the Cognitive Revolution too, the student appears passive and powerless over his mind, with his success at gaining understanding appearing to depend upon the teacher, his teaching methods, and the environment and conditions of learning he creates for individual students. However passionately the disciples of the Cognitive Revolution condemn behaviorism and ardently wish to recast teaching and learning outside the primitive bounds of "rat-in-a-box" psychology, their educational vision is nonetheless constrained by a stimulus-response mentality. "The choice of mode of presentation [of the lesson] can in many cases spell the differences between a successful and an unsuccessful educational experience," writes Gardner, showing very clearly the modern educationist emphasis on the teacher's responsibility to find the right lesson for each student.[2] One rarely finds an educational researcher considering the possibility that such attitudes actually harm students by leaving them theoretically unable to succeed unless they have the perfect teacher, the one who can create conditions of learning appropriate for each student's psychological profile.

I concentrate here on four different modern educational approaches that arose in the wake of the Cognitive Revolution. Briefly, these are their characteristics.

Left Brain, Right Brain (for the sake of brevity, it will be referred to as LBRB). The brain has two hemispheres, the left and the right, which communicate with each other through various nerve fibers, the largest being the *corpus callosum*. A hemisphere directs the movements of the arm and leg of the opposite side of the body. In most people, one hemisphere is dominant. Through the studies of brain-damaged patients and epileptics who have had the *corpus callosum* severed in order to halt debilitating and even life-threatening seizures, scientists have found that, for most people, the right hemisphere carries many (but certainly not all) functions of spatial skills and music, and processes information holistically, while the left hemisphere carries most of the functions of language and analysis, and processes information sequentially. LBRB fans argue that traditional education places far too much emphasis on the left-brain functions, leaving the right brain and its abilities undeveloped. The key to improving education, they claim, is to use certain teaching techniques that supposedly develop the propensities of the neglected right hemisphere. LBRB has mostly disappeared from the educational journals and teacher in-services, and the LBRB hoopla seems today a somewhat embarrassing fad, like eight-track tapes.[3]

Brain-compatible or brain-based learning. BB (for short) education seeks to use the brain's electro-chemical processes and its natural, evolutionary structure to enhance students' learning, and aims to eliminate school practices that obstruct the brain's natural functioning. Despite the immense complexity of the human brain, writes Eric Jensen, a proponent (he admits that some would even call him a zealot) of BB education, "It is extraordinary to think that today we know with impunity [sic], *how our brain naturally learns best.*"[4] Jensen and other advocates of BB education therefore call for a revolution in education, claiming that modern school and classroom practices make real learning—not just rote memorization—impossible. Brain-based education is currently a hot topic in education, and teachers attend in-services on it, as I have.

Learning styles and cognitive styles. Every individual is unique, of course, each being the result of a different combination of genes, raised by different parents in a different environment with a different history of stimuli and reactions to them, and a combination of different electro-chemical processes in the brain. Therefore each has his own learning or cognitive style. "Like individual differences among students, the possible variations in learning style are infinite," says one author who specializes in learning styles (henceforth referred to as LS).[5] Teachers, as with earlier teaching philosophies, are expected to identify these never-ending variations and make lessons appropriate for them.

Many differing theories aim to delineate the diverse learning styles among students. Some LS theorists posit that an individual processes new information through a dominant sensory channel; thus one can be a visual learner, an auditory learner, a tactile/kinesthetic learner, or can use different combinations of the senses. Some theorists also stress that people have definite preferences for environmental stimuli, preferring certain types of light, placement in a particular part of the classroom, a certain temperature, a particular time of the day for learning, and so forth. Others see students as global learners or analytical learners, while others see them as field dependent or field independent. Others seek to apply Jung's psychological types to the classroom in an attempt to shape curricula and methods in accordance with the student's type—introverted or extroverted, sensing or intuitive, judging or perceiving, and so on.[6] In any event, LS theorists predict academic success for students if teachers will adapt their teaching styles and methods, if not the curriculum itself, to their students' learning styles and cognitive types.

LS is not now the hot topic it was during the late 1970s and 1980s, when education researchers foresaw a revolution in education on LS theory. "It is nothing less than revolutionary to base instructional planning on an analysis of each student's traits," wrote James W. Keefe, a researcher in LS—though the revolution in fact started almost a century ago with Thorndike, Dewey, and Kilpatrick.[7] The theory of Multiple Intelligences has largely supplanted LS, but teachers today are still pressured to teach in accordance with students' different learning and cognitive styles, and students' failure to learn is not infrequently attributed to teachers' failure to match their presentation of the lesson to their students' learning styles.

Multiple Intelligences. This is the creation of Howard Gardner, professor of education at Harvard University, and is currently the rage in education. Gardner rejects the idea of a single, quantifiable intelligence as measured by traditional pencil-and-paper IQ tests. Such tests, he argues, rely upon an outdated and antiquated view of the brain and mind, and ignore recent research which shows that the brain's functions are somewhat localized—speech in Wernicke's area and Broca's area in the left hemisphere, music in the right hemisphere, and so forth.[8] Through studies of idiots savants and brain-damaged patients, researchers show that the regions of the brain carrying the functions of math, language, music, and other specialties are relatively autonomous. A mathematician who loses the ability to speak because of a stroke, for example, may nonetheless continue to do mathematics, or an idiot savant (like the character played by Dustin Hoffman in the movie *Rain Man*) may be utterly incapable of many basic intellectual functions necessary for survival yet still perform at high levels of mathematics. Consequently the brain seems to be composed of minibrains, each of which performs its specialty. That leads to the question: how can there be a single, unified theory of intelligence when there is not one brain but many brains, not one mind but many? Traditional pencil-and-paper IQ tests, Gardner argues (with much validity), far from measuring a person's overall intelligence, measure only the person's logical and linguistic abilities, thus leaving a very inaccurate and scientifically invalid assessment of the person's overall abilities. A mechanic, for example, who scores low on such a test yet can install a timing belt, is undoubtedly intelligent, despite what the test shows. An illiterate, uneducated farmer who can grow a large crop and survive on the land is obviously intelligent, no matter what the test indicates.

Gardner therefore created the theory of Multiple Intelligences (MI for short). He argues that we need a pluralization of intelligence, a definition that will take into account the many varied ways in which people act upon the world and understand it. He redefines intelligence as "the ability to solve problems, or to create products, that are valued within one or more cultural settings—a definition that says nothing about either the sources of these abilities or the proper means of 'testing' them."[9] He argues that there are at least eight intelligences, which all normal people have, and that individuals tend to understand the world and act upon it through their predominant or preferred intelligences. These eight intelligences are: (1) linguistic, the ability to use language, both written and spoken, to express oneself and to meet one's goals, as a poet or novelist does; (2) logical-mathematical, the ability to use numbers and numerical concepts, as a scientist, accountant, or engineer does; (3) spatial, the ability to perceive the visual world accurately, as an architect or artist does; (4) musical, the ability to notice and appreciate differences in tempo, tone, timbre, and so forth, as musicians, singers, and composers do; (5) interpersonal, the ability to notice and make distinctions among other individuals, and to use that knowledge as a politician, manager, or coach might; (6) intrapersonal, the ability to understand oneself and one's emotions, as a philosopher does; (7) bodily-kinesthetic, the ability to use one's body to express oneself and meet goals, as an athlete, singer, or actor does; and (8) naturalist, the ability to classify natural phenomena and species, as a biologist or a hunter does. Other MI writers have proposed other intelligences—existential, ethical, sexual, culinary.[10]

Gardner admits that there may be several hundred dimensions of the mind, but he has given his imprimatur only to the eight above. He notes, "These intelligences are fictions—at most, useful fictions—for discussing processes and abilities that (like all of life) are continuous with one another; Nature brooks no sharp discontinuities of the sort proposed here. Our intelligences are being separately defined and described strictly in order to illuminate scientific issues and to tackle pressing practical problems." He emphasizes that all normal people have all the intelligences: "All normal human beings have all of these potentials [the eight intelligences], but for both genetic and environmental reasons, individuals differ remarkably among themselves in the particular profiles of intelligence that they happen to exhibit at any given moment of their lives." He also declares, unequivocally, that "nearly every cultural role of any degree of sophistication requires a combination of intelligences." That is, every normal person has all the intelligences and uses many, if not all, of them in various combinations in the normal activities of life. A truck driver, for example, will show spatial intelligence as he keeps his truck a safe distance from other vehicles; bodily-kinesthetic intelligence as he maneuvers the truck through traffic without hitting other vehicles; linguistic intelligence as he converses on his CB radio; musical intelligence as he taps his thumbs on the steering wheel in rhythm with the music on the radio; intrapersonal intelligence as he maintains his sanity despite long hours alone on the road; interpersonal intelligence as he manages to avoid confrontations with other drivers; logical-mathematical intelligence as he succeeds in making a profit despite rising prices for diesel fuel and tires; and naturalist intelligence as he identifies the species of roadkill along the highway.[11]

In a time when some Progressive educational practices are on the

defensive and standardized tests and curricula assume increasing importance in educational policy and practices, MI theory and its creator provide hope for yet another revolution in education and clearly inspire
reverence and adulation among the Progressive faithful. Thomas R.
Hoerr, director of the New City School in St. Louis, believes that Gardner and MI have caused a paradigm shift, while Thomas Armstrong,
who writes on how to implement MI in the classroom, gushes, "At
times, I almost think of Gardner as an archeologist who has discovered
the Rosetta stone of learning."[12]

As we shall see, the four theories above share some educationist traits
and ultimately betray their descent from the Progressive Paradigm. They
show various degrees of anti-formalism and anti-intellectualism; they believe that teachers must individualize the curriculum and teaching
methods to the peculiar needs and characteristics of individual students,
so that learning will be natural, unstressed, unforced, and emotionally
fulfilling if not joyful; and they ultimately see the students as passive and
helpless, their success dependent upon the teacher's ability both to divine their individual needs and to construct lessons that meet them.

THE CONSTRAINED, INCAPABLE STUDENT

All these theories deriving from the Cognitive Revolution are based to
some degree upon a negative view of human abilities. Put bluntly, they
hold that students are incapable of achieving certain things. For example, students who are right-brain dominant cannot be expected to excel
in left-brain activities, for it goes against their very biology; or students
with an auditory learning style cannot be expected to use their visual
learning style at the same level of performance that other students do,
for doing so is unnatural and will result in stress and discomfort, if not
outright failure or psychological damage. Students with particularly
strong bodily-kinesthetic intelligence but weak mathematical-logical or
linguistic intelligences cannot and must not be expected to perform at
the same level in math and English as do students with average or strong
intelligences in those fields. Overall, students cannot be expected to

adapt to conditions not of their liking; they cannot be expected to change in ways that seem unnatural or cause them discomfort.

Gardner and others argue that the point of their research is to enable teachers to teach students through the channels by which the students learn most easily and efficiently. If, for example, a student with a strong bodily-kinesthetic intelligence could be taught physics in a way harmonious with his preferred intelligence, learning style, or dominant hemisphere, in order to capitalize on his strengths, he would learn physics easily and naturally.

One need not read far into the literature to find evidence that these cognitive theories regard students as incapable or their efforts constrained; one could even claim that all these theories as applied to education depend upon students' inabilities. Research shows, the educationists will say, that the students' brains, along with their abilities and inabilities, are to some extent biologically determined by their genetics and the environment in which the students were raised. Gardner, his followers in MI, and other writers on the cognitive theories emphasize that students cannot be expected to achieve reasonably high standards outside their preferred modes:

> In the heyday of the psychometric and behaviorist eras, it was generally believed that intelligence was a single unity that was inherited; and that human beings—initially a blank slate—could be trained to learn anything, provided that it was presented in an appropriate way. Nowadays an increasing number of researchers believe precisely the opposite: that there exists a multitude of intelligences, quite independent of each other; that each intelligence has its own strengths and constraints; that the mind is far from unencumbered at birth; and that it is unexpectedly difficult to teach things that go against early "naive" theories or that challenge *the natural lines of force within an intelligence and its matching domains.*[13]

Gardner also rejects the claim of Benjamin Bloom in *Developing Talent in Young People* "that the all-important determination of ability is training." Perhaps this is what Gardner disagrees with: "After forty years of intensive research on school learning in the United States as well as abroad," says Bloom, "my major conclusion is: What any person in the world can learn, *almost* all persons can learn *if* provided with appropriate prior and current conditions of learning."[14] (It is important also to note that Bloom finds that "almost any person" constitutes 95 percent of the population.) No, in modern cognitive theory a person is largely stuck with whatever type of mind he was born with, and his cognitive makeup is relatively immutable. Although Gardner expresses strong doubts about the extent to which a person's abilities are fixed and determined, he also makes statements like this:

> Reflecting their behaviorist heritage, some psychologists have been prone to assume that most any organism can, given proper training, learn to do most anything. . . . Similar claims have been made about human beings, such as the suggestion that anything can be learned at any age, in some useful form [this is a reference to famous remarks by Jerome S. Bruner]. More recent studies have come down, however, in harsh opposition to this optimistic cast of mind. An emerging consensus insists that each species—including ours—is specially 'prepared' to acquire certain kinds of information, even as it proves extremely difficult, if not impossible, for that organism to master other kinds of information.[15]

The mind is especially prepared to learn some things, like language, and children do so quickly, naturally, and easily. But, says Gardner, "By the same token, the difficulties most humans exhibit in learning to reason logically—particularly when propositions are presented in an abstract form—suggests no special preparedness in this area and perhaps even a predisposition to attend to the concrete specifics of a situation *rather than* to its purely logical implications." There is some truth to his statements. For example, after a certain age it is virtually impossible to learn a foreign language without showing the accent of the native language, and there can be no doubt that somehow unknown innate differences in brains do influence levels of performance. For the purposes of our public school system, however, such speculation is irrelevant. Not only are normal students' brains more plastic than adults' brains, and thus quite capable of changing as they grow, interact with their environment, and pursue goals; it would also be grossly unethical and scientifically naive for schools and teachers to promote the idea, and illegal to implement any plan, that some students, by virtue of their genetic heritage and up-bringing, are *incapable* of achieving reasonably high standards in math, English, history, sciences, and a foreign language. The United States would make great strides in social justice if *Brown v. Board of Education* came to encompass not just equality of opportunity but also *equality of expectations*. Gardner, with undoubted sincerity, protests that he does not want MI used as a political tool, but the danger for abuse is so great that our education system and the students in it would be better off with-out any such labels and speculation about innate abilities. We must con-tinue to embrace the article of faith among many educators that "Any child can learn."[16]

Whatever doubts Gardner may have about the flexibility and adapt-ability of the growing human brain, other authors on cognitive psychol-ogy in education do not share them. If not altogether impossible, change is seen as either too difficult to warrant the effort or unnecessary, despite the obvious fact that the very purpose of having schools is to induce changes in behavior and ways of thinking. One author who ap-plies Jung's psychology of types to the classroom advises that trying to change mental habits "is like trying to change the stripes on a tiger—like trying to change the grain in a piece of wood." Two other Jungians ask the reader to suppose that people's behavior "is just as inborn as their body build." Since Guild and Garger in their book on individual differ-ences make the dubious claim that individual differences in personality, learning styles, intelligences, and so forth are positive (being simple facts of life, they are value-neutral until people use them), we conclude that there is no expectation that people should change. Teachers and administrators in their workshops, Guild and Garger write, often say that the best part of learning about personality styles is "knowing that 'I'm OK!' "[17] If I'm okay, and you're okay, and everyone's okay, individ-ual differences necessarily being a positive thing, there is really no need to change, grow, and strive for improvement, especially when change goes against our very nature—or, more accurately, what is *perceived* to be our very nature. Psychology is not an exact science, and when a classroom teacher is facing twenty-five students in each of five or six classes a day, psychology's accuracy and utility are still more evanescent.

The function of the school system in these cognitive theories is therefore to identify a student's peculiar talent, help him develop it further, and assist him in learning through his strengths. If only the teacher will teach the subject in accordance with each child's natural strengths, each child will learn naturally and easily and live up to his potential. One author compares the student to a television: "The learner is like a television set which can receive information on several channels. Usually, one channel comes in more clearly and more strongly than the others. . . ." It is the teacher's job to keep clicking the remote control until he finds the channel by which the hapless, helpless, and passive student will receive a crystal-clear signal. With Dunn and Griggs defining learning style as "a biologically and developmentally imposed set of characteristics that make the same teaching method wonderful for some and terrible for others," we can see the absence of expectations that students should change in accordance with the demands of the situation, or overcome adversity. The teacher must find the natural, easy way for each student in the class to learn.[18]

Worse—to the educationist, at least—than the failure to progress academically is the possible psychological damage done to the student who must work outside his preferred cognitive styles. According to some researchers, both competence and self-esteem come from using natural stylistic traits: "If I'm naturally inclined toward certain patterns of behavior, I will be at my best in these areas. If I get strokes for these behaviors, I will feel good about myself. With a strong sense of self, I am in a better position to learn behaviors natural to other styles. If, on the other hand, my own natural traits are not valued, they will not develop to their fullest and I may wonder, 'What's wrong with me?'" Keirsey and Bates report Jung's claim that if the child is forced to live out of his nondominant types, "this falsification of type results in the individual's becoming disturbed in later life." The student cannot be expected to struggle to adapt his behavior or core personality and being to the demands of the environment; the environment must be modified so as to obviate the difficulty of change. One notes the inverse Darwinism—the environment is to be adapted to the organism, not the other way around. "In the future," prophesize Rita Dunn, Thomas DeBello, and their co-authors, "when others translate current research and add what will emerge over the next decade, the many different parts will form newer, better ways of helping students achieve more easily through, *rather than in spite of*, their many individual differences."[19]

Gardner expresses frustration when people confuse MI with learning-styles theory, but theirs is an understandable mistake when they read a statement like this: "My research has suggested that any rich, nourishing topic—any concept worth teaching—can be approached in at least five different ways that, roughly speaking, map onto the multiple intelligences. We might think of the topic as a room with at least five doors or entry points into it. Students vary as to which entry point is most appropriate for them and which routes are most comfortable to follow once they have gained initial access to the room. Awareness of these entry points can help the teacher introduce new materials in ways in which they can be *easily* grasped by a range of students. . . ."[20] One can clearly see that American education does not expect students to succeed in spite of difficulties and adverse circumstances; school is expected to be easy, struggle-free, and natural. The teacher must find the most suitable doorway or most clearly received channel for the students.

More pernicious than the teacher's daunting responsibility is the thought that students are incapable of overcoming their constraints, no matter how hard they try, or that overcoming constraints is not worth the trouble. The story "A Rabbit on the Swim Team," which was delivered to me and other teachers at a teacher in-service on MI, shows the currency of such theories in American education and society:

A RABBIT ON THE SWIM TEAM

Once upon a time, the animals decided they should do something meaningful, so they organized a school.

They adopted an activity curriculum of running, climbing, swimming and flying. To make it easier to administer the curriculum, all the animals took all the subjects.

The *rabbit* started at the top of his class in running, but developed a nervous twitch in his leg muscles because of so much make-up work in swimming.

The *duck* was excellent in swimming; in fact, better than his instructor. But he made only passing grades in flying, and was very poor in running. Because he was so slow in running, he had to drop swimming and stay after school to practice running. This caused his webbed feet to be badly worn, so that he was only average in swimming. But average was quite acceptable, so nobody worried about that—except the duck.

The *squirrel* was excellent in climbing, but he encountered constant frustration in flying class because his teacher made him start from the ground up instead of from the treetop down. He developed "charley horses" from overexertion, and so only got a C in climbing and a D in running.

The *eagle* was a problem child and was severely disciplined for being a non-conformist. In climbing classes, he beat all the others to the top of the tree, but insisted on using his own way to get there.

Each creature has its own set of capabilities in which it will naturally excel—unless it is expected or forced to fill a mold that doesn't fit.[21]

Unfortunately, MI, LBRB, and LS, and their belief in "the constrained student," fit well with American beliefs that talents or propensities are innate, genetically endowed, and relatively immutable, an odd sort of educational predestinationism for a country that once prided itself on its Calvinist, Protestant work ethic and "pick-yourself-up-by-your-bootstraps" tradition. Instead of stressing development and what students *can* achieve and make of themselves if they work hard enough, the cognitive theories reinforce the already prevalent notion in American education and society that students must do only what comes easily and naturally. It is futile, even harmful, for the rabbit to keep wasting precious time and effort in a pointless attempt to learn to swim, so why should we torture, say, an African-American kid with obvious bodily-kinesthetic intelligence, by forcing the kid to become proficient at reading and math?

In discussing the MI approach at the Key School in Indianapolis,

Mindy Kornhaber and Howard Gardner in fact consider the case of Kimberly, an African-American girl who excels at projects involving bodily-kinesthetic activities but who doesn't fare so well with standardized tests on math and English. Note the subtle anti-intellectualism: "What may be more surprising," the authors write about Kimberly, "is that this school success [in projects involving drama, singing, and dancing, her predominant intelligences] comes in the face of marginal results on IQ tests and a failing grade on the state's standardized test of math and English."[22] In other words, Kimberly is smart, but not in the subjects she is tested on. Obviously she cannot be expected to bring up her math and English scores to a reasonably high level that other children reach in formal math and English classes; instead of torturing this poor girl by forcing her to do something she has no knack for, she should stick to what she does best, which is singing, dancing, and acting. Math and English should be taught to her through bodily-kinesthetic activities or drama.

Since it is important that students identify their preferred modes—the lines of natural force, I suppose—so that they can more effectively manage their learning and how things are taught to them, the cognitive theories emphasize metacognitive activities: students are encouraged to think about how they think. For example, under Practical Intelligence for School, one of Gardner's projects, students in middle and high school are encouraged to think about their preferred learning styles[23] and their dominant intelligences. While classroom teachers are often desperate to have their students simply read the textbook and complete the assignment, Gardner and Krechevsky recommend that students read books about MI and LS—and various LS theorists have students taking tests to identify their predominant learning or cognitive styles. MI and LS thus increase the danger that these fictional or theoretical limitations will be accepted by students as hard scientific fact. Students in our educational system, which applauds "A Rabbit on the Swim Team" and never questions the natural-learning beliefs, lack the sophistication to realize that such "intelligences" and "learning styles" are merely artificial constructs, mere rules of thumb to describe the enormously complicated and imperfectly understood process of learning. Students are more likely to accept such assessments as the final, oracular truth on their abilities. After all, the *experts* trained in a scientific discipline have spoken.

The danger of pigeonholing as a result of these exercises is great. "I have a linguistic intelligence, I can't do math," students can and do say, for they hear such nonsense in society. People often say things like "I'm not a math person" or "I'm not a language person" to excuse their failures, or as facile excuses to obviate the struggle of learning and change. Once, when I was with a crowd of adults at a restaurant and it came time to pay the bill, one person—a teacher—excused her inability to figure out the tip (15 percent of the total) with the lame excuse, "I'm not a math person." It seems that I have heard students say innumerable times, "Reading/math/Latin/Spanish/chemistry/history [anything that doesn't come naturally or easily] just isn't my thing." "I guess Latin's just not his thing," I recently heard from one mother when she was excusing her son's failure. As she and her husband excoriated me for not meeting their son's individual needs, it came as no surprise to me that she was working on her master's in education. "That's just his way," explained another mother about her son's disruptive classroom behavior; it being immutable, she expected me and the rest of the class to be tolerant and accepting. One teacher told me about a tenth-grade music student who defended her inability to read music after four years of music lessons with the excuse that she was an auditory learner, not a visual learner, and therefore couldn't possibly be expected to learn to read music. Claudia Cornett, who specializes in learning-styles theory, admits the great danger of the theories: "Teachers could end up doing more harm than good if their use of the results of brain research for learning style development is simply to attach another label to each child. A learner cannot be reduced to a dominant brain hemisphere or a cognitive process." Yet as seen in the examples above, such labels provide very handy excuses for failure and lower expectations. The excuses may well salve people's self-esteem, but they ignore what is usually the reason, namely, a lack of will and tenacity, over which one *does* have control. Students expect—and are expected—to understand things immediately, easily, and naturally, if the teacher will only teach the subject in accordance with each student's peculiar intellectual profile or learning style.

Many students limit their accomplishments, intellectual growth, and understanding of the world because of such theories, for they do not consider the possibility that knowledge and the benefits of knowledge may come only with difficulty and diligence. Stevenson and Stigler, who have studied the Japanese and Chinese educational systems in order to explain the higher achievement of their students, argue that the pervasive emphasis on innate ability in the American system "lowers expectations about what can be accomplished through hard work. Whether children are considered to be bright or dull, the belief that ability is largely fixed leads parents and teachers to be reluctant to demand higher levels of performance from their children, and leads to a satisfaction with the status quo."[24]

The irony of this artificial, educationist-constructed helplessness is that Gardner himself admits that people *can* learn outside their preferred intelligences. In a statement that sounds remarkably like Bloom's beliefs, Gardner says, "What recent research has shown, virtually incontrovertibly, is that whatever differences may initially appear, early intervention and consistent training can play a decisive role in determining the individual's ultimate level of performance. If a particular behavior is considered important by a culture, if considerable resources are devoted to it, *if the individual himself is motivated to achieve in that area . . .* nearly every normal individual can attain impressive competence in an intellectual or a symbolic domain." The editors of *Multiple Intelligences: A Collection* show where they stand on the issue of students having to work hard to overcome deficiencies in their ability to read and write: they put into a textbox Gardner's description of a student who, because of the school's concentration on linguistic-mathematical intelligences, fails to develop in a preferred nonlinguistic-mathematical area and loses her self-esteem. Yet they omit from the textbox the rest of Gardner's words: "it might turn out that with a lot of extra help and practice in the area of literacy, the child will become good enough to get good grades and have an enhanced self-image, in which case a parent may feel vindicated." (Note that the benefits accruing from the student's increased effort seem to be only good grades, enhanced self-image, and the parents' feeling of vindication. What about the real purpose of

schools and the real importance of that particular student's improvement—the child's wider abilities and increased powers to understand
the world and succeed in it?)[25]

Gardner praises the Suzuki violin method, by which ordinary children learn to play at impressive levels of competence; that and widespread accomplished performance in music among the members of a
certain cultural group suggest "that musical achievement is not strictly a
reflection of inborn ability but is susceptible to cultural stimulation and
training." Similar comments are made about the widespread ability of
the Japanese at drawing—practically all Japanese adults, writes Gail R.
Benjamin, because of the training they undergo in school, can draw at
impressive levels. The Japanese put no stock in beliefs about innate abilities, believing instead that hard work and diligence produce success.
Since all normal people also speak a language and do mathematics at
some level of proficiency—all normal people have all the intelligences,
remember—it isn't a huge assumption that all normal students can
achieve at reasonably high levels in all subjects in a standard curriculum, provided they study and practice hard enough and endure whatever discomfort the learning process may present to them, and are
taught by competent teachers who present organized lessons that cover
the material in depth, with plentiful opportunities for practice. Gardner's key phrase, however, is "if a particular behavior is considered important." As we shall see, Gardner and other MI writers, true to the
tenets of the Progressive Paradigm, show education's ambivalence to the
three Rs. As Gardner puts it, the linguistic and logical-mathematical intelligences have been overvalued in our schools.[26]

Gardner admits that individuals *can* achieve without the lessons
being crafted to their personal, idiosyncratic learning styles or intelligences. "In fact," he writes, ". . . students have managed to learn even
when lessons are in no way tailored for them, presumably because most
curricula are redundant, and because the students themselves possess an
array of intellectual strengths and strategies on which they can draw." It
stands to reason that the more progress students make through hard
work in domains they find difficult, the wider the array of strategies they
will have, and the better they will be able to solve a wider array of prob-

lems they encounter in life and acquire a wider understanding of the world. All that is needed is the expectation that students must do what is necessary to succeed, and that they put forward the effort, sometimes light, sometimes grueling, necessary for success. Gardner is certainly aware of what people can accomplish through hard work, for he mentions how some people in Nigeria view talent, a statement worth quoting at length: "Among the Anang peoples in Nigeria, every individual is expected to be able to dance and sing well, to carve and to weave. The Anang recognize that a very few individuals may have talents superior to their fellows, but they firmly believe that no one lacks the requisite abilities to achieve in these aesthetic domains. As anthropologist John Messenger indicates, 'It is obvious that, to the Anang, *talent implies the possession of certain capabilities which anyone can develop if he sets out to do so.*'" (This "can-do" attitude is also commonly held in Japan.)[27]

LS theorists too admit that students can learn outside their preferred learning styles. Some even advise that students be *required* to learn outside their preferred styles. Although Anthony F. Gregorc admits that learning styles have an inborn, natural basis, which to some would argue their immutability, he nonetheless finds that students can learn outside their preferred cognitive styles. He even recommends that students be expected to do so, as "development of these [minor] proclivities," he writes, "is necessary because of the multivariate demands from our environment." Later he suggests, "[Learners] also need to learn how to add 'unnatural' behaviors, to adapt, cope with, and change themselves and their environment." Claudia Cornett has a similar opinion, for she argues that we should encourage the "flexing" capabilities of both teachers and students. "Learning to learn," she says, is the process of having students gradually increase their capacity to adjust their learning style to the teaching style and task. (Yet teachers are expected to know when it is best to teach each student according to his learning style, and when to expect him to flex—an expectation impossible to meet.) Gregorc, and Ramirez and Castañeda, and others are said to "advocate selective teaching of students through their *weaker* characteristics to build upon those. The Dunns [in contrast] insist that traits develop over time, and that students should always be taught through their strengths." Yet elsewhere

the Dunns also say explicitly that students can overcome their preferences if they are motivated and interested. That is, if they work and
study hard enough.[28]

Other LS theorists find that students' styles are more fluid than
people think, that they become more integrated with age. Young children are predominantly tactile-kinesthetic, yet as they mature they tend
to become auditory and then visual learners, and altogether they become more capable of using different styles, as called for by the situation. *"The modalities* [that is, learning styles]," write Walter Barbe and
Michael Milone, *"become more integrated with age.* In young children,
the modalities are comparatively independent from one another. As the
child grows older, however, maturation and experience contribute to integration of the modalities, and strategies are developed to transfer information from one perceptual channel to another . . . so there are more
adults than children with mixed modality strengths." The best students,
it appears, are the ones who can work from various modes: "Research
also indicates that some students have perceptual strengths in several
areas and that, almost without exception, these prove to be the high
achievers." The low achievers are stuck in one mode, predominantly
tactile-kinesthetic.[29]

It stands to reason, then, that the teacher should simply teach the
subject formally and in-depth to the class as a whole, in a manner conso-
nant with the discipline and its structure, providing much practice for
the students and tutoring before and after school. The students can and
need to adjust in order to develop into well-rounded individuals, capable in as many modes and disciplines as possible. The purpose of education is change, after all, in behavior and knowledge, so that a person will
be enabled to respond to the demands of the environment and the exigencies of life.

STUDENT HELPLESSNESS IN BRAIN-BASED EDUCATION

Brain-based education presents a peculiarly gloomy estimate of students'
abilities. Students could learn easily, effortlessly, and naturally, BB theo-

rists argue, except that schools and their practices make learning difficult, if not impossible.

One reason why students are prevented from learning in school lies
in the evolutionary structure of the brain, argues Leslie A. Hart, one of
the fathers of BB education. The foundation for Hart's theory is Paul
MacLean's theory of the triune brain, according to which the human
brain is composed of three brains that evolved, one after another and
one on top of the other, over time. The oldest and most primitive of
those brains is the Reptilian brain, which is responsible for instinctive
behavior. A second brain, higher than the Reptilian, is the Old Mammalian, which is responsible for the limbic system and emotions. Finally
the New Mammalian is the highest and most recently evolved, for it includes the prefrontal cortex, which is responsible for our ability to think
in abstractions, our personality, and so forth—in other words, what
makes us distinctly human.[30]

Hart concludes that learning in the typical classroom is impossible
because the practices of the typical school are antagonistic to this evolutionary brain. Teaching in the typical school, he claims, is aimed at the
most recent accretion to the brain, the New Mammalian and its intellectual and cognitive capacities. It ignores the needs and characteristics
of the Reptilian and Old Mammalian brains, thus causing them to
"down-shift," or switch into a sort of survival mode. "The implications of
this must be seen as staggering for anyone engaged in instruction: *the
brain we are dealing with was not 'designed' by evolutionary needs for
logic, manipulation of symbols, for dealing with tight, sequential struc-
tures or word-systems, which today constitute the main concerns of conventional schooling and much training.*" Further: "To expect this successful,
established brain to change its natural ways of working to conform to
schools—a very recent invention—or to readily accept demands that it
work logically seems to me obviously absurd." Elsewhere Hart declares
that the conditions of the normal classroom and school "are *brain-
antagonistic* conditions and under them, learning grinds to a halt.
School and brain are at loggerheads and the consequences are the learning failures, discipline problems, confrontations, frustrations, and boredom we see at every turn." In fact, Hart argues, schools actually harm

students by teaching them, and he makes some stunning pronounce-ments: "There is more than a little evidence (rarely looked at) that at least a considerable share of conventional teaching has *negative* results: it inhibits, prevents, distorts, or holds back learning."[31]

There must be a conspiracy afoot: "Some suppression of learning, deliberately and systematically, is essential to preserve the present graded classroom system," argues Hart. Traditional teaching techniques don't work; if they did, he polemicizes, "we should have millions of reports of such success; we have almost none."[32] (Apparently there are almost no individuals in the United States who read, write, do mathe-matics at various levels of competence, understand some of the history of the world and the country they live in, or converse in a foreign lan-guage they learned at school. Not to mention that most researchers in all the sciences in the United States attended public schools.)

For BB theorists, the solution to this problem is to teach informally and give students almost total freedom in school. That will allay their in-stinctive fears of captivity (Hart compares students in a typical school to inmates in a prison or mental institution) and remove the teacher's threatening mien. In the brain-compatible school, Hart argues, "Stu-dents will be set free . . . to move around, talk with many people, com-municate, calculate, explore interests, and work on real projects and problems rather than contrived assignments and busy-work." Hart's edu-cational vision is scarcely new—it is simply Dewey and Kilpatrick with a different name, something Robert Sylwester, another proponent of BB education, admits. His recommendations for implementing BB educa-tion in the classroom won't surprise his readers, he says, because the cognitive sciences are discovering all sorts of things that good teachers have always intuitively known. "What's important," he continues, "how-ever, is that our profession is now getting strong scientific support for many practices that our critics have decried." And here we thought they had scientific support long ago.[33]

Eric Jensen, who has written numerous books and given many teacher in-services on brain-based learning, also blames the traditional classroom and the behaviorist basis of instruction for students' failure to learn. "We are all great natural learners," he advises. "Failing children and failing schools are an indication of a faulty system, not a faulty brain. . . ." Jensen too finds that teaching actually harms students: "We are given as educators, budding Einsteins, Mozarts, Robert Frosts, and Helen Kellers, but traditional teaching methods often turn them into bored, frustrated, and disillusioned dropouts who never get a chance to experience their own greatness." Jensen does not explain how Einstein, Mozart, and Frost managed to succeed despite the brain-antagonistic methods of their training. Nor does he explain why Helen Keller—according to *The Miracle Worker*, at least—was making little progress in her free, uninhibited life of natural learning until Annie Sullivan, a very strict, no-nonsense teacher came along with some decidedly old-fashioned ideas about learning and teaching; only then, and with great struggle and strain, did young Helen begin to learn and progress.[34]

The reason why traditional school practices and teaching so effectively impede the learning process lies in the chemistry and functioning of the brain, argue Jensen and Sylwester. Students in a traditional classroom with a typical teacher experience great measures of threat, and threatening conditions cause the brain to release cortisol, which impairs learning by acting negatively upon the hippocampus, which plays an important role in memory. "While small amounts [of cortisol] can feel good and be a motivating source, too much depresses the immune system, tenses muscles, and impairs learning. Ultimately, high cortisol levels can result in feelings of despair or overwhelm [sic]." Because they are forced to be in school, under the teacher's power, in confined conditions, unable to move and talk and engage in normal activities, Jensen argues, students suffer stress and lowered immune systems. This impairs their ability to learn and fend off disease, which results in less ability to learn, causing still greater stress and lowered immune systems. "Such findings may help explain the viscous [sic] academic performance cycle most of us have become all too familiar with: More test stress means more illness and missed classes which eventually means lower test scores; and the cycle of failure continues." Such dire consequences are the result of excessive stress, for Jensen acknowledges that moderate levels of stress enhance learning.[35]

To create a brain-friendly learning environment, Jensen proposes that the teacher impose high standards (relative to the student's abilities, however, which in essence means no standards at all) but with just the right amount of stress: too little stress does not prompt people to change, while too much stress creates "feelings of despair or overwhelm." All threats must disappear, and students must feel totally comfortable in their surroundings. He advises teachers, "Avoid calling on learners unless they volunteer. Eliminate discipline policies that are fear or threat-based. Avoid score keeping, overt comparisons, or situations that cause embarrassment to students. Never threaten a student by saying you'll send them [sic] to a higher authority, kick them out, or call their parents." A teacher should also remove the threats of after-school work and unannounced pop quizzes. Instead, to encourage good feelings in the class (and thus promote the release of endorphins, which brings about pleasant feelings), Jensen offers this advice to teachers: "Post affirming messages on doors and bulletins that read, for example, 'My success is absolutely assured.' Suggest to your learners how interesting they might find the material. Communicate to them that learning is fun, easy, and creative. . . . Aim for orchestrating at least twenty positive messages per hour." It should be noted, of course, that if students believe their success is assured, they will feel no need to change or to exert themselves or strive and struggle. Necessity, not complacency, is the mother of invention.[36]

ANTI-FORMALISM REVISITED

The various approaches that follow from the Cognitive Revolution show, each in its own way, their descent from the intellectual and social philosophy and psychology of the Progressive Paradigm. Two of their characteristics are anti-intellectualism (sometimes subtle, sometimes not) and anti-formalism. Gardner and other MI writers fault traditional education for its overemphasis on the linguistic and logical-mathematical intelligences: "Although I name the linguistic and logical-mathematical intelligences first, it is not because I think they are the most important — in fact, I am convinced that all seven of the intelligences have equal claim to priority. In our society, however," says Gardner, "we have put linguistic and logical-mathematical intelligences, figuratively speaking, on a pedestal." Thomas Armstrong advises, "During the typical school day, every student should be exposed to courses, projects, or programs that focus on developing each of their [sic] intelligences, not just the standard verbal and logical skills that for decades have been exalted above other domains in American education."[37]

This subdued bashing of the concentration on language and mathematics is ironic, because while Gardner believes that all the intelligences are equal, he also admits that in our society the logical-mathematical and linguistic are crucial: "I don't think *any* intelligence is inherently more or less important than others. In fact, which ones are important changes over time. But in our society, the linguistic and logical mathematical are considered to be the most important, and the intelligences you ought to have if you just have one or two intelligences." Gardner also admits that the logical-mathematical will become even more important than it is now.[38]

Perhaps the most stunning pronouncement of anti-formalism in BB education comes from Robert Sylwester, when he compares students in a modern classroom to the mortals in Plato's myth of the cave. He urges teachers, "Extend your thoughts also to classroom *caves*—with students metaphorically chained to their desks, looking at the chalkboard up front that's filled with vertical, horizontal, diagonal, and curved lines that the curriculum combines into very limited verbal representations of just about everything that exists beyond the classroom walls."[39] Such thinking is typical of education's anti-formalism, bordering on anti-intellectualism, for it regards academics and book learning as actually retarding the development of the mind and hindering one's understanding of the world. The fact is, however, that it is chiefly by means of studying academic subjects—English, sciences, history, a foreign language, math, and so forth—that a person in a modern, industrialized nation best increases his understanding of the world, its forces, and its peoples and their actions, and hence his ability to act upon the world effectively and survive.

Sylwester offers many examples of his dedication to anti-formalism through recommendations for classroom activities and occasional anecdotes of his years teaching elementary school. For example, he advises that the teacher have the students study how much classroom space is needed by having them experiment with the distances between their desks. Or the class might experiment with the "classroom energy," or identify an exploratory space in the natural world that is the size of a television screen, and then regularly observe it. Overall he urges that teachers respond to the needs and interests of their students, and he gives an example of how he did so during his years in the classroom. When the Russians launched Sputnik in 1957, he realized that he knew nothing about rockets, nor did his students, but since it was a newsworthy topic he created an ad hoc unit on rocketry. Despite the lack of a curriculum for rockets, a textbook, or his own formal training, he devoted "several" weeks of class to the study of rockets, even though doing so "intruded seriously into the formal curriculum." Sylwester justifies this by saying that the students later called it the most memorable of the subjects he taught that year. Finally, he reports that in an informal survey he conducted, novice teachers and burnt-out veterans showed an untoward dedication to the curriculum while those teachers who were dedicated but secure in their position were more likely to depart from it. "Teachers who seemed a cut above the norm," he writes, were more likely to disregard the formal curriculum in order to meet students' needs and interests. How curious is our educational philosophy—the "better" teacher doesn't teach the subject. Is it any wonder that our students achieve so much less than students in other countries do, such being education's hostility to "mere knowledge"?[40]

In departing from the set curriculum, the teachers were undoubtedly benefiting the students. After all, Sylwester argues, "Stress and drug-related illnesses are part of the personal and social costs of educational and technological efforts to force our body/brain [Sylwester's term to denote the unity of the body and mind] to function well beyond its normal capabilities—whether it be to require students to use paper and pencil to solve math problems they don't understand and consider irrelevant, or to require them to use an equally incomprehensible computer program." Again the notion that studying and hard work at academics are bad for students' health. Sylwester sounds almost like G. Stanley Hall or Margaret Naumberg: "Because secondary schools are typically more beset by political pressures to excel, they are more oriented toward increasing the pressure on students during a decade [years ten to twenty of life] in which adolescents need to slow down, consolidate the explosive motor and social development of their first decade, and *discover themselves*." One wonders why educationists cannot imagine that school subjects might help students discover themselves—by testing their abilities and limits, and widening their understanding of the world they live in.[41]

INDIVIDUALIZED CONTENT AND METHODS
FOR NATURAL LEARNING

The various cognitive theories also share the Progressive beliefs in individualized education. All believe that without the teacher designing lessons for the peculiar needs and characteristics of each individual, students cannot be expected to succeed.

Gardner believes that we can figure out the predominant intelligences of children in early childhood, perhaps even in infancy, then construct an individualized educational regimen that capitalizes on the child's preferred modes of processing new information. This individualized regimen includes an apprenticeship which the child, in conjunction with the school's assessment specialist (trained in MI's methods), teachers, and parents chooses after the *third grade*. Gardner's visions for education through the use of students' multiple intelligences are based on the principal assumption that individuals are not alike "and that education can be more properly carried out if it is tailored to the abilities and the needs of the particular individuals involved." He sees educational success as arising *solely* from individualized curricula and individualized methods; he often waxes indignant about uniformity in American education.[42]

In discussing the assessment of students, Gardner declares, "There is in the country today an enormous desire to make education uniform, to treat all students in the same way, and to apply the same kinds of one-dimensional metrics to all. This trend is inappropriate on scientific grounds and distasteful on ethical grounds." Elsewhere he suggests, "Since we have thousands of different kinds of kids, probably school should be done a thousand different kinds of ways"—a statement that incidentally reminds us of the complexity of the students whose individual needs teachers are expected not only to identify but also accommodate. The feasibility of such an individualized education program is not discussed in useful detail. At one point Gardner casually rebuffs any objections that such individualization is utopian, claiming it is merely a matter of will; yet at another he admits that such an individualized education program is difficult to conceptualize, let alone achieve. Note, of course, that the individualization of curricula will have to be implemented in the absence of reliable, objective tests over "several hundred" possible dimensions of mind. Gardner also fails to discuss the possibility that an individualized curriculum and methods might prove unethical. With a gratuitous insult, he says, "Some teachers just don't want children to do too good a job or it makes them feel superfluous." Surely he will admit that some assessment specialists might, for example, track African-Americans into the bodily-kinesthetic apprenticeships, thinking that since the child is from such-and-such circumstances, he or she cannot possibly be expected to learn the same math and physics that a middle-class Asian or white child is expected to learn. Instead such children, showing natural ability at singing, dancing, and acting, should stick to what they do best and not trouble themselves over their lower levels of performance in English and math.[43]

This hostility to a uniform educational system for all is shared also by the Dunns and other LS writers. Lamenting the lack of different educational programs and teaching approaches for different students in a typical school today, the Dunns write, ". . . Children are forced to adjust their learning styles to whatever teaching approaches are used. This procedure may be damaging to their progress because it makes learning more difficult than it should be, causes frustration, and decreases a youngster's confidence in himself. Conversely, when a student learns in ways that are natural to him, the outcomes usually are increased academic achievement, improved self-esteem, a liking for learning, improved basic skills, stimulated creativity, and gradually increasing learner-independence." Therefore the Dunns envision a school that will offer many structural alternatives (traditional, open, free, alternative) and differing educational philosophies, so that students will receive lessons attuned to their learning styles. "The important thing to remember is that the placement of students [in an educational program at school] should be based on the way they learn, and not on the supposed value of a given program," they warn. Since the Dunns elsewhere note that students differ in respect to the times of day when they learn best, and that their schedules should therefore be constructed accordingly, one can imagine the monstrous boondoggle that counselors and administrators would face in seeking to satisfy all students' multifarious needs *just in scheduling.*[44] Yet the Dunns do not discuss the feasibility of such an individualized program or even the ethical and legal problems that it might create.

School personnel might conceivably meet the peculiar learning needs of a few students: some students whose energy levels are highest in the morning, for example, could have their most intellectually demanding courses scheduled then. The problem is that not all students can be so accommodated, thus leaving a great many parents and students angry and likely to seek redress through the courts for not being treated equally. Or, if two students in the same class are suddenly unable to tolerate the other's presence in the room, are they to have their schedules changed so that their peculiar learning style is not affected? If one student with a particularly acute olfactory intelligence cannot tolerate being in the same room with a student with a deficient hygiene intelligence, which one should be removed from the class? If special treatment is given to some, it must be given to all, something that is simply impossible as well as unnecessary. Students could learn to adapt themselves to conditions if our educational system expected them to learn and change despite the occasional discomfort.

Some authors argue that it is unfair to teach according to only one or two intelligences. For example, English class, though revolving almost exclusively around linguistic intelligence, should incorporate the other intelligences into its various lessons so that nonlinguistic students may also succeed in English. To teach English class in a way that requires students to use mostly their linguistic intelligence, or math class in a way that penalizes the students without a strong logical-mathematical intelligence, or basketball in a way that does not allow the non-bodily-kinesthetically adept to succeed, is unfair. "Concentration on only [math and language] . . . ignores the dominant strengths of perhaps the majority of children in the classroom," complains Thomas Armstrong. "If we treat everybody as if they [sic] are the same," says Gardner in an interview, "we're catering to one profile of intelligence, the language-logic profile. It's great if you have that profile, but it's not great for the vast majority of human beings who do not have that particular profile of intelligence"—though Gardner has stated quite clearly that all people have all the intelligences, and differ only in their relative strengths. This opinion is shared by LS writers. We read, for example, "While based in recognition of individual differences, a focus on learning styles can be a significant step for promoting *equity* in the schools. For instance, if the visual learner has less opportunity to learn than the auditory learner because of prevalent teaching behaviors, not only has that learner been shortchanged, but our society has been deprived of the optimum talents of that individual."[45]

In none of these cognitive theories are students thought to be *incapable* of learning outside their preferred or dominant style. It is simply to make things easier and more natural for the students that the teacher is expected to adapt his methods to their needs. There is nothing wrong with the teacher striving to make the students' learning easier or more efficient; helping students learn and meet their potential is the teacher's job. The damage appears when the application of cognitive theory promotes the idea that students are helpless and passive, able to succeed only under optimal conditions; does not encourage students to push themselves and overcome obstacles to success; and results in dumbing-down for all students or in perversions of the subject matter.

The BB people agree completely that schooling should be individualized. Sylwester goes to absurd lengths in calling for individualization for students: "Because mood significantly determines response, we might begin the day with interactive activities that provide a sense of how the various moods of students might affect their behavior. We might then *further adapt instruction to the moods of the participants.*" So much for a carefully planned lesson. Jensen believes that uniformity is brain-antagonistic and therefore causes problems. "We may be accidentally driving our learners crazy by stressing uniformity in the environment. . . . Many of our learners are underperforming due to restrictive classroom policies that conflict with their preferred learning style." He argues that teaching to only one or two intelligences demotivates students, and he vehemently rejects standardized testing. The only thing that matters in assessment—"how a student is doing compared to their [sic] previous performance!" He asks, "Shouldn't the student who is living with abuse, rage, brain insults, or distress, for instance, be evaluated on an individual basis?" Since Jensen also sternly denounces the idea of comparing one student's performance with another's (at one point he even compares testing students to uprooting a fruit tree to see if it is growing), one must point out that it is actually unfair *not* to let students know how they fare in comparison with others.[46] People tend to become easily satisfied with themselves and their current performance; seeing that others actually do something better can shock people from their complacency and inspire them to strive for improvement.

INDIVIDUALIZATION THROUGH MULTI-DISCIPLINARY PROJECTS

One way for the school to achieve individualization, argue the educationists, is to have the students engage in multi-disciplinary projects. The advantages of the projects (according to these various approaches) are obvious: first, the students have a great deal of choice in what topics to study and are thus more likely to be motivated to learn—or, in BB theory, they exercise more control; second, they are allowed to focus on the learning style or intelligence they find most congenial; and third, projects are "real-world" activities, involving the use of many intelligences and learning styles across domains and subject matters. In short, multi-disciplinary projects are education for the whole child, the Holy Grail of the Progressive Paradigm.

In Gardner's ideal MI school, for example, students learn academic subjects through projects; thus the students are able to learn through their preferred intelligences. "In the mornings, students study the traditional subject areas but in untraditional ways. Almost all the work in mathematics, social studies, reading and writing, and science takes the form of student projects. Students explore particular aspects of material in depth, addressing problems that confront professionals in the discipline." In the afternoon they work on the apprenticeships they chose as third-graders. MI writers apparently expect students to make bricks without supplying the straw, that is, to address problems that trained professionals work at in their daily work, but without the prior formal training. (I can imagine nothing more daunting, humiliating, and frustrating for a novice Latinist than to tackle a problem that occupies experts but without the expert's knowledge and training in grammar, literary analysis, social and literary history, culture, and so forth.) Gardner is also very Deweyan in his emphasis on having students work on projects that involve the wider community, though he admits that some topics need to be taught in fairly traditional ways. "It would be a mistake to consider projects as a panacea for all education ills, or as the royal road to a nirvana of knowledge. Some materials need to be taught in more disciplined, rote, or algorithmic ways," he writes. He acknowledges that while the Suzuki violin method works well with young children, older learners need a more structured approach, for the children in the Suzuki method do not learn to read music or learn music theory.[47]

Renate and Geoffrey Caine, who apply BB education to the classroom, argue that learning must include physical and social interactions, uses of language, and creative enterprises, and they too advocate the use of projects. In one example they describe the cross-disciplinary approaches a class might use to learn about the potato; another concerns the eagle. Reading about their proposed eagle project, one cannot but recall Kilpatrick's description of boys learning about castles and medieval warfare:

[Students] may explore nesting, feeding, and reproductive patterns and the eagle's ecological requirements, together with relevant information spanning several subject areas. They listen to recordings of the live eagle as it moves through the air, and they read literature featuring eagles. They study the eagle as a political symbol and its role in the arts. Students develop areas of expertise or experts are brought to class or are recorded or videotaped. Computer simulations and tracking programs are made available to students to help them identify where eagles are located and whether they are thriving. The mood that should prevail is that of a team of researchers or explorers engaged in a meaningful, exciting adventure.[48]

If only the students could engage in real, meaningful projects that were compatible with the true characteristics of their brains, their learning would come naturally. They would learn the subject in depth, without feeling strain or negativity. "Acquisition of natural knowledge is the result of the entire process [of adjusting new knowledge with old]. When immersion is orchestrated properly, including the fact that the learner is intrinsically motivated, the learner will have spontaneous and often unnoticeable shifts or flashes of insight—those 'aha's' that represent felt meaning," the Caines say. This view of the acquisition of knowledge is reminiscent of one of Dewey's idealistic views in *Interest and Effort in Education*, in which the student—almost as in Zen—becomes one with the problem and learns naturally. But the authors declare, teachers actually make it harder for students to learn, if not impossible: "Schools organized on the factory model [the standard slam today against the typical school] do not open doors to the future; they imprison students in their own minds."[49]

Jensen too advocates the use of multi-disciplinary projects in the classroom. In discussing the teaching of math, for example, he explains, "Brain-compatible learning means weaving math, movement, geography, social skills, role-playing, science, and physical education together." He omits language arts and social studies, but we understand what he means. One of his ideas reveals the dangers of a project curriculum: "So although a trip to China to learn about the country's political system is out of the question, asking your students to plan out such a trip is not. Of course, to accomplish the task, they will have to learn something about the political climate, geography, money, language, passports, weather, foods, people, and customs."[50] If the original purpose of the project is to learn about the political system in China, students doing research according to Jensen's recommendations will learn very little about the political system. They will be too busy learning about other myriad subtopics. The sometimes dry facts of Chinese communism will not command the attention students will pay to "related" topics such as food, customs, or money. Think about it this way: which is more likely to cause the release of endorphins into the brain and thus bring about a feeling of pleasure—the study of Chinese communism, the civil war between Mao and Chiang Kai-shek, the development of Chinese communism under Mao, and the differences between Marx's theory and its implementation under Mao; or eating Kung Pao chicken? Which is more likely to cause the release of negative amounts of cortisol? Which approach best responds to students' interests and needs?

The use of projects as a primary learning tool for students increases the risk that they will acquire a haphazard, slipshod education—a little of this, a little of that, without much continuity or depth, with the student never really learning the formal structure and fundamental concepts of a discipline, chiefly because he has never studied it formally. He learned about American history through his study of the eagle, or he learned of the culture of ancient Rome as it pertained to its use of the eagle on the army's standards, or he learned about the Chinese political system through wonton soup. Since the student's attention is so diffuse and scattered across many divergent subtopics during work on such a project, the intellectual sloppiness of our feel-good education system is fostered. Attention to detail and accuracy run counter to the spirit of American education and its anti-formalism biases, and the use of multidisciplinary projects promotes careless, superficial, shallow work. Jensen inadvertently proves my point about the great risks of intellectual sloppiness in natural learning. Discussing how people learn their native language naturally, he asks, "Is it possible to learn science, history, accounting, geography, math, life skills, literature, and the arts by default [sic]? Of course it is!"[51]

The haphazard manner of multi-disciplinary projects becomes more of a problem when we consider the individual teacher's ability to instruct well and to assess students' work fairly across so many disciplines. While education reformers of more modest expectations want students to be taught by teachers who know their subjects well, the project proponents apparently want teachers who know dozens of subjects tangentially related to the main topic. And while students may know the material, they may be incapable of demonstrating their knowledge in the traditional way; so they must be allowed a variety of means to show what they know. ". . . Just as the theory of multiple intelligences suggests that any instructional objective can be taught in at least seven ways, so too does it imply that any subject can be assessed in at least seven different ways."[52]

In lessons dealing with the novel *Huckleberry Finn*, for example, Armstrong would offer the following options so that students could use their various intelligences to exhibit their understanding: "Pantomime how you think Huck Finn would act in a classroom. If Huck were a musical phrase, what would he sound like or what song would he be?" or "Describe in a few words your personal feelings toward Huck Finn. . . ." He would give bodily-kinesthetic students in chemistry the assignment, "Orchestrate a dance showing different bonding patterns," an activity no doubt eagerly anticipated by those whose sexuality intelligence is so brutally repressed by puritanical teachers. Guild and Garger make similar recommendations for teachers, and they glowingly praise an English teacher who responded to the diversity among his students during their reading of Robert Frost's "The Road Not Taken." After the students had finished their lively discussion of the poem (livelier, of course, than the discussion in the class with a traditional teacher and lesson plan), the good English teacher gave them a choice of assignments for that night's homework: (1) memorize the poem, (2) illustrate it with a drawing, or (3) act out an example of its message. While not every reading assignment in English demands an essay, one must note that a writing assignment wasn't even offered, much less required. Similarly, in their description of how an English teacher taught the "novel" [sic] *Oedipus Rex* in accordance with her students' diverse learning styles, Dunn and Griggs describe the homework the students were assigned after reading or hearing the play (nonvisual students, in accordance with their learning styles, were not required to read it). The teacher distributed a crossword puzzle based on the play and encouraged the students to test themselves. For homework "she required the students to use all the information in the crossword puzzle in a creative way. Thus, students could develop a game, poster, book cover, poem, or drawing that included the information."[53]

One must ask: Are the students who do not like to write or who do not write well ever required to write a coherent essay? How will they ever learn to write coherently and formulate and refine their thoughts in writing if they are never required to write? We should not be surprised, then, when Dunn and Griggs mention how one teacher, to meet the diverse needs and cognitive styles of the students in her French class, did not require that they speak or understand French. "Some students found responding to oral questions difficult, so [the teacher] dramatized the meaning and asked students to respond in whichever modality they preferred."[54] But isn't a major goal of taking French, a modern language, acquiring the ability to converse in it? Society insists that students take many years of English in school so that they may learn how to read and write English, not so that they can improve their dancing, drawing, or singing. The reason for learning chemistry is to be able to work within the rules of the science of matter, not to improve one's dancing. The purpose of education is, after all, to change one's behavior and ways of thinking. The "multi-modal" assessments pose no harm, and even help, if they are used to inspire creative thinking or to bring some levity into the class. Yet if the students are still unable, say, to describe Huck's growth as a moral human being over the course of the novel, the assessments can be used to mask the students' ignorance, give a false sense of competence, and remove the necessity of going through the learning process. Since students' failure to learn is thought to constitute an admission of the teacher's failure to teach correctly, teachers and parents are often too eager to search for *any* sign of success, no matter how tenuous.

ASSESSING THE QUALITY OF INSTRUCTION

Another grave danger in such teaching practices concerns the quality of instruction and how accurate the information given to the students would be. Attempts to individualize instruction according to students' cognitive profiles increase the likelihood that everyone will receive poor lessons.

The Dunns' proposal for dealing with all of the numerous learning styles in the classroom offers a good example. First, it should be noted that most of the students in the typical classroom are auditory, visual, or mixed learners: according to one study, the breakdown is 30 percent visual, 25 percent auditory, 15 percent kinesthetic, and 30 percent mixed.[55] Thus most students in the classroom are capable of adapting, with varying degrees of ease, to a standard, whole-class lesson: the teacher explains the new concept in a brief lecture to the class as a whole (a method that suits the auditory learners particularly well) while writing key concepts and diagrams or graphics on the blackboard or overhead projector (which suits the visual learners very well), or while illustrating such points in a handout (for the visual students but also helping the tactile-kinesthetic, for it gives them something to touch and manipulate). Then the teacher shows sample problems which the class solves together. Despite the fact that most of the students are in tune to the predominant teaching methods, and the others can adapt with some effort, the Dunns advocate radically changing traditional classroom and school practice to meet *all* students' needs. Doing so, however, would be bad for *all* students' learning.

The first important change is that the teacher will not deliver lessons to the class as a whole. Instead the teacher will sort the students into groups, depending upon the results of their Learning Style Inventory or their personal preferences. "It is easy for teachers to post an assignment *with specific objectives* and say to the class, 'You may learn this alone, in a pair, or in a team of three or four, or with me. If you wish to work alone, sit wherever you will be comfortable in the room. If you wish to work in a pair, take a moment to decide where you will sit, but stay away from those needing to be by themselves." Students who are highly motivated or who like to work alone may be given Contract Activity Packages, so they can work alone. Other students will work together in teams or pairs, based upon their learning preferences, while those who need the most structure and guidance will work with the teacher. Since those who need the most structure and guidance are usually the students who do the worst in class, that particular group will likely be called the "dumb" or "bad" group by the other students, many of whom will resent the fact that the "dumb" or "bad" kids get all the teacher's time and attention while they, the responsible kids, are expected to learn by doing worksheets in class. The Dunns seem to think that because the responsible kids can work quietly and need little supervision, they don't need or deserve much help from the teacher. They certainly will not gain much benefit from the teacher's knowledge and expertise in the subject, for they will be reading the textbook and filling in the blanks on the worksheets while the teacher devotes his time and energy to the students who need the most supervision. In that classroom, the good students will rightly complain that they are being punished for being good.[56]

One student's comment about her class, which caters to different learning styles, reveals dangers that Dunn and Griggs do not discuss: "Can you imagine anyone wanting to learn these things by reading a book?" comments that enthusiastic learner whose needs have been met. "It's so much more fun with this board game and with your friend!" The danger is that the students will be too distracted by interacting with their friends to concentrate on learning the subject accurately and in depth, a danger heightened by the fact that accurate, in-depth knowledge (represented by the book and the teacher) is apparently regarded as irrelevant in the student's learning. Dunn and Griggs also advise that the teacher allow students to "bypass" the teacher's lesson if they feel it is incompatible with their learning style, so that they can learn the subject on their own, in a way they find most comfortable. This approach will surely increase the likelihood that the students will pick up bad habits in the subject, if they do not spend their time goofing off entirely. (Dunn and Griggs believe that the teacher's good classroom management skills will prevent such goofing off.) It is difficult to imagine the learning of more than a few students in such an LS classroom to be anything other than shallow, superficial, and naive, and the classroom itself to be chaos.[57]

In another example, Dunn and Griggs describe how one English teacher taught *Oedipus Rex*. The teacher divided the students into many different groups, according to their Learning Style Inventories. Some students read the play alone, some with a partner, others in a group; those who didn't read well or who were auditory learners listened to a tape of the teacher reading the play aloud; less motivated students read along with the teacher. The problem is this: literary language is not transparent. Even the best readers in the class will miss many nuances, subtleties, references to events within the play, references to contemporary or ancient history, and so on. I have found that students reading even a straightforward work like *To Kill A Mockingbird* fail to see and appreciate many of its nuances. For example, I have never had a ninth-grader who knew what Atticus means by "the crash" when he explains to Scout that "the crash hit them [country folks] the hardest." Similarly, students never realize—until I provide the crucial background information—what Scout refers to when she says, very early in the book, "Recently we had been informed that we had nothing to fear but fear itself"—an important reference because it tells when the story occurs and the circumstances of life in the United States and the South at the time. And, of course, the students never understand why Miss Caroline, whose head is full of Progressive education practices, discourages Scout from reading.[58]

If students, following the advice of Dunn and Griggs, read *Oedipus Rex*—a work far less accessible than *To Kill A Mockingbird*—by themselves, doing worksheets, they will miss much of what makes the play a glorious piece of literature. They simply do not have the background knowledge or critical ability to be left to their own devices. (If Dunn and Griggs themselves think *Oedipus Rex* is a novel, could high school students, reading the play on their own, be expected to do better?) Reading a play in class or discussing a literary work should be a group effort, so that the class as a whole can participate and benefit. The students who don't read well need to learn how to read and interpret literary language and learn the many wonderful pleasures that come from analyzing literature, and the students who do read well certainly need to improve their skills.

Suggested ways of implementing MI in the classroom are also perilous. In order to teach to every intelligence, Armstrong recommends that the teacher teach each lesson seven different ways, and he details his lesson plan for teaching punctuation: one day for linguistic intelligence, another day for mathematical intelligence, and so on. "All a teacher has to do is teach seven different ways on seven different days," he explains. At the end of seven days, ". . . the teacher would have presented the skill through every child's strongest intelligence and bolstered children's less-developed intelligences as well."[59] The only problem is that it now takes seven times as long to cover the material, and the students will therefore learn one-seventh as much as they might. The sacrifice in content poses no problem for educationists, for one frequently hears them claim that covering less material is better.

MULTIPLE INTELLIGENCES, LEARNING STYLES, BRAIN-BASED EDUCATION — WHY BOTHER?

Informed laypersons, accustomed to education's embarrassing susceptibility to fads, often greet new teaching methods and approaches with bemused skepticism. Like many educational vogues of the past, the approaches described in this chapter are not benign. They pose certain dangers to students, their intellectual growth, and their development as responsible, autonomous individuals.

By presupposing a one-dimensional student—like the duck, bearing the absurd expectation to run as a rabbit does—the theories inhibit students' growth. Students are not expected to push themselves to succeed and thus to expand their range of knowledge and abilities. Consequently their theoretical limitations become accepted as fact, and they become the victims of low expectations. Their vulnerability rises, for without a teacher capable of being all things to all students at all times, students are assumed to be incapable of learning and succeeding. Their ability to succeed, the quality of the conduct of their lives, is thought to be found outside their own actions and thoughts.

Is it fair, just, and kind to allow the young, who do not know better, to wait in vain, for their teachers to create the perfect conditions that will bring them educational success naturally and easily? Should we not make it clear to them that their success and happiness lie in what they do, in what they choose to think, and in how they adapt themselves to the circumstances of life? Should we not foster the attitude that they must create their own success, regardless of the circumstances?

6

PEDAGOGUE-CENTRIC EDUCATION: THE OMNIPOTENT/ INCOMPETENT TEACHER, THE IRRELEVANT STUDENT, AND THE "TEXTBOOK GARBAGE"

*I*f the present is the result of the past, modern educational thinking is no exception. It is a "low-brid" of three distinct currents of thought, which I have called the Progressive Paradigm. By one current, behaviorism, the teacher's responsibility is to provide the appropriate stimulus that will elicit from each student the desired response; the student is seen in a relatively passive and helpless role, his actions determined by the demands of the environment and the stimuli provided by the teacher, who is all-powerful because of his training in pedagogical science.

By another current, based on the theories of Dewey and Kilpatrick, students are expected to learn only what they feel a need to learn. Because compelling students to learn something they feel no need for might inflict on them grave psychological damage, all subjects must be learned in a natural way, through normal interactions and relations with one's environment, society, and peers, in the absence of compulsion, strain, and formal lessons on academic subjects.

The third current, from the child-cult advocates, is the idea that learning must be fun, emotionally fulfilling, a joyful, exuberant experience. Since learning academic subjects per se can scarcely fulfill these demands—the pleasures of exercising the intellect are more subtle and refined than those of dancing or playing games—and appears contrary to the needs and nature of youth, this thinking transcends mere anti-formalism and results in a deep and abiding distrust of, if not hostility to, academic subjects and the disciplined effort necessary for mastering them.

Because the Progressive Paradigm has set the terms by which our society thinks about education and youth, the continuing national debate over education reform inevitably devolves upon teachers and their teaching (that is, presenting lessons) as the ultimate source of students' academic success. Teachers, after all, are trained professionals in pedagogy, a scientific discipline, with the power—*if* they try hard enough, *if* they care enough, *if* they are not cynical, burned-out, public functionaries, protected in their incompetence by the teachers' unions, and *if* they will merely implement the latest pedagogical techniques devised by the experts in the colleges of education, acting in impartial, scientific rigor—to make learning natural and easy, even *fun* for students.

The student, on the other hand, merely *is*. The teacher must act and create, molding the student for bad or good, depending upon the teacher's ability to create learning activities that capitalize on the student's interests, abilities, and cognitive style, thereby allowing him to learn easily, naturally, and joyfully through his normal activities in daily life. The failure of our students thus appears to be proof positive of their teachers' incompetence. Considering all the findings of pedagogical science in the past hundred years—behaviorism, social psychology, the needs and nature of the young, with contributions from the cognitive sciences and brain science—many observers conclude from the disappointing results of our educational system that our teachers are simply lazy or incompetent.

It is time for Americans to consider the possibility that the problem of underachievement in the nation's public schools does not stem from the teachers and how they teach, but rather from elements of the Progressive Paradigm that make widespread academic excellence virtually impossible to achieve. It is time to consider the possibility that the chief beneficiaries of this pedagogue-centric educational philosophy are not the students but only the colleges of education and the people in them who promote the Progressive Paradigm.

EXPECTATIONS AMONG THE PUBLIC

Let there be no doubt about it: the United States looks to its teachers and their efforts, but not to its students and their efforts, for success in education. That being the accepted wisdom, students are free to do nothing more than wait for the teacher to create success for them. Education reform literature rarely contains the thought that our students are failing primarily because they do not study enough. So inbred is our educational thinking that discussions of students' failure to learn for reasons outside the teachers' control are found largely in studies dealing with schools in other countries.[1] Here is a sampling of the mind-set I am talking about:

> A pay raise for teachers is not justifiable for at least two reasons. The first is simply that the job of educating our children is not getting done.[2]

> At its National Education Summit last year, business people, educators and governors came out strongly for pay-for-performance for teachers. They realize that teaching is the most important factor in student achievement.[3]

> Whenever you have had a small teacher-student ratio, a strong principal and adequate facilities, children do well.[4]

I have no idea what course of study, what techniques of pedagogy or socialization produce well-educated children.[5]

The classroom teacher is the most important factor in the success of a student.[6]

The quality of our education system is determined more by the quality of the teaching that goes on each day than by any other single factor.[7]

Can there be more compelling evidence of the inadequacy of our teaching force?[8]

At a time when Americans view improving the quality of education as the most pressing issue confronting the nation, an overwhelming majority of the public considers improving the quality of teaching as the most important way to improve public education.[9]

I started [the book *Ed School Follies*] with the belief that at the center of the learning process stands the teacher capable of inspiring the student.[10]

The educational profession itself fosters the idea that teachers determine whether or not their students learn:

We have a curriculum that we want our teachers to teach and if they do that and they do that well, then their children are going to perform well on the assessments.[11]

What teachers know and do is the most important influence on what students learn.[12]

[In a review of Parker J. Palmer's *The Courage to Teach*:] . . . Palmer arrives at about the same [conclusion of the author of another book]. . . . Learning depends on the quality of the intellectual, emotional, and spiritual resources of the individual teacher.[13]

THE EXPERTS

The belief that teachers create or fail to create academic excellence for their students is fostered by today's education experts, who are the greatest devotees of the Progressive Paradigm. They may be found in the state education agencies, in the administration buildings of the public schools, and in colleges and schools of education in the universities. For all their talk about active learning, the educationists tend to see the student's role in learning as minor, if not insignificant. The following excerpt comes from a document handed to me and thousands of Texas teachers in an in-service on the Professional Development and Appraisal System. Note the seemingly insignificant role of the students in this state-of-the-art pedagogy:

Student Learning Occurs When . . .

A teacher is *well-advanced* in identifying the goals of student learning.

A teacher is *skilled* in teaching techniques.

A teacher is *skilled* in identifying student needs for planning and implementing instruction to assure student success.

A teacher is *effective* in professional and interpersonal communication skills.

A teacher is *adept* in improving the profession and maintaining professional ethics and personal integrity.

A teacher *understands* the depth and complexity of the curriculum.[14]

Note especially how passive the student is portrayed in the main clause, "Student learning occurs." The verb *occur* is intransitive, and its subject is *learning*, thus implying that the students have no role, or at most a minor one, in the creation of their knowledge. Grammatically speaking, of course, the word *student* could be omitted entirely and the sentence would nonetheless be complete, though still inaccurate: Learning just *happens* in the students' heads, as a result of the magic that teachers work, just as chemists mix chemicals or some pedagogical Merlin might wave a magic wand. Whether or not the students learn appears to result from what teachers, not what students, do. The teacher does this, the teacher does that, and somehow "student learning occurs."

From the example above, it would follow that students of a teacher who lacks all these good qualities will not learn. But this is patently false. People do learn, even quite complicated and abstract things, without teachers giving excellent lessons. We read, for example, that schools in Confucian-heritage cultures do everything that educators in the United States consider wrong, yet their students learn more than American students do. ". . . Perhaps we are seeing that when schooling [in China] is poor, good students are forced to generate their own self-regulated strategies for deep learning precisely in order to survive bad teaching," an observer writes. Chinese students manage to learn, and to learn in depth, despite bad teachers.[15] Many students in the United States frequently fail to learn even when they have a good teacher, one reason being that they are not expected to engage in the struggle that is sometimes—even often—necessary for gaining knowledge, and therefore don't strive for understanding. In accordance with expectations and educational theory, they wait for the teacher to produce learning in them. Needless to say, teaching is not the most important factor in student achievement. The student's will to succeed is the crucial factor, for that drive determines whether or not he will keep turning the matter incessantly in his head until he finds a solution. The teacher can influence, but not control, the student's actions and thoughts, and hence his learning. School systems not run according to the Progressive Paradigm (as in Japan, China, Europe, and some private schools in the United States) believe that students may have to struggle in order to succeed; students in our public schools are seen as having success created for them by their teachers and their teaching methods.

The idea that "student learning occurs" is not uncommon among educationists. One finds it a constant theme in the major studies on education reform that followed in the wake of A Nation at Risk, the landmark 1983 report from the National Commission on Excellence in Education, whose members had been appointed by Terrell Bell, secretary of education under Ronald Reagan. The commission used stirring words to shock the nation: "If an unfriendly power had attempted to impose on America the mediocre educational performance that exists today, we might well have viewed it as an act of war." The "rising tide of mediocrity" that the commission noted—decades of steadily declining SAT scores; American students placing last in international comparisons seven times, first or second never; high illiteracy rates among youth, as high as 40 percent among minority youth—were a result of lax requirements and low expectations. Thirty-five states, for example, required only one year of math for a high school diploma, while thirty-six required only one year of science; none had a foreign language requirement; the only statewide requirement for graduation in California was two years of physical education. In thirteen states, half the units required for graduation were electives, and many students chose courses such as "Bachelor Living."[16]

All these major studies betray varying degrees of allegiance to the Progressive Paradigm. In so doing they perpetuate low academic achievement and the growth and power of the colleges of education.

THE CARNEGIE FORUM: A NATION PREPARED

The Carnegie study on improving teaching acknowledged the problems in public education, and its title showed its authors' confidence in the measures proposed to overcome them. One notes with dismay the wording the authors use in describing the problem: "It is no exaggeration to suggest that America must now provide to the many the same quality of education presently reserved for the fortunate few." As do many Americans, the authors assume that teachers *provide* students with a good education; a good education results, in other words, from what teachers do. The students themselves are irrelevant or inconsequential factors in their success. In fact schools can provide only the *opportunities* for an education. Learning and understanding are mental processes achieved by an individual through his own thinking. Readers who may argue that I am excessively nitpicking, a too critical reader (that the authors really meant "provide educational opportunities for the students to capitalize on, by diligence and effort"), should consider this statement: "School," write the Carnegie Forum authors in their discussion of the importance of our education system in the functioning of a democratic society, "*must provide a deeper understanding* necessary for a self-governing citizenry." Can understanding be *provided* by one person to another? Understanding is something a person *achieves* through the use of his intellect, and educators above all should recognize that. Yet the Carnegie authors and many others believe that teachers achieve excellence in education for the students.

Later on in the report one reads, "Textbooks cannot do it [that is, bring the mass of citizens up to the lofty new academic standards]. Principals cannot do it. Directives from state authorities cannot do it. Only the people with whom the students come in contact every day can do it." The authors entirely omit the students and their responsibilities and necessary efforts from the list, and conclude, "Though many people have vital roles to play, only the teachers can finally accomplish the agenda we have just laid out." Later in the document, the authors tell how altruism and pride motivate "those often unnoticed teachers who extend themselves to *achieve much* for their students and their schools. But the system's rewards do not go to those who *produce the most achievement for the students* and the greatest efficiency for the taxpayer." The sheer frequency of such nonsensical phrases by American educational experts should give us serious pause. Why are students consistently portrayed as so helpless, so incapable of learning except under utopian conditions? Who benefits from that way of thinking?[17]

(It is worth noting that the authors of *A Nation at Risk,* true to the best traditions of American public education as a means of individual improvement, are much more realistic about the respective roles that teachers and students play in education. "Our society and its educational institutions seem to have lost sight of the basic purposes of schooling, and of the high expectations and *disciplined effort* needed to attain them," they write. On the next page they state, "Part of what is at risk is the promise first made on this continent: All, regardless of race or class or economic status, are entitled to a fair chance and to the tools for *de-*

veloping their individual powers of mind and spirit to the utmost. This promise means that all children *by virtue of their own efforts, competently guided,* can hope to attain the mature and informed judgment needed to secure gainful employment, and to manage their own lives, thereby serving not only their own interests but also the process of society itself." Later in the document, one reads, "Our goal must be to develop the talents of all to their fullest. Attaining that goal requires that we *expect* and *assist* all students to work to the limits of their capabilities." It is clear that the educationists, on the other hand, think that students can succeed only to the limits of their *teachers'* capabilities, an outrageously false and self-serving presumption, however flattering it may be to teachers and the trainers of teachers.[18])

The Carnegie Forum's plan for reforming education calls for an entirely new breed of teachers. The authors quote from Theodore Sizer's *Horace's Compromise* the belief that improving American secondary education "absolutely depends on improving the conditions of work and the respect for teachers" and, in an egregious non sequitur, declare that improving teachers' professional environment will itself lead to improvements in teachers' performance (which, of course, will result in improved student achievement).[19] The key to education reform, they believe, is "the professionalization of the teacher work force" through more education classes taught by education professors. It is necessary to quote at length the qualifications and responsibilities of the Young Turks of this new, reformed education (note the similarity to the job description given by Kilpatrick):

> Teachers should have a good grasp of the ways in which all kinds of physical and social systems work; a feeling for what data are and the uses to which they can be put, an ability to help students see patterns of meaning where others see only confusion; an ability to foster genuine creativity in students; and the ability to work with other people in work groups that decide for themselves how to get the job done. They must be able to learn all the time, as the knowledge required to do their work twists and turns with new challenges and the progress of science and technology. Teachers will not come to the school knowing all they have

to know, but knowing how to figure out what they need to know, where to get it, and how to help others make meaning out of it.[20]

Such mismash reveals quite clearly that the Carnegie Forum writers have little or no interest in teachers teaching basic subjects and subject-matter-set-out-to-be-learned. "In schools where students are expected to master routine skills and acquire routine knowledge, the necessary skills and knowledge can, to a degree, be packaged in texts and teachers can be trained to deliver the material in the text to the students with reasonable efficiency. But a much higher order of skills is required to prepare students for the unexpected, the non-routine world they will face in the future."[21] With this sort of language the Carnegie Forum authors are setting teachers up for failure, for Americans are, with a great deal of justification, more and more expecting substantial, quantifiable results from schools. One should note that the emphasis on basic knowledge and formal instruction, which the Carnegie writers and educationists in general so disdain, produces success in schools not devoted to the Progressive Paradigm.

The educational vision of the Carnegie Forum writers is best seen toward the end of A *Nation Prepared,* where they present "Schools for the 21st Century: A Scenario." It reads like a Deweyan fantasy, for all the aspects of the Progressive Paradigm are implemented, along with a little postmodern political correctness to bring it up to date. Subject-matter-set-out-to-be-learned is relegated to its proper place, on the pedagogical sidelines. Most members of the professional teaching staff of the fictional school have been certified by the National Board for Professional Teaching Standards and are therefore well trained in the best that modern scientific pedagogy has to offer. An Executive Committee of Lead Teachers, all with professional rank in the National Board for Professional Teaching Standards, coordinates academic affairs and helps teachers improve their teaching. The teachers have much time for collaborating with the Lead Teachers, other teachers, and members of the community in establishing goals for the school and tailoring the curriculum to meet the diverse needs of the students and the community. The teachers' objectives must "reflect what the teachers themselves thought they could and should accomplish for the students."[22] The students described in one class are involved in a group project, which involves community issues and representatives of the community. The students have learned so much from a project the year before that when a political columnist from the town's daily paper appears for a seminar, they are able to point out his mistakes, which he says he will acknowledge in a later column. Local colleges and universities have developed partnerships with the school to help students keep up with the school's demanding curriculum, which, of course, is taught through projects according to the needs and interests of the students, not as subject-matter-set-out-to-be-learned.

The curriculum itself is not strictly adhered to; the teachers adapt it to the needs and characteristics of the students and the community. For example, students in one small group aim to assess the toxicity of the pollutants in an open sewer. The students, according to the authors of the scenario, "are working on the project with the city's environmental agency, a local firm that specializes in the analysis of toxic materials, and their teachers of chemistry, biology and social studies. They know that all this work is intended to help them prepare for their statewide test in science, but they know also that their social studies teacher has designed the project so they will be well prepared for that part of the social studies examination that deals with students' grasp of conflicts in public policy."[23]

The school shows other characteristics desired by the educationists. Computers are abundant; the school has many high-achieving minorities, both among the student body and the faculty; the students are engaged in "genuine creativity" (as opposed to the fake creativity in the bad schools); even a poet from the community arts center gets involved to teach them creative problem solving. Teachers are held accountable for the learning of the students. Consequently the students are brilliant and happy, the teachers are fulfilled and have high morale, and the members of the community are satisfied with the school, for the students rank among the best in the state on standardized tests, despite the lack of a formal curriculum taught as such. "This is not a utopian vision," the authors inform us.[24] Perhaps.

THE HOLMES GROUP: *TOMORROW'S TEACHERS*

The thought that the teacher determines all student success is the theme of another "teacher quality" document written after A *Nation at Risk*. The Holmes Group, a consortium of education deans, writes, ". . . American students' performance will not improve much if the quality of teaching is not much improved. And teaching will not improve much without dramatic improvements in teacher education." The Holmes Group too shows unwavering allegiance to the Progressive Paradigm and expects teachers to achieve academic excellence for students, despite the paradigm's hostility to formal academic training and subject-matter-set-out-to-be-learned.[25]

That the nation's teachers are not creating the proper conditions to produce learning in students is obvious to the education deans. However much they would be embarrassed by their intellectual consanguinity with G. Stanley Hall, and would disavow his goofier ideas, their criticism of American teachers sounds remarkably like his. It continues the long, demoralizing, and ultimately pointless American tradition of bashing teachers for failing to meet impossible expectations. "The last five years of reports on high schools present a dismal account of high school teaching," write the deans in one of their many polemical statements. "Most of it is dreary. Teaching consists chiefly of either dull lectures or fact-oriented workbook assignments. Most teachers exhibit no deep grasp of their subjects, nor any passion for them. Their pedagogy is as sadly lacking as their grip on the material."[26] Again, the notion that *if only* the teachers would do this, or *if only* the teachers would do that—make learning fun, create playful learning games, or make learning the subject vital to the students' felt needs and desires, etc., etc.—students would learn. The students are failing to learn, it appears, because the teachers are boring. This type of criticism should sound familiar, for it could have been taken from the works of Hall, Naumberg, Rugg and Shumaker, Kilpatrick, Dewey, or Meriam.

Good teachers of today are bothered, write the Holmes Group authors, "by mounting evidence that many of this country's teachers act as

educational functionaries, faithfully but mindlessly following prescrip-
tions about what and how to teach." What the teachers are doing to earn
such disparaging words is teaching the curriculum in the textbook.
American teachers are not singled out for blame, however, for the members of the Holmes Group lash out at their colleagues in the arts and
sciences departments as well: "The undergraduate education that in-
tending teachers—and everyone else—receives is full of the same bad
teaching that litters American high schools." (Note how the education
deans presume that they alone are competent arbiters of good teaching
and intellectual achievement; note as well that the basis of their standards is the Progressive Paradigm.)[27]

The Holmes Group members take particular aim at the belief

> that whether or not learning takes place [note again the preposterous
> wording] in any particular class is primarily an outgrowth of the students
> who happen to be there. The teacher's responsibility is only to develop
> and deliver lessons in some reasonable fashion; the onus for learning
> rests with the students. The characteristics of the student group and the
> individuals in it thus influence the lesson and mode of delivery only
> modestly. . . .
>
> This conception [of teaching] blithely overlooks one of the most
> critical aspects of quality teaching—the extent to which the lesson is ap-
> propriate for the particular students for whom the teacher is responsible
> and for whom the lessons should be crafted.[28]

Yet the fact is that in those schools where the responsibility for learning rests primarily with the students, their performance far surpasses that
of schools run according to the Progressive Paradigm. During the American Occupation, reports Nobuo K. Shimahara, the Japanese tried the
Deweyan experience-based and student-centered system, but it was
widely criticized—"the chief contention being that student performance
had deteriorated"—and ultimately abandoned. Catholic schools in the
United States, which show little influence of the Progressive Paradigm—indeed, many parochial schools have been founded precisely as
alternatives to Progressive education—show impressive results: higher
student achievement in mathematics and verbal ability, extremely low

dropout rates, and higher percentages of graduates going to college and succeeding there, despite the low socio-economic status of their students. The British and Canadians, on the other hand, have tried Progressive practices and, like the Japanese, have made changes because of low academic performance.[29]

The educationists do not expect students to struggle through the learning process. They believe that truly professional teachers would understand "the core ideas in the subjects they teach [why not expect teachers to have expert knowledge, one must wonder], the likely learning problems children encounter at different ages, and the multiple ways by which *teachers can overcome these problems.*" Note the language: the authors do not state "the multiple ways by which teachers can *help students* overcome those problems." Students are expected only to be in class; everything else falls upon the teacher's back, for he must *overcome the students' problems.* This type of thinking is not restricted to the deans of education: "It's reasonable to assume that high quality teachers will possess the strong verbal and quantitative skills needed to recognize *and correct* the weak verbal and quantitative skills of their students," writes an author in a publication with conservative political leanings. A teacher can easily show students their mistakes, how to correct them, and offer practice on correcting such mistakes, but ultimately the student must strive for improvement and do what is necessary to succeed.[30]

When the Holmes Group authors delineate the critical aspects of quality teaching, they reflect the child-centered nature of their educational philosophy: the teacher is expected to construct lessons in accordance with the students' needs and abilities, not what teachers want them to learn or what the curriculum dictates. One of many problems with that approach is that standards become meaningless and irrelevant. The criterion for success becomes the degree to which the student's needs have been met, and the focus of the classroom becomes the meeting of the child's needs, not mastery of the prescribed curriculum. The education deans even chide their colleagues in the academic departments of the universities for "the preoccupation with 'covering the material.' "[31]

In arguing for better-qualified teachers, they explain, "The entire formal and informal curriculum of the school is filtered through the minds and hearts of classroom teachers, making the quality of school learning dependent on the quality of teachers."[32] There is much truth to the first part of the statement: teachers do largely determine what they do in the classroom—how much of the subject to teach and in what manner to teach it, and what topics within the subject to stress. But they are supposed to be teaching in accordance with the student's felt needs and abilities, and thus they "filter" the subject, or psychologize it, as Dewey put it. Is it best for the curriculum to be "filtered" through teachers who gauge their teaching according to their students' needs and abilities? State boards of education are demanding more and more that teachers teach the curriculum, and advocates for minorities rightly insist that teachers should expect as much of students of color as they do of middle-class white or Asian students.

The net result of the filtering process is an enormous and unfair variation across the country in what teachers and administrators expect students to achieve. If students are lucky enough both to be born into a well-educated family that values learning and to attend a school with other similarly motivated students, the teacher will hold high expectations of the students and will teach the subject in great depth and quality—according to their needs, interests, and abilities. But if the students are not so motivated, or not as naturally bright, or attend a school where the community expects little from the students, the teacher will be expected to meet their needs and dumb-down the curriculum. Students who are not likely to go to college are not perceived by themselves, their teachers, and society to have much need to learn academic subjects, and the teacher, to meet their nonacademic needs (to get the diploma while doing as little work as possible) will hold them to lower standards. To force them to work hard against their wishes creates negative attitudes and makes the teacher's job miserable every day. Consequently low-performing and minority students in the United States are pitied in a patronizing and pernicious way, and are not expected to work as hard because, the thinking goes, they may already have unhappy lives of poverty and broken homes, and it is cruel to make them work hard in a futile endeavor, like meeting high standards—academic content being irrelevant anyway.[33]

That such thinking reinforces race and class differences, and helps perpetuate a permanent underclass, is not often discussed by the educationists. To many, the fact that the students are underachieving indicates that they are more helpless. Consequently underachieving students are usually expected to do less work and are seen as more helpless and passive, more prone to being a victim. We must create success for them because they cannot possibly be expected to create their own success through diligent effort and with competent guidance. In contrast, the lockstep Japanese system, with its national curriculum and intensive focus on formal academic subjects, uniformity in teaching methods, and emphasis on students' hard work and perseverance, is far more egalitarian than the democratic system in the United States. Expectations in Japan are the same across the country, all students have equal access to the materials that will be covered on the tests, and the quality of teaching is nearly uniform. Similarly, Coleman and Hoffer found that Catholic schools in the United States enroll a much higher percentage of students in the academic track and, despite their adherence to formal academic studies and traditional teaching methods, more closely approximate the democratic ideal of the public school, as they do more to diminish the deleterious effects of poverty, broken homes, and racism. Students in the public schools of the United States, however, whose ability to learn is seen as being restricted by their teachers' ability to teach in accordance with their needs and wants, are lucky if they have a well-educated family and a demanding teacher who ignores much of what he learned in the education courses. Students are simply out of luck if their teachers take their ephemeral whims more seriously than their long-term needs.[34]

While the Progressive Paradigm places the onus for student success on the teacher, successful students see the job as their own. Laurence Steinberg and associates conclude: "Successful students, on average, are more likely to attribute their academic accomplishments to hard work and their occasional failures to a lack of effort. Unsuccessful students, in contrast, are more likely to see their performance as due to factors that are beyond their personal control."[35] The greatest influence on a student's academic achievement, found Coleman, is not the teachers or the curricula but the student's family and peers, for they lay the basis of the attitudes that seek success. Our educational experts promote an educational philosophy that is doomed to fail.

WHAT MATTERS MOST

Still another study published in the wake of A Nation at Risk conveys the same message: better teachers will produce smarter students. We must therefore improve the quality of our teachers in order to improve the quality of education in the United States. "A caring, competent, and qualified teacher for every child is the most important ingredient in education reform," write Linda Darling-Hammond and her fellow authors. They refine the idea later: "Policymakers are just beginning to grasp what parents have always known: that teaching is the most important element of successful learning."[36]

The authors paint a portrait of a teacher creating learning in the students, with the students themselves being irrelevant, or some type of indifferent soil that will sprout learning depending upon the generative qualities of the teacher's instructional practices. The different skills held by good teachers, write the authors, "make the difference between teaching that *creates learning* and teaching that just marks time." Learning is seen as something that happens in one's head because of what others or the environment does. This is not mere semantic nitpicking on my part. Teachers, write the educationists, "must themselves know more about the foundations of subject areas, and they must understand how students think as well as what they know in order to create experiences *that produce learning*." Note the assumption that learning results from what others do, not what the students themselves do: the experiences "create learning." Much later in the study, while describing the improvements made at some schools, the authors write, ". . . here we describe how both elementary and secondary schools have redesigned staffing to greatly enhance teaching and teacher collaboration and *pro-*

duce greater success for students." This same wording—"produce greater success" for students—is repeated in other contexts. If statements to that effect were rare in our nation's discussions on education, they could be attributed to sloppy writing; but our educational philosophy is pervaded by sloppy thinking—the idea that by virtue of the methods they use, teachers "create learning" in the hapless students.[37]

Educationists will argue that the teacher creates learning by manipulating the environment and the lesson according to the individual student's needs, wishes, abilities, and community influences, and in that way "produces learning." Teachers with National Board Certification were praised in one report because they "adjust their practice based on students' interests, abilities, skills, and backgrounds." Darling-Hammond, et al., also suggest that because European and Asian teachers receive more extensive training in both content and pedagogy, it makes for their students' superior learning. Yet teachers in other countries, especially in Japan, are not expected to tailor-make lessons for the needs of individual students, and the teaching style at the secondary level is predominantly one of lectures on formal academic subjects—a practice severely criticized (and sometimes rightly so) in our schools as "teacher talk" or "chalk talk." Japanese students are also expected to work hard for success in terms of formal academics, not to wait for their teachers to "produce greater success" for them on the basis of their interests and perceived needs.[38]

Despite my criticism, *What Matters Most* is the only report among those cited in this chapter that addresses the need for students to work harder. "In addition to all the efforts teachers must make to teach to new standards, students will need to work hard to meet them," the authors write. Note the wording used at the end of the study, when the authors address students: "Students may think they have no role to play in implementing the recommendations of commissions such as these. But students *are* America's future, and it matters greatly that you take your education seriously . . . think about how you can contribute to your learning and that of others. We urge students of all ages to seek to understand and appreciate what your teachers are trying to accomplish. . . ."[39]

"What your teachers are trying to accomplish" implies that students have a back-seat role in the attainment of educational excellence—yet it is far more than many writers on education issues admit.

THE GOODLAD FORMULA

One of the most visible and prolific educationists today is John I. Goodlad, professor emeritus of education at the University of Washington and author of dozens of books and articles about education. Since our society almost without fail sees its educational problems as stemming from the failures of teachers, Goodlad, as do the authors of the reports discussed in this chapter, urges massive overhauls of the colleges of education in order to revamp teacher training. In two of his books, *Teachers for Our Nation's Schools* and *Educational Renewal: Better Teachers, Better Schools*, he offers his plan. He proposes the creation, at universities, of Centers of Pedagogy, independent of the colleges of education and thus free from many bureaucratic regulations and legislative interference in curriculum. The centers will also award their own degrees, a B.A. or B.S. in pedagogy and a D.Paed. Their faculties will be composed of three different groups: education professors, who are experts in learning, teaching, educational theory, and the function of schools in a democratic society; professors of arts and sciences, who will oversee the general education of the teacher candidates and help train them in subject matter; and faculty from partner schools, who will model the new teaching techniques for the teacher candidates and enculturate the teacher candidates into the teaching profession.[40]

Goodlad is thoroughly devoted to the Deweyan vision. The names he gives to the schools attached to a fictional Center of Pedagogy—Dewey Primary School, Dewey Middle School, and Dewey Upper School—demonstrate his allegiance. His ideal school is Deweyan through and through, and accordingly deemphasizes academics in favor of socialization and other nonacademic goals. Goodlad finds fault with the teachers college's perceived role in American society: "The most critically important omission [in this role] is a vision that encompasses a good and just society, the centrality of education to the renewal of that society, the role of schools bringing this education equitably to all, and the kind of preparation teachers require for their stewardship of the nation's schools."[41]

In accordance with his Deweyan vision of education, Goodlad and his research team formulated the four dimensions of teaching: (1) "facilitating enculturation of students" to political and social democracy; (2) providing access to knowledge; (3) building an effective teacher-student connection; and (4) practicing good stewardship of the schools. He and his team then judged teacher training institutions by how well these ideals were inculcated in the teacher candidates. They "looked for well-designed, well-constructed houses of teacher education and found roofs missing, doors hanging loose, and windows broken."[42] They did not consider that the Deweyan foundation might be cracked.

Despite the existence of hundreds of institutions that train teachers and educational researchers, staffed by thousands of professors of education (and more education specialists appearing daily—between five thousand and seven thousand doctorates in education every year, more than in any other field); despite the fact that 16.5 percent of all bachelors' degrees held in the United States are in education; despite the support of billions of dollars in financing over the past 150 years; and despite the publication each year of thousands of books and journals, and papers by blue-ribbon commissions concerning problems in education, teacher education in the 1990s, Goodlad writes, like medical education before the famous Flexner report, "is something not yet seriously attempted." Hence his proposal for the new Centers of Pedagogy, to educate the new breed of teachers. We are to assume that the new Centers of Pedagogy will not repeat the mistakes of the past, but one finds that Goodlad's solution to the problem of underachievement among students is in fact the drunkard's cure for a hangover—a little of the hair of the dog that bit you.[43]

Goodlad blames teacher training for the failures of our schools, and we are to believe that superior training in the latest findings in pedagogy will make better teachers—and, true to the tenets of the Progressive Paradigm, that better teachers will produce smarter students. Apparently today's teachers, with their faulty training and their allegiance to a rigid curriculum and formal knowledge as presented in textbooks, just are not getting the job done: "The common inability of secondary school teachers, particularly of mathematics, social studies, science, and English (as compared with the arts, physical education, and vocational education) to interest students in their subjects is well documented." The student, of course, is seen here as passive; the teacher is expected to solve the student's problems. Teachers shouldn't feel unfairly singled out for criticism, however, for Goodlad also chastises his colleagues in the arts and sciences departments at universities for failing to do their jobs as professors: "There is a never-ending job to be done in reminding arts and sciences professors that those academic deficiencies among incoming freshmen are due in some considerable degree to their failure to contribute adequately to the education of the teachers who taught these young people."[44]

Yet Goodlad is a rarity, for he argues that the teachers colleges already devote *too much time* to teaching teachers nuts-and-bolts information such as subject matter and how to teach it to students and manage the classroom. Prospective high school teachers in particular, he writes, "need much more preparation in the role of schools in a democratic society, human cognition and development, both general and content-specific pedagogy, their responsibilities as moral stewards of schools, and curricular and organizational alternatives in schooling." Teachers in the new pedagogy centers will be trained less in helping individual students and more in stewardship of the schools and the situation in which the school is located. "Attention to the stewardship of schools is largely missing in teacher education. We found [in the study of teacher education institutions] almost the whole of practice-directed preparation to embrace individual pupils, groups of pupils, and classes, not whole schools."[45]

Since schools are part of the social environment and the community, improving a school will require improving the community, and teachers and educators of the future will be expected to engage in active inquiry regarding public affairs. In other words, the job of teachers and education professors, in Goodlad's vision, far supersedes teaching academic subjects to young people. The job now is to be an activist in identifying and resolving the community's problems: "This inquiry [into the public context of the school] goes far beyond determination of the present nature of this context [that is, what goes on within the school's walls]. It is, rather, historical, philosophical, and—yes—judgmental. A center of pedagogy can no more be neutral in its relationship to the public context than a school of public health can stand above the health of its community." The irony of such pedagogue-sponsored censorship of public affairs is that Goodlad himself has acknowledged that teachers and the schools suffer from inappropriate, excessive demands. His grandiose expectations set teachers up for still more failure, for teachers end up becoming responsible not only for helping students learn but for creating a just and good society.[46]

Goodlad's plan for an educationist social critique is entirely consistent with the Deweyan vision of the schools. Here are the words of R. Bruce Raup and fellow authors Dewey and Kilpatrick: "If we have followed where the argument inevitably leads, the school and the educator will accept fully the challenge to assess the social order in the interest of the education of the young. There will be no institution, no custom, no practice which will be outside the field of their potential subject matter." The authors of A *Nation Prepared* also envision teachers playing an active political role, for part of the process by which one becomes a Lead Teacher involves being an advocate for the young.[47]

With social goals prevailing over academic and intellectual goals in Goodlad's vision, proponents of back to basics find merely an echo of the anti-formalist element of the Progressive Paradigm. Teachers trained in Goodlad's new pedagogy will be better able to meet the students' needs; these will be teachers "who see curriculum content as means, not ends, and who are prepared as educators, not trainers. Teacher educators must not be unwitting accomplices in the advocacy of unexamined ideologies in the schools." In this melancholy lament, Goodlad shows clearly that formal academic knowledge ranks very low in his priorities: "In general, the ubiquitous curriculum makes subject-matter content the end. Students will be tested in it many times, by both teacher-made and standardized tests. Subject matter is what teachers are expected to deliver. This is what teacher education is to prepare teachers for. So it has been, and so it is. But this is not what could and should be." As a good Deweyan, he bashes the idea of learning subject matter for itself. And he praises Gardner's Multiple Intelligences, in which "Students are intensively engaged in making meanings rather than in picking through the textbook garbage for clues to the tests they are about to take." He bashes strict curriculum guides, arguing that the better, looser curriculum guides "are more likely to remind teachers of broad expectations for schools and point out that the subjects are a means to their attainment. They emphasize the importance of teachers' being professionally prepared to exercise judgment in deciding what and how to teach."[48]

Instead of using standardized tests and various instruments to assess students' academic knowledge, Goodlad writes, the real measure of a school's worth should be how productive it is of human goodness. "Surely our best schools," he declares, "should be those most committed to and productive of human goodness." He elaborates: "But in recent years in particular, we have witnessed a surge of corruption in high places on the part of many much-schooled individuals. We should give serious consideration to the hypothesis that we have got it all wrong with respect to the criteria of excellence most commonly used to judge the quality of our schools." (One is reminded of Kilpatrick's words that without education in the right social attitudes, "a merely bookish education may be a menace.")[49] One must ask: Are teachers expected to root out original sin? I have no doubts that educationists are willing and eager to do the research on how teachers should do so.

In any event, Goodlad's vision of emphasizing goodness is already in place in schools. There exists a subtle expectation that teachers will not fail students who try a little and are pleasant, yet fail to meet minimal standards. The traditional objection is, "But Johnny/Janey is such a nice kid"—with further explanation about how good the kid is at some other subject.

One's already flagging confidence that the new, improved teacher in Goodlad's vision will be able to teach students academic content in greater depth and with greater efficiency falls further when one sees the knowledge base that Goodlad proposes for training teachers. "There is a knowledge base," Goodlad informs us, "that is potentially relevant and powerful for teaching, but it has not yet been rendered useful. It is now encapsulated in the annals of scholars and largely inaccessible to the practitioner. Indeed, it is sufficiently inaccessible to the practitioner and obscured from the layperson to cause both to question its existence." Strange that the new Centers of Pedagogy themselves do not yet know how teachers should teach, despite more than a century of educational research conducted with scientific rigor and impartiality. Goodlad seems not to be embarrassed by this shell game: in the first year at the fictional university in the fable that ends *Teachers for Our Nation's Schools*, the students who are there to obtain their teaching certificates "realized early on that much of the curriculum emerged as they progressed, on a weekly and even daily basis." The experts in "scientific" pedagogy, with their "potentially relevant and powerful" knowledge base, with which they intend to revolutionize American classrooms and establish a good and just society, are winging it, flying by the seat of their pants, doing exactly what the harried, ridiculed, and incompetent schoolteacher of lore is doing: staying one chapter ahead of the students. But at least the incompetent schoolteacher has a textbook for guidance; the education experts are teaching from notes hurriedly compiled before class and still warm from the Xerox machine.[50]

So much for expert guidance. Supposing that Goodlad's recommendations will be implemented—he is an expert in education, and he receives grant money from numerous philanthropic organizations for his research—the students in our public schools will continue to fail to learn basic facts. For this failure the teachers will be flailed, on one hand by the educationists for teaching subject-matter-set-out-to-be-learned, and on the other hand by conservative critics for not teaching subject matter and correcting students' errors in spelling and punctuation, and so forth. The public, enraged at the gross ignorance of the students, will consult the experts in education, who will blame the teachers and chant the monotonous and customary refrain that with more research and money they will find the answer, and recommend massive changes in the way teachers are taught to teach. So the cycle continues.

Hope is on the horizon, however. In words that should remind us of the potentially relevant and powerful knowledge base that is inaccessible and obscured from view, the Holmes Group authors proclaim, "Within the last twenty years . . . the science of education promised by Dewey, Thorndike, and others at the turn of the century, has become more tangible. . . ."[51] But as "the promise of science of education is about to be fulfilled," they lament, current efforts at reform are bypassing modern education research. There is hope yet.

7

WHERE EDUCATION SUCCEEDS: THE ABSENCE OF THE PROGRESSIVE PARADIGM IN JAPAN

For decades the United States has rightly prided itself on providing free secondary education to all students, and for being the first country to offer it to all students, regardless of class or family income. The fact that inequalities have existed because of race and funding does not gainsay the fact that the United States was a model for the rest of the world. The United States is no longer alone in providing free secondary education to its citizens, however, and report after report has shown that the educational system in the United States ranks among the worst in the industrialized nations. Recently the Third International Mathematics and Science Study (TIMSS) showed how American twelfth-grade students were superior only to those of Cyprus and South Africa. Statistics presented by Harold Stevenson and James Stigler in *The Learning Gap* show that at the fifth-grade level, the worst Chinese and Japanese students surpass the best American students in mathematics, and rarely do the top students in America rank among the world's highest-achieving students. The poorest-performing students in Japan far surpass the poorest-performing students in the United States. So demanding is the Japanese high school, writes Thomas P. Rohlen, that a Japanese high school diploma may be the equivalent of an average bachelor's degree in the United States. I was mortified as an undergraduate when I met students from Germany, who were undergraduates and not majoring in American Studies, and realized that they knew much more about the history of the United States than I did. Similarly, Rohlen finds that Japanese students learn more about the history of the United States than American students do.[1]

It is not superior teachers, superior genetics, or more money spent on education that makes other schools superior to American schools, but rather differences in attitudes about how one succeeds and why one goes to school. Japanese schools, in short, do not operate according to the Progressive Paradigm. Consequently the study of Japanese schools in particular offers an enormous contrast in attitudes toward youth, school, and the acquisition of knowledge. As an outgrowth of a different intellectual tradition and a largely homogeneous culture, the Japanese system cannot be a model for the American. Our diversity of races and cultures, and our intellectual, social, and political traditions, require and foster debate, individualism, and creative thinking in ways peculiarly American. Yet those American traditions stand in contrast to another American tradition, one not so great or deserving of preservation: the tendency to accept as inevitable low academic achievement among most of the students in our public schools. Our students achieve far below what they could and should, and our schools do not command respect internationally, unlike our universities. Studying Japanese education can force us to confront our assumptions.

While haranguing my own students for poor performance, I sometimes tell them that American students usually place last, or close to last, in international comparisons. Most are surprised, for they tend to believe they are getting a great education—they have high self-esteem, they make good grades, they have passed the most recent standardized test of basic literacy or numeracy, and they use computers and calculators at school. Others are not surprised, as some read the newspapers or watch the news. Some in this latter group protest that in other countries not all students go to school, something they hear from many teachers, administrators, and parents. (The charge is almost entirely without merit.) When finally they see that they are not learning as much as average students in other countries, they usually respond that teachers in Japan, China, Korea, or Germany are better, make learning fun, "inspire" the students to study, use computers to make learning easier, use better books, and so forth. Again, the students simply repeat things they hear in our culture, which is pervaded by the idea that students' learning depends upon the teachers' teaching or upon factors outside the students' own control.

Along with many parents, administrators, and researchers on blue-ribbon commissions, students believe that teachers in other countries are simply better. They rarely consider that through their own actions, students themselves determine whether or not they learn and succeed. Occasionally a student will comment that students in other countries learn more because, according to expectations, they simply study more and work harder for success. One student who had migrated to the United States from Taiwan, for example, commented that when he was in sixth grade there, students were called to the teacher's desk to answer a question. Those who gave the correct answer were allowed to return to their desks while those who answered incorrectly received a rap on the knuckles with the teacher's ruler and were given another question to answer. In his ninth-grade mathematics class in the United States, the student said, he was doing material that he had done in sixth grade in Taiwan. While the teacher's method of dealing with students who made errors was certainly objectionable, the expectations were not.

INTENSIVE CONCENTRATION ON SUBJECT MATTER

The Japanese school system differs from the American in ways that have enormous influence on student achievement. First, it is highly centralized. The Ministry of Education (Monbusho) has created a rigid, formal curriculum which all public schools must follow. The curriculum dictates the number of hours to be allotted each week to each subject, grade by grade; teachers can be fired for not following it. Japanese students go to school 240 days a year (30 of which are devoted to nonacademic festivals, such as a nationwide Sports Day), which includes a half day on Saturdays. Over the six weeks of summer vacation and the shorter winter vacation, the students have homework, and the mothers make sure the students do it. Monbusho does not control the schools through micromanagement, as local school boards take care of hiring and administration, yet they are responsible for implementing Monbusho's guidelines. Funding is roughly equal from school to school, as is the quality of teaching, since teachers must be licensed by Monbusho before they can be hired, and teachers are frequently transferred from school to school. Textbooks are of nearly equal quality, since they must meet Monbusho's strict guidelines before they can be approved for purchase by the local districts.[2]

Education is compulsory through the ninth grade, and all students in the public schools (which are more highly regarded than the private schools) are taught exactly the same curriculum from grades one through ten. No allowance is made for individual differences. Slow learners are expected to work harder to keep up (they might be encouraged by a sign on the wall with the inspirational message "The slow bird must start out early"), and fast learners are expected to help the slow. The curriculum itself is quite demanding—so demanding, in fact, that the teachers themselves talk about their system being 7, 5, 3—only 70 percent of the elementary students, 50 percent of the junior high school students, and 30 percent of the high school students can satisfy the curriculum's high expectations. Yet teachers follow it like a bible, for the students are tested on their knowledge.[3]

Completion of the ninth grade marks the end of compulsory education in Japan, but 96 percent of the students go on to high school (for which the parents must pay a nominal fee), and 70 percent of those choose the academic high schools rather than the low-status vocational schools—which, incidentally, suffer the highest dropout rates in Japan; the dropout rate at the academic schools is low. The high school graduation rate is almost 90 percent, on a curriculum that is intensely demanding. By comparison, only 69 percent of U.S. high school students graduate from high school, most of them having studied a curriculum that is substantially, even laughably, easier. Japanese high school students even in a humanities track have reported taking calculus, and Harry Wray writes that the curriculum for students in the vocational track is more demanding than that taken by all but the top 25 percent of students in American public schools.[4]

During their school years Japanese students face two crucial tests on the Monbusho curriculum, and those tests bear heavily on their future. The first, during the ninth grade, determines whether or not they will be accepted by the high school of their choice. Students seek to go to the high schools that produce the highest number of students passing the admission tests of the top universities, Tokyo University being the flagship. The second big test comes during their senior year at high school, for it determines whether or not they will be accepted by the university of their choice, and upon that may well rest their whole future adult life — much rides upon going to the "right" university. Consequently Japanese students face strict accountability from grade eight on. Critics of "high stakes" tests in the United States, which are usually little more than tests of basic literacy and numeracy, and which students may take six or seven times in order to secure their high school diploma, would be boggled by the Japanese program. For Japanese students, two tests, one taken when they are fifteen years old, and the other when they are eighteen, literally determine their future.

The day of the test, notes Gail Benjamin, is not a good day to have a cold or the flu: students who fail the exam for the high school of their choice may not attend another public high school (they must go to a private high school), and students who fail the entrance examination of the college of their choice become *ronin*, literally "masterless samurai." They must wait a year to try another time, or seek admission to a private university, which is less prestigious and very expensive. Financed by their parents, many *ronin* spend that year in study at a *yobiko*, a private cram school that helps students prepare for their next attempt to pass the university entrance exam.[5]

The Japanese educational system does not offer many second chances, so the pressure is on the students to perform. Yet the Japanese regard their system as fair, because the students know that the tests will cover the material in the Monbusho curriculum, as described in the textbooks and taught by the teachers. Thus all students have an equal opportunity to do well on the exams, and Monbusho created the national curriculum for the very purpose of insuring a fair opportunity for all.[6] The Japanese system is ultimately more democratic than the American system with its widely divergent curricula and expectations, for *all* Japanese students are given equal opportunity to master the material for the examinations. The Japanese do not see their school system as engaged in social engineering; they see it as an arena for fair competition.

Competition on the admissions tests is fierce: "What Americans might regard as the lunatic fringe—students memorizing whole English dictionaries or doing seven hours of preparation a night for a year—actually sets the pace in this sort of competition," writes Thomas Rohlen. The students do not bear that pressure alone, however, for the whole society is focused on education: "Anyone who has lived in Japan becomes aware of the great interest (bordering on obsession) that the Japanese have in education," writes Wray. Seeing that their small island is poor in natural resources, the Japanese know that their chief wealth lies in capitalizing upon their human resources. They must be smart if they are to survive. Since 1868, the end of feudalism, the Japanese have seen themselves as having to catch up with the West, and despite their economic success since the end of the Occupation after World War II, they still see their civilization as being on the brink of survival. Consequently education is a deadly serious business, and despite the success of their educational system, the Japanese are still harshly critical of it. Results of the national tests are dissected in the media, and profiles of the three thousand students admitted to Tokyo University each year are published in the press, with accounts by their proud parents of "how their son or daughter suffered the grueling work necessary to pass the examination." Many thousands of *juku* and *yobiko*, cram schools, do a thriving business across the nation, helping students who are caught up in the frenzy of "examination hell."[7]

Mothers are called *kyoiku mama*, education moms, who become

their children's personal academic trainers of sorts, as their most important job is to wheedle, coax, cajole, harangue, shame, and otherwise per-
suade or manipulate their children to study in preparation for the test.
The mothers' social reputation rests on how well their children do on
the exams, and the Japanese mother "is virtually totally responsible for
seeing that her children succeed in school." Very early in their children's
lives the mothers begin training them to concentrate and to persist
with single-minded effort. Merry White tells of Japanese mothers in
Riverdale, New York, who bought copies of their children's textbooks to
keep at home so they could study along with their children. So well did
the Japanese students in the Riverdale schools perform that, though they
had started the year knowing little or no English, by the end of the year
they were at the top of their classes in all subjects.[8]

Since the Japanese child's future is decided, quite literally, upon two
exams, and the mother's social status depends upon her child's academic performance, the mothers pressure teachers to be hard on the students, in order to increase their chances of doing well on the tests.
"Easy" teachers jeopardize students' future and social standing. When
Monbusho advised that the Saturday half-days at school be canceled so
that the students could have more time for fun and relaxation, the parents objected. Instead of sending the children to school on Saturday
mornings, they sent them to *juku* to make up for the lost time. The intense pressure on students to do well comes not from the teachers and
Monbusho but from students and parents themselves, who see the vital
connection between education and economic and social success.[9]

EXPECTED TO ACHIEVE

The Japanese show their earnestness for success in education in many
ways. The schools themselves are simple, drab, uninspiring buildings,
and at the secondary level have little color or festiveness about them.
Flashes of color on the walls of the elementary schools come from the
children's artwork. The buildings lack central heating or air condition-

ing, the only source of heat being a kerosene heater, which many students object to using because they prefer to show how tough they are. Benjamin observes that even at some elementary schools, students who wear long pants during the winter are ridiculed by some teachers: "Stoically enduring cold has long been a means of character building in Japan." The bathrooms lack air conditioning and heating entirely, despite the cold of the Japanese winter. The message to the students is that school is not a place for fun and games. The Japanese could afford more attractive and better-equipped schools, but they believe that Spartan conditions more effectively convey to students the idea that learning and comfort are not related, that the primary purpose of going to school is serious study. The Japanese clearly focus on students doing what is necessary for success, and firmly believe that students must learn to thrive despite obstacles and inconveniences, for overcoming such obstacles makes one hardier and a better person.[10]

In reading about Japanese education, one is repeatedly struck by the expectation that the students must work hard for success, in contrast to the United States where the *teacher* is expected to work hard to find a way for the students to succeed. The theme is repeated and restated in a variety of ways:

> The famous exhortation, "Pass with Four, Fail with Five" means that if one is so lax as to sleep five hours rather than four, one will fail in the exams.[11]

> Chinese and Japanese societies allow no excuses for lack of progress in school; regardless of one's current level of performance, opportunities for advancement are always believed to be available through more effort. High scores on a test are interpreted as a sign of diligence. Low scores are not regarded as a sign of stupidity, but simply as an indication that the student has not learned what will ultimately be possible through persistence and hard work.[12]

> When one asks a Japanese why a student does poorly, particularly in mathematics, one of most [sic] common responses she receives would be, *benkyo busoku*, or lack of study.[13]

. . . Japanese language teachers note that American university students assume that their lack of comprehension of subject matter is the teacher's fault. Asian students believe that they themselves are the problem.[14]

. . . Everyone is given the same chance to do well on the examinations; failure to do so is a result of not trying hard enough.[15]

[Devoting hours to drills and tests in mathematics in Japan] is a rather drudging process requiring a great deal of patience and perseverance. And supporting the process at home stands literally an army of parents who encourage the child to exert every effort to study mathematics in order to pass the examination.[16]

Effort and self-discipline are considered by the Japanese to be essential bases for accomplishment. Lack of achievement, then, is attributed to the failure to work hard, rather than to a lack of ability or to personal or environmental obstacles.[17]

It is the student who must meet the standard in foreign countries. Responsibility for failure is primarily placed on the students, and only secondarily on the teacher.[18]

What makes a student strive to succeed is perseverance or diligence—*gambaru* in Japanese. The concept of *gambaru* is so important that Duke devotes a whole chapter of his book to it. The spirit of *gambaru*, he says, "engulfs every facet of society. . . . One must sacrifice in order to succeed on the examinations. One must devote many hours of sheer drudgery to learn mathematical equations, to memorize the new ideographs of the language, or to repeat over and over again the meaning in Japanese of the English vocabulary lists required of all Japanese junior high school students." Such diligence and perseverance are expected of the students: ". . . Every, yes, every school in a multiplicity of ways encourages the students to gambare from the first year onward. . . ." One of the few displays in Japanese classrooms, writes Gerald LeTendre, is a motto like "Never Give Up!"[19]

Japanese students are expected to survive with what is available and to adapt themselves to conditions, not to have conditions adapted to their needs and interests. Unlike American students, writes Wray, Japanese students "do not establish unrealistic expectations that learning will be fun, interesting, or exciting, but rather that it will be difficult and require some suffering." When asked what he expected of school, one Japanese student from a highly successful school answered simply, "Studying." American educational philosophy, on the other hand, expects teachers to provide stimuli that will overpower the students' sense of boredom or so inspire the students to learn that they will be swept up in a torrent of educational ecstasy and learn naturally, without having to experience stress and discomfort. The Japanese see that a young person's learning to tolerate stress and challenges leads to moral and social growth; American educational philosophy sees the same thing as damaging to the psyche. (Unfortunately, it is American educational philosophy and psychology that are damaging: Steinberg et al. found that "the longer [an immigrant] student's family has lived in this country, the worse the youngster's school performance and mental health.")[20]

The Japanese place little emphasis on innate ability, believing that effort is far more important: "Most Japanese parents and educators are unshakably optimistic that virtually all children have the potential to master the challenging academic curriculum, provided they work hard and long enough." Clearly, the primary source of students' academic success in Japan is not the teachers and their scientific teaching methods or ability to meet students' idiosyncratic needs, but rather the *students* and their drive and determination to meet high standards and to adapt. Gail Benjamin calls the Japanese educational philosophy "the 'anyone can do anything' school of thought." The sharp divergence between Japanese and American thinking about the reasons for academic success may also be seen in this observation: "Students in higher tracks [in Japanese schools] seemed more likely to be regarded as *gambatteru*, 'working hard,' than *atamagaii*, 'smart.'" Yet in the United States, students in the higher tracks are regarded as "gifted and talented," words that imply natural, immutable abilities and qualities, over which one has little control. "Differences in student achievement [in Japan] are thought to result largely from the level of effort, perseverance, and self-discipline, not from differences in individual ability," write Leestma, Bennett, et al.[21]

The students learn to work diligently and assiduously in their pursuit of excellence. American researchers describe how they aimed to test the perseverance of children from different countries by giving them a math problem that could not be solved. After trying the problems with several children, Japanese researchers convinced the Americans to discontinue the experiment because the Japanese children simply wouldn't quit working on the problem.[22] American students, typically, rely upon intuition rather than painstaking attention to detail and effort, and tend to give up very quickly. After all, the children cannot be expected to overstep the bounds of self-effort, as Colonel Parker put it, or to risk developing negative attitudes toward the subject, as Dewey and Kilpatrick warned. And anyway, it's the teacher's job to teach in accordance with each individual student's peculiar learning style or intelligence so that the student/television set will receive a crystal-clear signal or so that the learning will be in tune with the lines of natural force.

That emphasis on perseverance, diligence, and self-denial is part of the Confucian moral heritage. The learning environment that flows from it, reports John Biggs, "predispositions [one] to put in effort and to seek meaning; to persist in the event of boredom or failure; and to foster the kind of interaction between teacher and student, and student and student, that engages higher rather than lower cognitive processes." In Japan, education is seen as a matter of morals, and success shows how virtuous one is, how much suffering one has endured in the pursuit of success. The Japanese believe that facing struggles, such as difficult exams, promotes the development of character: "entrance examinations are believed to be important to character formation. They assume that children cannot achieve maturity unless the growth process from childhood to adulthood is challenging spiritually and emotionally." They also believe that through facing such obstacles and overcoming them, one becomes a fuller, more developed human being, a belief that reminds one of James's attitudes about the heroic individual and doing one's all in order to live a fuller, more meaningful life. James's Victorian values, of course, were regarded as somewhat old-fashioned by his contemporaries, as Japanese values may seem to many Americans today.[23]

The hard work and diligence that Japanese students dedicate to mastering their academic subjects show up in their conduct in school and in their study habits after school. Report after report shows that Asian students—and students from all over the world, for that matter—study more than students in the United States do. Japanese students are assigned large amounts of homework from the first grade on, and over summer and winter vacations, and they do it carefully. Reports differ on the quantity of homework done by students in other countries, but the consensus is that American students do less than one hour of homework per night, with students in other countries putting in at least two hours per night. According to Steinberg et al., students in other countries study four hours a day outside school, while American students study one. Tony Dickensheets, who lived with a Japanese family for a year, reports that the family's teenage son, through the course of the school day, *juku* classes, and studying, spent sixteen hours a day on schoolwork. Since many students also participate in *juku*, the amount of studying by Japanese students is impressive, but such hard work is recognized as a sine qua non for their high educational achievement.[24]

Students are expected to control themselves and do what is necessary in the pursuit of academic excellence. They are trained in the early grades to be responsible for their own and other students' behavior. Before the teacher begins teaching, the day's student leader (the leadership of the class rotates among the students) calls for quiet among the students. Thus the teacher does not have to spend valuable time and energy getting the class ready for the lesson. Students are trained in early childhood to behave with dignity and to cooperate with others. So well do they learn self-discipline that the schools do not find it necessary to hire substitute teachers for short-term absences. Benjamin tells how the *first-grade* class to which her daughter belonged had no substitute teacher when the regular teacher was absent. Instead, teachers from nearby classrooms popped in every now and then to make sure that the class was all right. The first-grade class was unsupervised for most of the day, and the principal informed Benjamin that having no substitute for a class that young was not unusual. Similarly, her son's fifth-grade art class (of forty-five students) went to the park with only one adult—the teacher—supervising them, even though many of the students were expected to be out of the teacher's sight as they drew and painted.[25]

Likewise, the authors of *Japanese Education Today* report that bad behavior reflects poorly on a school's reputation, and since each Japanese secondary school has its distinctive uniform, one can instantly tell by the uniform which school a student attends and immediately report instances of misbehavior to school officials. One reads of a study-hall class that is totally unsupervised by teachers, and the various clubs at the school, to which almost all students belong, are largely unsupervised by the club sponsors. Students eat their lunch, unsupervised, in the classrooms while the teachers eat in the teachers' lounge.[26] In the United States, public school teachers may invite serious trouble for leaving their students unsupervised merely to go to the bathroom, and there should be no doubt that many American high school students cannot be left alone in the classroom and trusted while the teacher is gone. After all, many American students cannot control themselves even when the teacher is *in* the classroom.

Japanese students are expected to memorize huge amounts of information in preparation for their exams. Much of the secondary curriculum seems to be in-depth memorization (as opposed to rote, mindless memorization, though some observers believe it is the latter) of facts. Students are expected to master the material, and the teachers make little or no effort to elicit their interests or tailor their lessons to meet the students' needs. The demanding Monbusho curriculum and the impending tests drive the class, even the entire school system, and the teacher plows through the curriculum, regardless. Students learn attention to detail and perfectionism, a good example of which is their memorization of the almost two thousand Chinese ideographs prescribed by Monbusho. The process by which they memorize them is noteworthy: not only must they learn the ideographs, they must also learn to write them putting the strokes in a certain order. (While the Japanese believe that each repetition of an act contains something new to learn, the attitude of American schools can best be found in Dewey's remark: "Monotony means that growth, development, have ceased.")[27]

"In Japan, if the child gets 99 out of 100 right," White writes, "the teacher will still say, 'Not perfect, but it could be so if you *really* pay attention.'" Singleton observes that during parent-teacher conferences in Japan, whether the student is at the top of the class or the bottom, the teacher inevitably advises, "I think a little more persistence would be good."[28] Asian teachers rarely praise students for correct answers and even consider it harmful to a child's character to praise without outstanding cause. Teachers in the United States, on the other hand, are severely criticized by administrators during evaluations for not reinforcing good behavior with ample praise.

Contrast the Asians' relentless demand for excellence with the timid thinking of American society and its educational system. In a syndicated advice column, a mother asked a psychologist for advice about her daughter, who was in the third grade.

> School has been very easy for her until now, and she has been a straight-A student with very little effort. Although this sounds like every parent's dream, I am concerned. On her own, my child now expects to make all A's—in other words, she expects perfection. So what happens the day she really has a challenge? What happens when she has to put in the effort and doesn't make the grade?

The question itself is troubling: the girl isn't having such problems now, but she *might* someday have them—though one can be sure that her life story has not been one of constant success without occasional failures and the need to try again. The psychologist's response is also troubling: she tells the mother that people, like Linus in the comic strip "Peanuts," have their security blankets, and her daughter's security blanket is perfectionism. "Children who hold on to the blanket of perfection are doomed to let it go because they must face their own imperfection," she writes. Her advice to the mother:

Have your child cut out several Linus cartoons, or draw a picture of herself holding a "security blanket." Ask your child to write down in each blanket what makes her feel secure. The blankets could read, "being with Grandma and Grandpa" or "sleeping with my teddy bear" or "being chosen for the basketball team" or even "making straight A's."

As your child names these blankets, help him or her understand how life will make these blankets change. Demonstrate by writing your "adult security blanket" list, such as "having a job" or "providing a good home" or "knowing I can pay my bills."

For a child holding on to the blanket of perfection, a parent must help her understand that security cannot be found in the impossible. Although she does not have to let go of her blanket right now, she has the opportunity to find new blankets, such as "I'm proud of effort regardless of grade."[29]

The poor little girl will learn from this orgy of psychological meddling that excellence and perfectionism are *bad.* Since the girl knows that Linus is silly for dragging around the security blanket and sucking his thumb, the adults must be telling her that perfectionism and excellence are silly, childish, and unnecessary, a foolish habit she should grow out of. Teachers and administrators in American public schools and colleges of education who hold similar views effectively preclude the possibility of academic excellence. Further evidence comes from advice given to teachers on how to deal with students who experience difficulty in reading. How can we help such students? It's easy, according to this in-service program:

FIND A WAY FOR STUDENTS TO USE THEIR SPECIAL TALENTS

Completing art projects

Building three-dimensional models or projects

Demonstrating and/or discussing hobbies

STRESS VERBAL PARTICIPATION

Reduce reading requirements

Provide tapes of content area textbooks

Do not require students to read aloud

REDUCE WRITTEN WORK ASSIGNMENTS
   Substitute oral reports for written
   Accept work dictated by student and written by parent or tutor[30]

The problem with such suggestions is that they effectively relieve the student of struggling to do what is necessary to improve his ability to read. While not requiring the student to read aloud during class is sensibly humane (the other students might laugh at him for his halting reading), the other "solutions" mean that the student will never improve his ability to read, for he has been relieved of the necessity of reading. The student may feel better, not having to struggle, but how likely is it that he will learn to read better when he isn't required to read? School systems in other countries expect their students to go through the learning process, even when it is not fun or pleasant.[31]

LIKING THE WORK

One telling aspect of the Asian emphasis on creating one's abilities and self through diligence and hard work is students' attitudes toward school. Despite the rigors and pressures they face at school, the many hours a week they must spend in intense study and concentration, the sometimes absurd restrictions and pressure for conformity (in Japanese schools only one menu item is offered for lunch; all students must wear the same color backpack or ride the same color bicycle; many schools prohibit the wearing of jewelry while many junior high schools prohibit watches; students are prohibited from riding motorcycles after school or even on summer vacations; and schools generally prohibit students from working part-time jobs and from dating), Asian students have a more positive attitude toward school than American students do. Going to school and studying are a central part of their lives, something that can be said of only a fraction of American students, whose after-school hours often have nothing to do with school. "If anything, Asian children's frank enthusiasm about school . . . would suggest that studying hard may lead to a feeling of accomplishment and mastery that actually enhances their self-image and their adjustment to school," write Stevenson and Stigler. The statement recalls James's words about the positive worth of having an effect on the world and making the most of one's life. Steinberg et al. in fact suggest that many American students' disengagement from school "is not a reaction to too much pressure or to classes that are too difficult, but a response to having too little demanded of them and to the absence of any consequences for failing to meet even these minimal demands."[32]

Perhaps the reason American students dislike school (they rank near the bottom among students internationally in their favorable attitudes toward school) is that they are disillusioned. Our culture tells them that "learning should be fun," that ideally they should be enjoying absolute freedom, and that their teachers can and should make them smart and happy. Since those important expectations of school are unfulfilled, our students must be constantly disappointed and resentful when they not only experience little fun at school but also learn very little of substance because their incompetent teachers are failing to do their job and meet the students' needs. One study shows that more teenagers in Japan than in the United States believe that man has control over his destiny. American teenagers, schooled according to a behaviorist philosophy that emphasizes the helplessness of the individual in facing his environment and genetics, are more likely to view man as being "helpless in the face of forces at work in the world." As Steinberg et al. have shown, the better students in the United States believe they succeed because of their efforts and fail because of lack of effort; American educational thinking, however, holds that the environment and the teacher's methods—not the student's will and determination to succeed—produce learning in the hapless, passive student. Despite bad press, the teenage suicide rate in Japan is in fact lower than in the United States, and the United States, which has terrible problems with teenage drug and alcohol abuse, pregnancy, and juvenile delinquency, can scarcely claim that its lax education system makes for happier, better-adjusted teenagers. According to American educational thinking, Japanese students should have disintegrated personalities and brains ravaged by the stress of school—yet the converse seems to be true.[33]

TEACHING IN JAPAN

Japan's educational success is rightly touted in the United States, where many look to Japanese teachers for models of excellence in teaching. Many Americans unhesitatingly believe that Japanese students are smarter than American students because the teachers there are better. It is undoubtedly true that the average Japanese teacher is better educated than the average teacher in the United States. Japanese teachers are graduates of their own demanding high schools and are required to earn majors in their teaching fields (not general education degrees); they do not come from the bottom of their high school and college classes.

Yet Japan's schools owe their success to the fact that their students strive to meet the high expectations of their parents, teachers, and society. The teachers merely teach the subject matter. The teacher's job, at the junior and senior high school levels, at least, is simply to deliver the material, mostly through a lecture format, using the textbook and the Monbusho curriculum as a guide, and students pay attention and work the problems. The emphasis is on the textbook and the subject matter, pure and simple, the "subject-matter-set-out-to-be-learned," as Kilpatrick derisively referred to it, or "the textbook garbage," in John Goodlad's memorable words. The students are already motivated by the major tests and encouraged by their parents and society, so the teacher is free to teach the subject in a formal, in-depth manner. Rohlen writes, "Japanese high school teachers do not evidence much feeling of need to stimulate their students." They do not bear the multitude of demands that American teachers routinely bear: they feel no necessity to make the lesson emotionally relevant, to captivate the student, or to create a lesson so entrancing that the student cannot help but learn. Even though Japanese teachers can be fairly certain that the students' previous teachers taught the curriculum, they are not expected to create individualized lessons (since there may be thirty-five students in elementary classes and forty-five in secondary classes—even fifty to sixty per class in the private schools—individualizing lessons is impossible, just as it is in the United States). Japanese teachers are also free of annoying problems such as discipline and negotiating with students over passing and failing grades, for Japanese schools rarely hold students back; the entrance examinations will ferret out the incompetent.[34]

The Japanese student is expected to do what is necessary to succeed, and that means paying attention in class and working for success, even when it is not interesting or emotionally fulfilling. Japanese classrooms at the secondary level are not very thrilling places:

> To a foreign observer, the kokugo [Japanese language] class, especially at the upper school levels, can be deadly dull.[35]

> The mathematics classes especially at the junior and senior high schools are, from U.S. perspective, deadly repetitious but also, significantly, deadly serious.[36]

> American elementary school students, watching a videotape of a Japanese mathematics lessons, inevitably react to the pace: They perceive unbearable slowness.[37]

"It is not uncommon for an Asian teacher [of *elementary* mathematics] to organize an entire lesson around the solution of a single problem," write Stevenson and Stigler. In such a situation, typical American high schools students would be misbehaving out of boredom, and their teachers condemned for not varying instruction. To the Chinese, the ideal qualities of a teacher are simply the ability to explain things clearly and to be enthusiastic.[38]

Not only are American teachers expected to do far more than Japanese teachers—inspiring students to learn, making learning fun, and meeting students' needs while covering the subject in great intellectual depth so that the students will attain the higher stages of learning and thinking—they are also paid substantially less for doing so, receive less respect (the Japanese word for teacher, *sensei*, is a term of equal respect whether denoting a first-grade teacher or a professor), and are subject to all sorts of criticism for failing to accomplish the impossible. First-year teachers in Japan generally earn more than first-year businessmen, engineers, pharmacists, and others, and after age fifty-three teachers earn more than those at similar points in their careers. Proponents of teacher accountability will argue that Japanese teachers are paid so well and enjoy so much respect because they produce such a good product. Yet it should be obvious by now that Japanese students and parents produce the superior product. Japanese teachers teach to high standards, but the most important factor in Japan's educational success is that the students keep up with the teacher and do what is necessary to succeed. While Japanese teachers may take the blame when students fail in their academics and general behavior, they receive tenure from their first day on the job and "cannot be fired for anything short of gross or illegal misconduct."[39]

Japanese high school teachers teach fifteen hours a week, similar to teachers across the industrialized world. Teachers in Beijing also teach three hours a day, unless the teacher is a homeroom teacher. Danish elementary school teachers teach eighteen hours a week, and Danish secondary teachers about sixteen. Teachers in Germany teach about twenty hours a week while teachers in the United States teach almost twenty-five hours a week. American secondary teachers teach, on the average, 943 hours per calendar year, while the mean from school systems across the world is 662 hours per year.[40]

The veteran teachers of today in the richest nation on the planet can recall the days when they taught six classes a day with no preparation time during the school day. And elementary school teachers have had to fight long and hard for a thirty-minute lunch in which they do not have to watch over the children. The demanding schedule has its effects on teachers' energy and dedication: "The notion that an American teacher can prepare three to five intellectually challenging and instructionally appropriate lessons each day, with perhaps ten to fifteen minutes to prepare each lesson, is patently absurd," writes Richard McAdams. Stevenson notes that Asian teachers are more enthusiastic than American teachers in their teaching, but

> Teachers [in Japan and China] are able to summon this amount of energy for teaching because they spend fewer hours being directly in charge of the classroom than do American teachers. Asian teachers are incredulous, in fact, when told that American teachers are typically re-

sponsible for their pupils throughout the school day. Although Chinese and Japanese teachers spend as much time at school as American teachers, they have much more time available during the day for preparing lessons, working with individual children, and conducting other class-related activities outside the classroom.[41]

Nor do Japanese teachers spend much time and energy dealing with student motivation, discipline, and grading. "The [Japanese] teacher's job is teaching, not classroom management," writes Benjamin matter of factly. But in the United States the teacher expends far too much energy in classroom management (I have seen veteran teachers reduced to tears after being overwhelmed by the frustrations of the job, and I have overheard students brag and laugh about how their class made a teacher quit or cry.) After all, the teacher is expected to solve all problems and be all things to all students. It is helpful to recall Kilpatrick's words that the teacher is responsible for everything that goes on in the classroom. "The workday of the American teacher," writes McAdams, "proceeds at a frenetic pace and with bone-crushing intensity." Teaching in the United States is a brutally demanding job *if* the teacher wishes to do the job well. The unreasonably heavy workload, writes McAdams, "creates a numbing exhaustion in the more conscientious teachers." The way to survive the job is, quite simply, just to punch the clock and pass every student, no matter how incompetent.[42]

No wonder that for every open teaching position in Japan there are five applicants, even in mathematics and sciences (some observers put the figure higher), while every August schools in the United States scramble to find teachers for their classrooms, many of whom must teach out of their field. American teachers tend to quit within three to five years of entering the classroom; those who survive the first years often suffer burnout as they toil in vain to find the magical teaching methods that will enable their students to learn without experiencing stress, frustration, or boredom.[43]

It is worth debating whether Japanese teachers are more effective than their American colleagues. Not often mentioned in the headlines declaring that Japanese students score much higher than American students on various tests is the fact that a large part of the Japanese student's academic experience is simply memorization, and the Japanese teacher's job at the secondary level is merely reading notes to the class. The American educational system is superior to the Japanese method because of its emphasis on thinking rather than simple memorization, but the American system overdoes it, condemning all memorization of facts in favor of abstract "thinking skills" for which facts are supposedly unnecessary. The American system expects students to engage in more analysis and creative problem-solving than their scanty store of basic knowledge allows. Harry Wray, who has taught in an American secondary school and at a private Japanese university, tells how on essay tests the Japanese students typically write terrible answers, as they have learned only to memorize, not to think: "Good American eighth-grade students," he argues, "may write longer, better essay examinations than many Japanese college students."[44]

There is good reason to consider it a miracle and a testament to American teachers' abilities and dedication that our students learn the little they do. Much is made of the fact that Japanese students go to school at least 30 more days a year than American students' 180 days. But that figure of 180 days scarcely represents 180 hours of intense teaching and studying in each class; the time spent on quality instruction in American schools is substantially less. Days must be subtracted for teacher and student illness or absence; standardized tests; movies in class or other nonacademic activities; days before major holidays; or community problems that may disrupt learning. One elementary teacher told me that her principal had instructed the teachers to collect the textbooks a month before the end of school so that they would have more time to complete an inventory before the last day of school. I remained shocked at such an extravagant waste of instructional time until the principal at my own school urged teachers to have the students turn in their textbooks two weeks before the end of the year—thus leaving the students without their textbooks *before final exams.*

Thus the number of hours spent on study and learning by American students is small indeed, probably half that of Japanese students. And the American student—if he reads the textbook—will be distracted by the unnecessary clutter in the book while the Japanese student's book is smaller and more concentrated, with few distractions in the text. Going to school is more than a full-time job for Asian students, as they study after school, over weekends and vacations, and study intently while in school; for many students in the United States, however, going to school is a part-time job.

Overall it is amazing that American students learn as much as they do, a fact pointed out by the Japanese and Chinese teachers who have observed American schools. Teachers in the United States deserve praise for the little that many of their students learn.[45]

8

WHAT IS TO BE DONE?

Blaming teachers for the failure of American students to meet high academic standards, and expecting their scores to improve solely through improved teaching methods, reveals the clash of two incompatible idea systems in American educational thinking. On the one hand we want our students to excel in tests of formal academic knowledge; on the other hand we expect such formal academic excellence to be produced by teachers as they individualize lessons and even the curriculum so that students will learn naturally and joyfully.

But these principles, which form the basis of the nation's thinking about learning at school, academic subjects, the nature of young people, and the role of the teacher, are hostile to formal academic content and even the cultivation of the intellect. They subvert the hard work, diligence, and discipline necessary for students if they are to meet high standards in academic subjects. In the United States, teachers are expected to do what is necessary to enable students to meet the standards that are met in other nations (such as Japan) by the intense, arduous, and diligent work of the students themselves, adhering to a rigid and formal national curriculum. Moreover, American teachers are expected to operate in a modified Deweyan framework, in which there is supposed to be no fixed curriculum, no study of academic subjects per se, and certainly no feelings of compulsion or strain experienced by the students, for such negative feelings are thought to inflict grave psychological damage on the young. Educational excellence must therefore be achieved by teachers and their teaching methods, regardless of what students do. This belief is held both by conservative critics of education and by the educationists. Conservatives demand that the teacher find a way to produce results; when exasperated teachers note that they cannot be held responsible for failures of the family, they are accused of laziness and union-supported incompetence. The education experts argue that if only lazy, incompetent, and cynical teachers would meet students' needs or implement the latest suggestions for reform, all would be bliss.

If our society truly wants its students to meet high academic standards, it must change its thinking about education. It must look to successful systems and successful students for answers, not to the Progressive Paradigm. The successful systems in Japan, China, Germany, France, and Catholic and some private schools in the United States provide models in both behavior and attitudes for our public schools, and the top 15 percent of students in our public schools show the traits that students in general should emulate if they wish to succeed. While our public education system need not slavishly adhere to the manners and methods of these other schools, it must nonetheless recognize their effective practices and adopt them. Creative adaptation works in other areas of American life; it should be no different in education. A remark by the superintendent of schools of the city of Vienna summarizes the attitudes Americans must have: "In Austria, children (and their parents) know exactly what the school expects of them. It's not entertainment, not 'edutainment,' but the old-fashioned task of learning."[1] Needless to say, children and their parents in the United States do *not* know what is expected of them—the teacher is charged with setting expectations according to student needs, interests, and abilities—but they *do* expect to be both entertained and edutained, not to be doing the old-fashioned task of learning. (As Dewey would say, they expect to do what a situation calls for, with the consequence being learning.) Such being the confusion, incoherence, and lack of focus in our public schools, how could students possibly succeed in meeting formal standards?

To solve the problem of underachievement in our schools, here is what we need. (My suggestions are applicable chiefly to junior and senior high schools.)

The creation of a challenging, rigorous national curriculum, with concrete, explicit statements of what students will be expected to learn in core courses in each grade—English, a foreign language, math, science, history, American government, and so on—and with textbooks that present information accurately and efficiently, with a minimum of distraction. The curriculum would spell out in detail the facts and concepts that a student must know in a subject at every level, and explain clearly how those facts and concepts are applied in more abstract ways. The national curriculum would help to level the playing field by giving all students—regardless of where they live, how often they move, or what their parents, teachers, or administrators think of their abilities or the value of school subjects—equal opportunity to acquire knowledge and equal expectations of achievement. For their own good, all students, regardless of race, class, geographical locale, or mobility of their parents, would be expected to meet a certain standard—which should be reasonably high and challenging—in the core academic subjects.[2]

The national curriculum would be accompanied by end-of-course tests in all subjects, which the students would have to pass in order to earn credit for the course. A final graduation exam (like the *Abitur* in German schools, *le baccalaureat* in French schools, or the university exams in Japan) would reinforce among students the idea that one learns the material as a lifelong possession, not something to be forgotten upon completion of the exam.

To be worthwhile, the end-of-course tests would have to contain questions about facts and basic concepts. Because of its anti-formalist past, the American educational system has an irrational, even hysterical fear of having students memorize facts, though the creation of deeper understanding is impossible without a store of facts and basic concepts. The tests would also need to probe for deeper understanding of the material. The excesses of the Japanese system should be avoided.

As a benefit of the tests, students could begin to see the teacher as a coach who would help them gain an understanding of the material and enable them to pass the test, rather than as an enemy imposing seemingly arbitrary standards. Teachers who now demand much of their students are not infrequently regarded by them (and their parents, and even some administrators) in something of an antagonistic light. The end-of-course test over the year's material could very well unite the teachers and their students against a common enemy, the impartial test, which would be given uniformly to students across the country. Students would be more likely to see the teacher as an ally in their struggle to pass the test than as someone who, in enforcing seemingly arbitrary standards, jeopardizes their good grades, eligibility for extracurricular activities, and chances of graduation. Such is the relationship between teachers and students in Japan, for example, and observers of other educational systems, in describing the benefits of a national curriculum and test, note that the relationship between teacher and students is not as hostile as in American schools, even though standards are much higher.[3]

A test-based national curriculum would also create an objective standard by which students, their parents, and other interested parties across the country could compare student performance. It is an ugly and disgraceful fact that the current system of letter grades, in the absence of an absolute, objective standard, is grossly unfair. That a student has earned an A in Spanish, for example, does not mean that the student has mastered the material in the Spanish curriculum, nor does a B in Marine Science show that the student has mastered most of the material for that class. The A student in Spanish might very well know less Spanish than a student who earned a C in Spanish in the classroom next door, under a tougher teacher; the B student in Marine Science might know nothing about the subject while a student with a D under a different teacher or in a different school might know a fair amount about Marine Science. The current system of letter grades penalizes students who choose difficult courses with demanding teachers, for such students are more likely to earn lower grades than students who choose electives taught by the "cool" teachers who don't expect their students to sweat and struggle to meet high standards. Because grades are such a crucial factor in class rank, eligibility for extra-curricular activities, and the awarding of scholarships, one must conclude that good students deserve something better: a grading system not arbitrary and inaccurate. The current system, because of the "Lake Wobegon Effect" (the term that describes how most students in U.S. schools are above average), also gives mediocre students good grades they don't deserve, and thus a false sense of competence. Finally, the letter-grade system penalizes demanding teachers, for teachers who have high expectations of their students and insist that they work hard for an A or B are more likely to face angry parents at conferences. Many students resent having to work hard for good grades when students in Mr. So-and-so's class have such an easy time—they all get A's and never have to study! The tough teachers in American schools must often waste an inordinate amount of time and energy defending their adherence to high standards; eventually, many simply lose their idealism and give up, having grown weary of incessant complaints from students, parents, and even administrators. The absolute, objective test would relieve the nation's demanding teachers of a great burden and perhaps compel "easy" teachers to tighten their standards and work harder on their teaching.

As an added incentive to high performance, students should be rewarded for meeting high standards on end-of-course tests. Since the Constitution delegates educational matters to the states, the federal government could not enforce a national curriculum. Yet it could create such a curriculum and devise the tests, with the requirement that students who wish to apply for financial aid from the federal government must pass such tests. Perhaps the minimum grade for passing a course and earning credit toward graduation would be 65 percent, while 75 percent would be the minimum grade for applying for federal financial aid. Poor but good students might receive more financial assistance for college than equally good but affluent students.

American schools must change student attitudes by making clear the purpose of being in school. Students must understand that going to school is their job, something most do not now realize. Many students, thinking it is the teacher's job to do what will "make" them smart, feel little need to take their classes seriously. End-of-course tests and an altered view of how success is achieved would help students focus their efforts and give them a feeling that school is a real mission, one that demands seriousness of purpose, dedication, and diligence. If they study more diligently, they might even come to enjoy learning and the feeling of real accomplishment.

Students should be told in plain language why they must take academic courses in school, why society has decided that they must learn math, English, the sciences, a foreign language, history, and social studies. Most students do not understand why they must learn these subjects; they tend to think of school only in terms of a future job. Some say they must learn such things in order to be well-rounded individuals, which is not a bad answer. But students should begin learning from their earliest school days that academic subjects are the primary means to understanding world civilization. These disciplines are essential to the development of an educated person who will be the equal of all other educated persons in America's republican democracy. To many Americans, academic subjects seem to be required because of mere tradition.

Changing what is expected of students will simultaneously change the attitudes of teachers, improving the morale and status of the teaching profession. The knee-jerk tendency in the United States is to charge teachers with incompetence for any perceived failure of their students or their schools. Considering what teachers are expected to do—make students smart without causing them stress, and make their time at school a joyful, emotionally fulfilling experience—teachers cannot but fail and thus incur society's contempt. Placing responsibility for learning on the students, and expecting teachers only to present competent lessons (as teachers in Japan and other countries are expected to do), might retain many of the large percentage of teachers who leave within the first three years, and might reduce the burnout factor among veterans.[4]

At the same time we change the relative responsibilities of teachers and students, we should reduce the number of hours teachers teach per day. So important is such a change that Stevenson and Stigler make it their first recommendation for changing the schools. Teachers in the United States should teach the same number of hours that teachers in other countries do—approximately four a day or slightly less, instead of five or more.[5] Reducing teaching hours will relieve teachers and also make it possible to lengthen the school day so that teachers can require failing students to attend tutoring sessions. Many teachers do not tutor as willingly as they should, one reason being that at the end of the day they are exhausted and have lesson plans to make, tests and quizzes to grade, and paperwork to complete. With more time during the day for noninstructional work, teachers can be required to tutor students who want and need help. Mandatory after-school tutoring for failing students should take precedence over all extra-curricular activities.

Our educational system must look to students and what they do as the fount of success. A few of the authors quoted in this book have noted the irony that in the United States, though famous for our work ethic, in our schools we don't expect students to work at their studies. One observer noted that to study the relationship between school success and character development, he had to go to Japan.[6] We must change our attitudes about school, the nature of young people, and how one achieves in academics. No school reform will succeed without a far-reaching transformation that goes beyond teachers and curriculum. We need also to change the attitudes of the education experts, who continually promote an unworkable and unfeasible educational philosophy and then flay teachers for their inability to meet impossible expectations.

Education is so important to the United States that we expect teachers, who are professionals trained in pedagogical science, to get the job done. We sincerely want all students to learn so that they may lead good, productive lives. But teachers, parents, and adults cannot do it for them. The nation is looking for educational excellence in the wrong place, in the actions of teachers. We must instead expect students to create their success, give them our full support and guidance in their labors, encourage and expect them to try again with renewed effort and persistence when they fail, and reward them for success.

NOTES

Preface: Maybe If You'd Sing and Dance, We'd Learn This Stuff

1. William F. Buckley, "A Second Generation of Know Nothings?" *Houston Chronicle*, October 6, 1998, 22A. Rita Dunn, Jeffrey S. Beaudry, and Angela Klavas, "Are Schools Responsible for Students' Failure? A Synthesis of the Research on Learning styles," in *Report of the New York State Board of Regents' Panel on Learning Styles* (ED 348 407), 1988, p. 34, emphases in original. Gerald Grant, "It's the Teachers, Stupid!" review of Diane Ravitch, *Left Back: A Century of Failed School Reforms*, *http://www.educationnext.org/unabridged/2001sp/grant.html*.

2. "The Teachers We Need and How to Get More of Them: A Manifesto," in *Better Teachers, Better Schools*, eds. Marci Kanstoroom and Chester E. Finn, Jr. (Washington, D.C.: Thomas B. Fordham Foundation, 1999), p. 5.

3. National Commission on Teaching and America's Future, *What Matters Most: Teaching for America's Future* (1996), pp. vi, 2. In the interest of economy and style, I use *he* and *his* to refer to a generic third person. I fully recognize the percentage and importance of women and girls in society and schools. National Commission on Teaching and America's Future, *Doing What Matters Most: Investing in Quality Teaching* (1997), p. 9. See Richard D. Kahlenberg, "Learning from James Coleman," *The Public Interest*, Summer 2001, p. 62. In an interview, Coleman declared flatly: "A child's learning is a function more of the characteristics of his classmates than those of the teacher." See James S. Coleman, Thomas Hoffer, and Sally Kilgore, *High School Achievement: Public, Catholic, and Private Schools Compared* (New York: Basic Books, 1982), pp. 190–191. For a discussion of whether or not teachers and their qualifications in education make a difference, see Christopher J. Lucas, *Teacher Education in America: Reform Agendas for the Twenty-first Century* (New York: St. Martin's Press, 1997), pp. 84, 118, 136. See Dan D. Goldhaber and Dominic J. Brewer, "Teacher Licensing and Student Achievement," in Kanstoroom and Finn,

eds., *Better Teachers, Better Schools*, pp. 93–96. See also Laurence Steinberg, with B. Branford Brown and Sanford M. Dornbusch, *Beyond the Classroom* (New York: Touchstone, 1997), pp. 138ff. Recruiting New Teachers, Inc., *The Essential Profession* (1998), pp. 1, 10. Alief ISD Staff Newsletter, *The Outlook*, May 1999; repeated in May 2000.

4. J. E. Stone, "National Council for Accreditation of Teacher Education: Whose Standards?" Kanstoroom and Finn, in *Better Teachers, Better Schools*, pp. 213–213. The entire sentence reads, "The product of teaching, learning, could not be used as an indicator [of teachers' teaching ability] because student learning is influenced by preexisting differences in student knowledge, skills, backgrounds, motivation, and other characteristics." Since learning is so heavily influenced by preexisting conditions—all outside of the teacher's control and purview—is it not inaccurate to call learning "the product of teaching"? The most one can say is that a student's learning is *influenced* by teaching, but hardly *produced*.

5. *The Rolling Stone Illustrated History of Rock and Roll*, 3rd ed. (New York: Random House, 1992), p. 408.

6. U.S. Department of Education, National Center for Education Statistics, *The Condition of Education 1999*, Tables 27, 153. Steinberg et al., *Beyond the Classroom*, p. 19. U.S. Department of Education, National Center for Education Statistics, *The Condition of Education 2002*, Table 113.

7. U.S. Department of Education, National Center for Education Statistics, *The Condition of Education 1999*, Tables 124, 384. National Center for Education Statistics, *The Condition of Education 2001*, Indicator 22. U.S. Department of Education, National Center for Education Statistics, *The Condition of Education 2001*, Indicator 20.

8. Web page of the Texas Education Agency on March 16, 1998: "Providing Leadership to Achieve Excellence in Education for all Students."

Chapter 1: William James and Pre-Progressive Educational Thinking

1. *The Oxford Companion to the Mind*, ed. Richard L. Gregory (New York: Oxford University Press, 1987), s.v. "William James." Ralph Barton Perry, *The Thought and Character of William James: Briefer Version* (New York: George Braziller, 1954), p. 200. Merle Curti, *The Social Ideas of American Educators* (New York: Charles Scribner's Sons, 1935), p. 443. Arthur I. Gates, "Contributions of Research to General Methods of Instruction," *The 37th Yearbook for Study of Education* (Bloomington, Ill.: Public School Publishing Co., 1938), p. 81.

2. Linda Simon, *Genuine Reality: A Life of William James* (New York: Harcourt Brace and Co., 1998), pp. 125ff. William James, "The Dilemma of Determinism," in

The Will To Believe (New York: Dover Publications, 1956), p. 150. Simon, *Genuine Reality*, p. 127.

3. Gordon W. Allport, Introduction to William James, *Psychology: The Briefer Course*, ed. Gordon W. Allport (Notre Dame: University of Notre Dame Press, 1985), p. xiii.

4. William James, *The Principles of Psychology*, 2 vols. (New York: Dover Publications, 1950), I, 8; II, 330.

5. James, *Psychology: The Briefer Course*, p. 237. James, *Principles of Psychology*, I, 122.

6. Ibid., I, 496; I, 234.

7. Ibid., I, 219, I, 288.

8. Ibid., I, 403–404; I, 420; I, 139, emphasis in original.

9. Ibid., I, 589.

10. Ibid., I, 424.

11. Ibid., I, 122. E. D. Hirsch, Jr., *The Schools We Need and Why We Don't Have Them* (New York: Doubleday, 1996), p. 150.

12. William James, *Talks to Teachers* (New York: W. W. Norton and Co., 1958), pp. 94, 39, 95.

13. Diane Ravitch, *Left Back: A Century of Failed School Reforms* (New York: Simon and Schuster, 2000), pp. 41ff; also Theodore Sizer, *Secondary Schools at the Turn of the Century* (New Haven: Yale University Press, 1964), passim. W. T. Harris, "The Curriculum for Secondary Schools," *NEA Proceedings*, 1894, p. 503. As described by Lawrence A. Cremin, *The Transformation of the School* (New York: Alfred A. Knopf, 1961), p. 19.

14. James, *Talks to Teachers*, pp. 101, 99, 98, 85.

15. Ibid., p. 131.

16. James, *Principles of Psychology*, II, 578–79.

17. James, *Talks to Teachers*, pp. 51–52, emphasis in original.

18. James, *Principles of Psychology*, I, 424, emphasis in original.

19. William James, "Is Life Worth Living?" in *The Will to Believe*, p. 47.

20. James, *Principles of Psychology*, II, 569, emphases in original.

21. James, ibid., I, 123. James, *Talks to Teachers*, pp. 111, 63, 62, emphases in original.

22. James, *Principles of Psychology*, I, 127, emphasis in original.

23. Coleman et al., *High School Achievement*, p. xxvi. James J. Shields, Jr., Introduction to *Japanese Schooling: Patterns of Socialization, Equality, and Political Control*, ed. James J. Shields, Jr. (University Park, Pa.: Pennsylvania State University Press, 1989), p. 3.

24. James, *Talks to Teachers*, pp. 23–24, 21.

25. Ibid., pp. 45, 46, 84.

26. Paul Woodring, Introduction to *Talks to Teachers*, by William James, p. 13. James, *Talks to Teachers*, p. 40.

27. James, *Talks to Teachers*, pp. 67–68.

28. Ibid., pp. 47, 75, emphases in original.

29. Ibid., pp. 106–107.

30. Ibid., pp. 83, 124, 127–128. As quoted in Simon, *Genuine Reality*, p. 322.

31. Woodring, Introduction to *Talks to Teachers*, p. 15.

32. See Chapter 7 on Japanese education.

Chapter 2: The Progressive Paradigm, Part One

1. Randall Collins and Michael Makowsky, *The Discovery of Society*, 6th ed. (Boston: McGraw Hill, 1998), pp. 19ff.

2. Frederick Lewis Allen, *Only Yesterday* (New York: Harper and Row, 1964), p. 164.

3. *Time*, January 2, 1961.

4. Geraldine Joncich, *The Sane Positivist: A Biography of Edward L. Thorndike* (Middletown, Conn.: Wesleyan University Press, 1968), p. 154.

5. John M. O'Donnell, *The Origins of Behaviorism: American Psychology, 1870–1920* (New York: New York University Press, 1985), pp. 73ff., 132; Daniel W. Bjork, *B. F. Skinner: A Life* (New York: Basic Books, 1993), p. 79; and Morton Hunt, *The Story of Psychology* (New York: Doubleday, 1993), pp. 242ff.

6. John B. Watson, *Behaviorism* (New York: W. W. Norton and Co., 1970), p. 2. John B. Watson, "Psychology as the Behaviorist Views It," *Psychological Review* (20) 1913, p. 158.

7. Watson, *Behaviorism*, p. 22.

8. O'Donnell, *Origins of Behaviorism*, p. 227.

9. Watson, *Behaviorism*, p. 104.

10. Ibid., pp. 303ff, 183; see also B. F. Skinner, *Walden Two*, passim. Cremin, *The Transformation of the School*, p. 200. See also Christopher J. Lucas, *Teacher Education in America*, pp. 101ff.

11. Thorndike later qualified his findings and admitted that the study of Latin could hold some value. Other Progressive educators, however, misused his research in their crusade to rid the schools of Latin. See Ravitch, *Left Back*, pp. 64–69. Joncich, *The Sane Positivist*, pp. 335, 489, 348.

12. O'Donnell, *Origins of Behaviorism*, p. 167.

13. Edward L. Thorndike, *Educational Psychology: Briefer Course* (New York: Teachers College, Columbia University, 1917), p. 174. Edward L. Thorndike, *Education: A First Book* (New York: Macmillan, 1912), p. 97.

14. Thorndike, *Education*, pp. 70, 257, 66. Thorndike, *Educational Psychology: Briefer Course*, p. 174.

15. Thorndike, *Education*, p. 60, emphasis in original.

16. Edward L. Thorndike, "The Contribution of Psychology To Education," *Journal of Educational Psychology* (1) 1910, p. 6.

17. Thorndike, *Education*, p. 258. Teachers College at the time was "an institution pervaded with messianic zeal," writes Samuel Tenenbaum in *William Heard Kilpatrick: Trailblazer in Education* (New York: Harper and Brothers, 1951), p. 63.

18. Allen, *Only Yesterday*, p. 165. Joncich, *The Sane Positivist*, pp. 529–530. E. G. Boring quoted in O'Donnell, *Origins of Behaviorism*, p. 207. Louis Berman, *The Religion Called Behaviorism* (New York: Boni and Liveright, 1927), passim.

19. Howard Gardner, *The Mind's New Science: A History of the Cognitive Revolution* (New York: Basic Books, 1985). Bjork, *B. F. Skinner*, pp. 192, 201, 214.

20. B. F. Skinner, *Beyond Freedom and Dignity* (New York: Bantam Books, 1972), p. 21. B. F. Skinner, *About Behaviorism* (New York: Alfred A. Knopf, 1974), pp. 162, 149, 168. B. F. Skinner, *Science and Human Behavior* (New York: Free Press, 1965), p. 160.

21. Skinner, *About Behaviorism*, p. 189. James, *Principles of Psychology*, I, 6.

22. Skinner, *Beyond Freedom and Dignity*, pp. 96, 201–202.

23. Skinner, *Science and Human Behavior*, pp. 116, 240, emphasis added. Skinner, *Beyond Freedom and Dignity*, p. 71.

24. James, *Psychology: The Briefer Course*, p. 318.

25. Skinner, *Science and Human Behavior*, p. 123, emphasis in original. Skinner, *About Behaviorism*, p. 105.

26. Hugo Muensterberg, *Psychology General and Applied* (New York: D. Appleton and Co., 1916), pp. 370–371, emphasis added.

27. Skinner, *About Behaviorism*, p. 181. Skinner, *Science and Human Behavior*, pp. 91, 32. Edward L. Thorndike, "The Foundations of Educational Achievement," *NEA Proceedings*, 1914, p. 204: "Human beings . . . are not indifferent clay to be molded at will by the teacher's art."

28. Skinner, *Beyond Freedom and Dignity*, p. 72.

29. Skinner, *Science and Human Behavior*, p. 28. Thorndike, *Education*, p. 102. Thorndike, *Educational Psychology: Briefer Course*, pp. 175, 379. Joncich, *The Sane Positivist*, p. 531.

30. Skinner, *Science and Human Behavior*, pp. 17, 19. Skinner, *About Behaviorism*, p. 209.

31. Skinner, *Science and Human Behavior*, p. 321. Bjork, *B. F. Skinner*, p. 100.

32. Skinner, *Science and Human Behavior*, p. 427. Skinner, *Beyond Freedom and Dignity*, p. 147. Joncich, *The Sane Positivist*, p. 533.

33. Thorndike, *Educational Psychology: Briefer Course*, p. 171.

34. Skinner, *Science and Human Behavior*, pp. 89–90, emphasis in original.

35. Bjork, *B. F. Skinner*, p. 219.

36. Ibid., p. 221.

37. Skinner, *Beyond Freedom and Dignity*, p. 196.

38. Quoted in Cremin, *Transformation of the School*, p. 19.

Chapter 3: The Progressive Paradigm, Part Two

1. Kenneth E. Hendrickson, Jr., ed., *Essays and Commentaries in American History*, vol. II. (Lanham, Md.: University Press of America, 1982), p. 159. Herbert Croly, *The Promise of American Life* (Indianapolis: Bobbs-Merrill, 1965), p. 6.

2. Cremin, *Transformation of the School*, p. 100. Alan Ryan, *John Dewey and the High Tide of American Liberalism* (New York: W. W. Norton and Co., 1997), pp. 43–44.

3. William H. Kilpatrick, "Dewey's Influence on Education," in Paul Arthur Schilpp, ed., *The Philosophy of John Dewey*, 2nd ed. (New York: Tudor Publishing Co., 1951), p. 464.

4. Tenenbaum, *William Heard Kilpatrick*, p. 185.

5. Lawrence A. Cremin, David A. Shannon, and Mary Evelyn Townsend, *A History of Teachers College Columbia University* (New York: Columbia University Press, 1954), pp. 221. 246. For a fuller treatment of Progressive education, see Diane Ravitch, *Left Back* or *The Troubled Crusade* (New York: Basic Books, 1983), or Cremin, *Transformation of the School*.

6. Henry Steele Commager, *The American Mind* (New Haven: Yale University Press, 1950), p. 45.

7. John Dewey, "My Pedagogic Creed," in *John Dewey: The Early Works, 1882–1898*, vol. 5 (Carbondale: Southern Illinois University Press, 1972), p. 93. John Dewey, *Human Nature and Conduct* (Carbondale: Southern Illinois University Press, 1988), p. 89. Merle Curti, *The Social Ideas of American Educators* (New York: Charles Scribner's Sons, 1935), passim. The arrogance of Dewey, Kilpatrick, et al., increased, if not engendered, the contempt and antagonism that many Americans feel for public education, an antipathy that weighs most heavily upon teachers—the most visible and vulnerable targets in the schools—despite their lack of power within the administrative structure of the public education systems and the colleges of education. Note the expectations that educational experts foisted (and, to some extent, still do) upon teachers in their daily work, no matter how obnoxious to public opinion and the teachers themselves: "Within schools," commented Kilpatrick, "a socialized outlook must bring a more socialized schoolwork, and the responsibility for effecting this should be principally with the teachers." Thus arose "the caricature of the radical pedagogue using the school to subvert the American way of life," as Cremin put it.

8. John Dewey, "Psychology and Social Practice," in *Philosophy, Psychology and Social Practice*, ed. Joseph Ratner (New York: G. P. Putnam's Sons, 1963), p. 295. John Dewey, "From Absolutism to Experimentalism," in *The Philosophy of John Dewey*, ed. John J. McDermott (Chicago: University of Chicago Press, 1981), p. 7. William Heard Kilpatrick, *The Foundations of Method: Informal Talks on Teaching* (New York: Macmillan, 1926), p. 172. Tenenbaum records that *The Foundations of*

Method sold more than 61,000 copies (p. 209). L. Thomas Hopkins, *Integration: Its Meaning and Application* (New York: D. Appleton-Century Co., 1937), p. 51.

9. Kilpatrick, *The Foundations of Method*, p. 321. John Dewey, *The School and Society* and *The Child and the Curriculum*, two volumes in one (Chicago: University of Chicago Press, 1990), p. 34.

10. John Dewey, *Individualism Old and New* (London: George Allen and Unwin, 1931), p. 14. To be fair to Dewey, one should note when the book was published. John Dewey, "Ethical Principles Underlying Education," *The Third Yearbook of the National Herbart Society 1897.* (Chicago: University of Chicago Press, 1907), p. 8. John Dewey, "The Need for Social Psychology," *Psychological Review* (24) 1917, p. 272. John Dewey, *The Public and Its Problems* (Athens, Ohio: Swallow Press, Ohio University Press, 1991), pp. 158, 176.

11. Dewey, "The Need for Social Psychology," p. 273.

12. Dewey, *The School and Society* and *The Child and the Curriculum*, pp. 28–29.

13. This need for the discovery of the people was voiced not only by Dewey but by Herbert Croly (*The Promise of American Life*, p. 145) and Walter Lippman (*Drift and Mastery*); Dewey himself discusses it in *The Public and Its Problems*, pp. 32ff, 126. William Heard Kilpatrick, *Education for a Changing Civilization* (New York: Macmillan, 1937), pp. 70, 71.

14. John Dewey and John L. Childs, "The Social-Economic Situation and Education," in William H. Kilpatrick, ed., *The Educational Frontier* (New York: D. Appleton-Century Co., 1933), p. 71. Croly, *The Promise of American Life*, pp. 387, 407. Croly was editor of *The New Republic*, a Progressive journal to which Dewey contributed after 1914. John Dewey and Evelyn Dewey, *Schools of To-morrow* (New York: E. P. Dutton and Co., 1915), p. 63.

15. Dewey, *The School and Society* and *The Child and the Curriculum*, p. 15. See also Dewey, "Ethical Principles Underlying Education," pp. 15–17. Dewey and Dewey, *Schools of To-morrow*, pp. 125–126. Cremin reports that within ten years of its publication, *Schools of To-morrow* saw fourteen printings (Lawrence A. Cremin, "John Dewey and the Progressive-Education Movement 1915–1952," in Reginald D. Archambault, ed., *Dewey on Education: Appraisals* (New York: Random House, 1966), p. 11).

16. Ravitch, *Left Back*, pp. 123–129, 162–237, and *The Troubled Crusade*, pp. 47ff; for a treatment with particular verve and wit, see Richard Mitchell, "The Seven Deadly Principles," in *The Graves of Academe* (New York: Fireside Books, 1981), pp. 69–91. The principles have not been repudiated: Harry Wray relates that he and fellow teacher candidates were required to memorize the "Seven Cardinal Principles of Education" (Harry Wray, *Japanese and American Education: Attitudes and Practices* [Westport, Conn.: Bergin and Garvey, 1999], p. 233). The 1940s saw the education establishment issue a report of a similarly anti-academic and anti-intellectual

nature, *Education for All American Youth*, in which the major goal was "life adjust-ment." See Ravitch, *Left Back*, pp. 324ff. Tenenbaum, *William Heard Kilpatrick*, p. 104. William Heard Kilpatrick, "The Theories Underlying the Experiment," *Teachers College Record*, March 1919, p. 100.

17. Kilpatrick, *Education for a Changing Civilization*, pp. 111–112.

18. John Dewey, *Democracy and Education* (New York: Free Press, 1966), pp. 18–19, 11.

19. Ibid., p. 76. John Dewey, "The University Elementary School: History and Character," as quoted in Arthur G. Wirth, *John Dewey as Educator: His Design for Work in Education (1894–1904)* (New York: John Wiley and Sons, 1966), p. 197.

20. Dewey, *The School and Society* and *The Child and the Curriculum*, p. 26. Dewey and Dewey, *Schools of To-morrow*, p. 315. Dewey et al., *The Educational Frontier*, p. 67, 301. See also *Democracy and Education*, pp. 136–137.

21. John Dewey, "Progressive Education and the Science of Education," *Progressive Education* (V) 1928, p. 198.

22. Dewey, *The School and Society* and *The Child and the Curriculum*, pp. 91–92. Dewey, "My Pedagogic Creed," p. 87.

23. Dewey and Dewey, *Schools of To-morrow*, p. 108.

24. Dewey, *The School and Society* and *The Child and the Curriculum*, pp. 22, 60. Tenenbaum, *William Heard Kilpatrick*, p. 141, n. 11. John Dewey, *How We Think* (Boston: D. C. Heath and Co., 1933), pp. 46–47; *Democracy and Education*, p. 241. Ryan reports that *How We Think* "was a staple in the diet of progressive teacher training colleges" (*John Dewey*, p. 73), and that despite Dewey's hatred of blind devotion to dogma and unquestioned acceptance of others' beliefs, William Heard Kilpatrick used *Democracy and Education* as a bible at Teachers College.

25. When students are aware that they are studying and learning, he states, "Just in the degree in which they are induced by the conditions to be so aware, they are *not* studying and learning. They are in a divided and complicated attitude" (*Democracy and Education*, p. 174). One must wonder if it is ever acceptable for an individual to do something without being aware of his actions and motives and their consequences. Dewey, *The Public and Its Problems*, p. 154.

26. Dewey, *The School and Society* and *The Child and the Curriculum*, p. 203, emphasis added. It is easy for Dewey to write "it is easy" because, like many educationists and critics of education, his experience in a real school under real circumstances is minimal. He taught for only two and a half years before leaving for the greener pastures of higher academia. As a professor, Dewey's method of conducting his classes was entirely contrary to his advice for teachers: "[Dewey's] practice . . . ," recalls Kilpatrick, "was to come to the class with a problem on his mind and sit before the class thinking out loud as he sought to bring creative thinking to bear on his problem." William Heard Kilpatrick, "Personal Reminiscences of Dewey and My Judgment of His Present Influence," in Archambault, ed., *Dewey on Education*, p. 3. Physician, heal thyself!

27. Dewey, "Progressive Education and the Science of Education," p. 204.

28. Dewey, *Democracy and Education*, p. 132.

29. Ibid., p. 180.

30. Dewey, *Experience and Education* (New York: Collier Books, 1938), p. 27.

31. Dewey, *How We Think*, p. 40.

32. Dewey, "Plan of the University Primary School," in Wirth, *John Dewey as Educator*, p. 303.

33. Dewey, *Interest and Effort in Education* (Boston: Houghton Mifflin Co., 1913), pp. 95–96.

34. In December 1993, ten years after the publication of A *Nation at Risk*, I attended an in-service entitled, "The Courage to Succeed: A New Look at Underachievement," in which we teachers were admonished to encourage students in the direction of their interests, not ours, to let them set their own standards, and to let them learn at their own pace. Like most educationists, the presenter failed to consider a basic question: What do we do if, say, a first-grader learning the alphabet decides that the pace most suitable for him is learning one letter of the alphabet each year? As will be seen in Chapter 6, Deweyism is surviving well in today's colleges of education. John Dewey, "Interest in Relation to Training of the Will," *First Yearbook of the National Herbart Society 1895*, Second Supplement (Chicago: University of Chicago Press, 1903), pp. 24–25.

35. William Heard Kilpatrick, "The Project Method," *Teachers College Record*, (September 1918), p. 323.

36. Kilpatrick, *Education for a Changing Civilization*, pp. 117–118.

37. Dewey and Dewey, *Schools of To-morrow*, p. 301.

38. Dewey, *Interest and Effort in Education*, p. 7. Dewey, "My Pedagogic Creed," p. 85. Dewey, *The School and Society* and *The Child and the Curriculum*, p. 123. Kilpatrick, "Dewey's Influence on Education," p. 458. Kilpatrick, *The Foundations of Method*, pp. 311, 78ff.

39. Dewey, *The School and Society* and *The Child and the Curriculum*, pp. 159, 201. Kilpatrick, "Dewey's Influence on Education," p. 455. Dewey, *Interest and Effort in Education*, pp. 21, 35.

40. Dewey and Dewey, *Schools of To-morrow*, p. 56. Dewey, *Human Nature and Conduct*, p. 86.

41. The stress can be seen in the fact that at the Laboratory School at the University of Chicago, which was run by Dewey's wife in accordance with her husband's philosophy, teachers were quite unhappy—Mrs. Dewey was "a bad boss and was much too hard on her teachers" (Ryan, *John Dewey*, p. 154). See also Brian Patrick Hendley, "John Dewey and the Laboratory School" in *Dewey, Russell, Whitehead: Philosophers as Educators* (Carbondale: Southern Illinois University Press, 1986), p. 35. One might also compare the high percentages of teachers leaving within the first three years (National Center for Education Statistics, *The Condition of Education 1999*, Table 73).

42. Cremin, *Transformation of the School*, p. 168.

43. Kilpatrick, *The Foundations of Method*, p. 278. Kilpatrick, *Education for a Changing Civilization*, pp. 112–113. It is worth noting that Kilpatrick uses the verb "learn" as a noun (*The Foundations of Method*, pp. 281, 291). Kilpatrick's peculiar style may have been the inspiration for Mortimer Smith's remark that educators' writings "sound as if they had been badly translated from the German." (Mortimer Smith, *And Madly Teach* [Chicago: Henry Regnery Co., 1949], p. 5).

44. Kilpatrick, *Foundations of Method*, p. 253. Dewey, *How We Think*, p. 35.

45. Gordon W. Allport, "Dewey's Individual and Social Psychology," in Schilpp, ed., p. 281. Dewey had written similar thoughts in "Psychology and Social Practice," in Ratner, *Philosophy, Psychology, and Social Practice*, p. 304.

46. Dewey, *How We Think*, p. 51, 53, 87, 90, 187–188, 236; "What Do We Mean by Progressive Education?" *Democracy and Education*, pp. 51, 77; "How Much Freedom in New Schools?" in *John Dewey: The Later Works, 1925–1953*, vol. 5 (Carbondale: Southern Illinois University Press, 1984).

47. "*What Do Teachers Teach?* A Survey of America's Fourth and Eighth Grade Teachers," Center for Survey Research and Analysis, University of Connecticut (New York: Center for Civic Innovation, Manhattan Institute, September 2002), Executive Summary. For one example, Douglas Carnine, "Why Education Experts Resist Effective Practices" (Washington, D.C.: Thomas B. Fordham Foundation, April 2000), pp. 5–7. This topic is explored in more detail in Chapters 6 and 7.

48. Harold W. Stevenson and James W. Stigler, *The Learning Gap: Why Our Schools Are Failing and What We Can Learn from Japanese and Chinese Education* (New York: Touchstone, 1994), pp. 145–146. See also U.S. Department of Education, National Center for Education Statistics, *The Condition of Education 1999*, Table 398. I admit that the work I did on "The Lesson Cycle" when I was obtaining my teacher's certificate was very helpful for teaching. Learning the format certainly didn't require twelve credit hours of education classes, though, and most of the requirements seem to have been imposed to provide jobs for education professors.

49. Center for Survey Research and Analysis, "*What Do Teachers Teach?*" pp. 5–7. U.S. Department of Education, National Center for Education Statistics, *Schools and Staffing Survey 1990–1991*, Table 6.1. *Different Drummers: How Teachers of Teachers View Public Education*, Public Agenda, 1997, pp. 9–16.

50. Lawrence A. Baines and Gregory Kent Stanley, "Disengagement and Loathing in High School," *Educational Horizons*, Summer 2003, pp. 165–168.

Chapter 4: The Progressive Paradigm, Part Three

1. Allan Nevins and Henry Steele Commager, *A Pocket History of the United States* (New York: Washington Square Press, 1981), pp. 290–291.

2. See E. D. Hirsch, Jr., *The Schools We Need*, especially pp. 71–91.

3. John Dewey, "How Much Freedom in New Schools?" p. 320. For the poor educational backgrounds of administrators, see Paul A. Zoch, "Our Uneducated Educators," *Wilson Quarterly* 23 (4) Autumn 1999, pp. 60–68.

4. Jack K. Campbell, *Colonel Francis W. Parker: The Children's Crusader* (New York: Teachers College Press, 1967), pp. 87, 100–102.

5. Ibid., pp. 107, 160, emphasis in original.

6. Ibid., pp. 170, 207. Lelia E. Partridge, *Notes of Talks on Teaching Given by Francis W. Parker* (New York: E. L. Kellogg and Co., 1883), pp. 21–22.

7. Dorothy Ross, G. *Stanley Hall: The Psychologist as Prophet* (Chicago: University of Chicago Press, 1972), p. 103.

8. Ibid., pp. 9–10, 79, 143, 145–146. See also Ryan, *John Dewey*, p. 71.

9. Ross, G. *Stanley Hall*, p. 207.

10. Ibid., p. 288. G. Stanley Hall, *Aspects of Child Life and Education* (Boston: Ginn and Co., Athenaeum Press, 1907), p. iii. G. Stanley Hall, "The Contents of Children's Minds on Entering School," in *Aspects of Child Life and Education*, p. 3.

11. Ross, G. *Stanley Hall*, pp. 292, 279, 118. See also O'Donnell, *Origins of Behaviorism*, p. 164. Dewey, "the uselessness and the danger for the teacher of miscellaneous scraps of child study," in "Psychology and Social Practice," ed. Ratner, p. 296. Later he trashed "the latest fad of pedagogical theorists—the latest panacea peddled out in school journals or teachers' institutes," p. 303. See also "Criticisms Wise and Otherwise on Modern Child Study," *NEA Proceedings*, 1897, pp. 867–868.

12. G. Stanley Hall, "New Departures in Education," in *Health, Growth, and Heredity: G. Stanley Hall on Natural Education*, eds. Charles E. Strickland and Charles Burgess (New York: Teachers College Press, 1965), p. 95.

13. G. Stanley Hall, "Child-Study and Its Relation to Education," in *Health, Growth, and Heredity*, p. 88.

14. G. Stanley Hall, "New Departures in Education," *Health, Growth, and Heredity*, p. 96.

15. Francis W. Parker, *Talks on Pedagogics* (New York: John Day Company, 1937), pp. 1, 7, 18.

16. G. Stanley Hall, *Educational Problems*, 2 vols. (New York: D. Appleton and Co., 1911), II, 80; I, 188; I, 339. See George Boas, *The Cult of Childhood* (Dallas: Spring Publications, 1990) for more information. Boas quotes *Encore de l'Immaculée Conception* by Victor Hugo, in which the poet discovers in an infant's babbling "un sens profond et grand/sévère quelquefois," p. 55. Hall, "The Contents of Children's Minds on Entering School," in *Aspects of Child Life and Education*, p. 23.

17. Matthew 18:1–4. Partridge, *Notes of Talks on Teaching*, p. 169. Parker, *Talks*, p. 16, emphasis added.

18. Parker, *Talks*, p. 2.

19. Ibid., pp. 83, 286, emphasis added. "If we wish to keep [attention] upon one and the same object, we must seek constantly to find out something new about [it]." James quoting Helmholtz, *Psychology: The Briefer Course*, p. 94.

20. Parker, *Talks*, p. 87, emphasis in original. In a strange prelude to the reading wars, Parker advocates what would now be called the "whole word" method, and he opposes phonics for its "soul-deadening" qualities, arguing that a phonics-based method will result in permanent mental weakness. A teacher in the Dewey school notes, "The effort to make out words by sounding during the first months of reading is likely to result in a fatal division of attention" (quoted in Wirth, *John Dewey as Educator*, p. 164), and Kilpatrick calls phonics "soul-killing."

21. Parker, *Talks*, p. 89. James, *Principles of Psychology*, I, 219, emphasis in original. It is also worth noting that James might well have been chastising Parker when he faulted "some authorities on teaching" for believing that geography began and ended with the neighboring hill; Parker believed that geography was the focus of all school studies.

22. Parker, *Talks*, pp. 90, 279, 252–253, 271, 329.

23. Hall, *Educational Problems*, I, viii, emphasis added.

24. Hall, *Youth: Its Education, Regimen, and Hygiene* (New York: D. Appleton and Co., 1906), pp. 79, 116, 80, 113.

25. Hall, "The Story of a Sand Pile," in *Aspects of Child Life*, p. 155, emphasis in original.

26. Hall, *Educational Problems*, I, 68–69; I, 43; I, 20. Hall, "Coeducation in the High School," in *Health, Growth, and Heredity*, p. 184.

27. Hall, *Educational Problems*, I, 96–97, 109, 133, 134. Harold Rugg and Ann Shumaker, *The Child-Centered School: An Appraisal of the New Education* (Yonkers-on-Hudson, N.Y.: World Book Co., 1928), p. 169. Cremin calls it "the characteristic progressive work of the twenties" (*Transformation of the School*, p. 183).

28. Rugg and Shumaker, *The Child-Centered School*, p. 231. Margaret Naumberg, *The Child and the World: Dialogues in Modern Education* (New York: Harcourt, Brace and Co., 1928), pp. 277, 40. While an undergraduate at Columbia University, Naumberg studied philosophy with John Dewey and was president of the Socialist Students' Club.

29. Junius L. Meriam, *Child Life and the Curriculum* (Yonkers-on-Hudson, N.Y.: World Book Co., 1920), pp. 222, 316, 13, 147.

30. Parker, *Talks*, pp. 157, 104, 259–260, 254.

31. Ibid., p. 88, emphasis added.

32. Hall, *Educational Problems*, I, 158. Hall, *Youth: Its Education, Regimen, and Hygiene*, pp. 238, 119.

33. Naumberg, *The Child and the World*, p. 13. Herbert S. Jennings, "The Biology of Children in Relation to Education," in *Suggestions of Modern Science Concerning Education* (New York: Macmillan, 1925), p. 42.

34. Hall, *Educational Problems*, I, 546; I, 511, emphasis added. Like many others in the late nineteenth and early twentieth centuries, Hall firmly believed that many students, by virtue of their genetic makeup, were incapable of academic achievement. See Ravitch, *Left Back*, pp. 72ff. Overt racial discrimination has been aban-

doned in schools, yet it has been replaced by grotesquely low expectations of students from low socio-economic levels. Hall, *Youth: Its Education, Hygiene, and Regimen,* p. 314. Sizer, *Secondary Schools,* p. 120; Ravitch, *Left Back.*

35. Jennings, "The Biology of Children," p. 40. Naumberg, *The Child and the World,* pp. 3, 311, 265–266, 81.

36. Meriam, *Child Life and the Curriculum,* pp. 50, 160, 217, 147, 40, 436, emphasis in original.

37. Rugg and Shumaker, *The Child-Centered School,* pp. 25, ii, 306, emphasis added. Such active discouragement of children from reading is memorialized in Harper Lee's *To Kill a Mockingbird.* One should recall from the novel or movie that Scout feels she must read clandestinely, lest Miss Caroline find out.

38. Hall, *Educational Problems,* I, 631. He makes a similar argument in *Youth: Its Education, Regimen, and Hygiene,* p. 314: "The rule should be to keep nothing that is not to become practical; to open no brain tracts which are not to be highways for the daily traffic of thought and conduct; not to overburden the soul with the impedimenta of libraries and records of what is afar off in time or zest, and always to follow truly the guidance of normal and spontaneous interests wisely interpreted."

39. Hall, *Educational Problems,* II, 274.

40. Many of his errors in Latin are ones that a reasonably competent third-year student should notice. *Educational Problems,* II, 583: *meninisse* should be *meminisse;* in *Educational Problems,* II, 264, *feminia* should be *feminea.* In *Youth: Its Education, Regimen, and Hygiene,* p. 8, *cogitari* should be *cogitare,* and p. 76, *valare* should be *valere.* Hall also comments that the Roman author Quintilian recommended medieval epics for moral growth, a recommendation that would have required a great deal of prescience on the part of Quintilian, since he lived centuries before the start of the Middle Ages. See "The High School as the People's College," in *Health, Growth, and Heredity,* p. 145. Hall, *Educational Problems,* II, 295.

41. Rugg and Shumaker, *The Child-Centered School,* p. 323. Naumberg, *The Child and the World,* p. 262. Meriam, *Child Life and the Curriculum,* p. 10. Oddly enough, modern critics of a conservative intellectual bent are far more critical of the education system than of the teachers. Teachers have no stronger allies than Diane Ravitch or E. D. Hirsch, Jr. (who dedicated *The Schools We Need* to them). Parker's most vocal critic on the Cook County Board, who fought against him for an academic curriculum, also advocated pensions for teachers and higher salaries.

42. Campbell, *Colonel Francis W. Parker,* pp. 121, 166, 156, emphasis added. Merle Curti reports that teachers were paid less than manual laborers (*Social Ideas of American Educators,* p. 252). See also National Center for Education Statistics, *The Condition of Education 1999,* Tables 39 and 82. Not until 1959–1960 would the average American teacher earn the princely annual salary of $5,000; that would be in 1959–1960 dollars, however.

43. Ross, *G. Stanley Hall,* p. 107. Ross also records that Hall had very little contact with children in the course of his scholarly life (p. 292). Because of the loving

detail Hall lavishes on girls in their early teens, we are perhaps justified in calling him the Humbert Humbert of educational psychology. Hall's Romantic views on women can be seen in these weird statements: "Only the woman's soul knows what flowers really mean" (*Educational Problems*, I, 9), and a girl's soul "may prove to contain most of the secrets of the universe" (Ibid., II, 16, 15).

44. Ibid., II, 616.

45. Ibid., I, 265.

46. O'Donnell, *Origins of Behaviorism*, p. 163. See also Joncich, who reports that by 1898 Clark University had conferred more than half of all the doctorates in psychology granted by American universities (*The Sane Positivist*, p. 154).

47. Hall, *Educational Problems*, II, 248.

48. Ibid., II, 604, 247–248.

49. Ibid., I, 629.

50. See Ravitch, *Left Back*, pp. 387ff. National Commission on Teaching and America's Future, *What Matters Most*, p. 2.

51. See Ravitch, *Left Back*, for more on the opposition. Edward Lee Thorndike, *Principles of Teaching* (New York: A. G. Seiler, 1917), p. 57. Geraldine M. Joncich, ed., *Psychology and the Science of Education: Selected Writings of Edward L. Thorndike* (New York: Teachers College Columbia University, 1962), p. 25.

52. Cremin, *Transformation of the School*, p. 288.

Chapter 5: The Revolving Revolution

1. Howard Gardner, *The Mind's New Science: A History of the Cognitive Revolution* (New York: Basic Books, 1985), p. 15.

2. Howard Gardner with Tina Blythe, "A School of the Future," in Howard Gardner, *Multiple Intelligences: The Theory in Practice* (New York: Basic Books, 1993), p. 73.

3. Sally P. Springer and Georg Deutsch, *Left Brain, Right Brain* (New York: W. H. Freeman and Co., 1981), p. 4. Robert Sylwester, *A Celebration of Neurons: An Educator's Guide to the Human Brain* (Alexandria, Va.: Association for Supervision and Curriculum Development, 1995), p. 6.

4. Eric Jensen, *Brain-Based Learning* (San Diego: The Brain Store, 2000), p. 2, emphasis in original.

5. David E. Hunt, "Learning Style and Student Needs: An Introduction to Conceptual Level," in *Student Learning Styles: Diagnosing and Prescribing Programs* (Reston, Va.: National Association of Secondary School Principals, 1979), p. 27.

6. Pat Burke Guild and Stephen Garger, *Marching to Different Drummers* (Alexandria, Va.: Association for Supervision and Curriculum Development, 1985) is a good introduction to the many theories of learning styles.

7. James W. Keefe, "School Applications of the Learning Style Concept," in *Student Learning Styles*, p. 131.

8. Howard Gardner, *Frames of Mind: The Theory of Multiple Intelligences*, 10th anniversary ed. (New York: Basic Books, 1993), passim. *Frames of Mind* has been called the "Bible" of MI theory.

9. Ibid., p. x.

10. *Frames of Mind* originally listed seven intelligences; Gardner added the "naturalist intelligence" in 1996. Thomas Armstrong, *Multiple Intelligences in the Classroom* (Alexandria, Va.: Association for Supervision and Curriculum Development, 1994), p. 13.

11. Howard Gardner, "Intelligences in Seven Phases," in Gardner, *Multiple Intelligences*, p. 228. Almost a century before the birth of LS and MI, William James had this to say on this very topic: "There is no reason, if we are classing the different types of apperception, why we should stop at sixteen rather than sixteen hundred. There are as many types of apperception as there are possible ways in which an incoming experience may be reacted on by an individual mind." James then tells the story of a little boy who, when seeing Niagara Falls for the first time, could exclaim to his mother only, "Is that the kind of spray I spray my nose with?" On that basis, James says, we might as well classify it and call it "rhinotherapeutical apperception" (*Talks to Teachers*, p. 112). Gardner, *Frames of Mind*, p. 70. Gardner with Tina Blythe, in *Multiple Intelligences*, p. 71. Howard Gardner with Joseph Walters, "A Rounded Version," in Gardner, *Multiple Intelligences*, pp. 26–27.

12. Thomas Armstrong, "Multiple Intelligences: Seven Ways to Approach Curriculum," in *Multiple Intelligences: A Collection*, ed. Robin Fogarty and James Bellanca (Palatine, Ill.: IRI/Skylight Publishing, 1995), p. 254. Thomas R. Hoerr, "Introducing the Theory of Multiple Intelligences," *NASSP Bulletin*, November 1996, p. 8.

13. Gardner, *Frames of Mind*, p. xix, emphasis added.

14. Howard Gardner with Joseph Walters, "Questions and Answers About Multiple Intelligences Theory," in Gardner, *Multiple Intelligences*, p. 48. Benjamin S. Bloom, "The Nature of the Study and Why It Was Done," in *Developing Talent in Young People*, Benjamin S. Bloom, ed. (New York: Ballantine Books, 1985), p. 4. Teachers are well familiar with Bloom, as during their training they learn his "Taxonomy of Educational Objectives."

15. I assume that Gardner is referring to "the proposition that the foundations of any subject may be taught to anybody at any age in some form." Jerome S. Bruner, *The Process of Education* (Cambridge, Mass.: Harvard University Press, 1960), p. 12. Gardner, *Frames of Mind*, pp. 38–39. Bruner's work provides the theoretical basis for constructivism, which is very Deweyan.

16. Gardner, *Frames of Mind*, p. 39. Gardner and Joseph Walters, "Questions and Answers," p. 47.

17. Gordon Lewis, *People Types and Tiger Stripes* 3d ed. (Gainesville, Fla.: Cen-

ter for Applications of Psychological Type), 1993, p. 1. David Keirsey and Marilyn Bates, *Please Understand Me: Character and Temperament Types*, 5th ed. (Del Mar, Calif.: Prometheus Nemesis Book Co., 1984), p. 4. Guild and Garger, *Marching to Different Drummers*, pp. x, 23.

18. Linda VerLee Williams, *Teaching for the Two-Sided Mind* (New York: Touchstone, 1986), p. 145. Rita Dunn and Shirley A. Griggs, *Learning Styles: Quiet Revolution in American Secondary Schools* (Reston, Va.: National Association of Secondary School Principals, 1988), p. 3.

19. Guild and Garger, *Marching to Different Drummers*, p. 77. Keirsey and Bates, *Please Understand Me*, p. 16; see also Lawrence, *People Types and Tiger Stripes*, p. 149. Rita Dunn et al., "Learning Style Researchers Define Differences Differently," *Educational Leadership*, February 1981, p. 374, emphasis added.

20. Gardner, *Multiple Intelligences*, p. 203; *Frames of Mind*, p. 334; and Mindy Kornhaber and Howard Gardner, "Varieties of Excellence: Identifying and Assessing Children's Talents," in Fogarty and Bellanca, eds., *Multiple Intelligences: A Collection*, p. 119. The frustration is expressed in Howard Gardner, "Multiple Intelligences as a Partner in School Improvement," *Educational Leadership*, September 1997, p. 21.

21. Dr. Lynell Burmark, "Reaching Every Learner: Multimedia and Multiple Intelligences," in-service given at Alief Independent School District (October 11, 1999).

22. Kornhaber and Gardner, "Varieties of Excellence," in Fogarty and Bellanca, eds., *Multiple Intelligences: A Collection*, p. 103. It would be rash of me to accuse Kornhaber and Gardner of "soft bigotry," but if *I* were Kimberly's father, and a school official told me that *my* African-American daughter's natural gift lay in singing, dancing, and acting, I would be contacting an attorney.

23. Howard Gardner and Mara Krechevsky, "Approaching School Intelligently: Practical Intelligence at the Middle School Level," in Gardner, *Multiple Intelligences*, pp. 122ff.

24. Claudia E. Cornett, *What You Should Know About Teaching and Learning Styles* (Bloomington, Ind.: Phi Delta Kappa), ED 228235 (1983), pp. 25–26. Stevenson and Stigler, *The Learning Gap*, p. 112.

25. Gardner, *Frames of Mind*, p. 316, emphasis added. Gardner as quoted in Robert J. Kirschenbaum, "An Interview with Howard Gardner," in Fogarty and Bellanca, eds., *Multiple Intelligences: A Collection*, p. 18.

26. Gardner, *Frames of Mind*, p. 112. Gail R. Benjamin, *Japanese Lessons* (New York: New York University Press, 1997), pp. 153ff. Howard Gardner, "Probing More Deeply into the Theory of Multiple Intelligences," *NASSP Bulletin*, November 1996, p. 2.

27. Gardner, *Frames of Mind*, pp. 389, 234, emphasis added.

28. Anthony F. Gregorc, "Learning/Teaching Styles: Their Nature and Effects," in *Student Learning Styles*, pp. 22, 26. Cornett, *What You Should Know About Teach-*

ing and Learning Styles, p. 19. Dunn et al., "Learning Style Researchers Define Differences Differently," p. 373, emphasis added. Rita S. Dunn and Kenneth J. Dunn, "Learning Styles/Teaching Styles: Should They . . . Can They . . . Be Matched?" *Educational Leadership*, January 1979, p. 240.

29. Walter B. Barbe and Michael N. Milone, Jr., "What We Know About Modality Strengths," *Educational Leadership*, February 1981, p. 379, emphasis in original. Rita Dunn, Kenneth Dunn, and Gary E. Price, "Identifying Individual Learning Styles," in *Student Learning Styles*, p. 53.

30. Leslie A. Hart, "The Three-Brain Concept and the Classroom," *Phi Delta Kappan*, March 1981, pp. 504ff. See also Leslie A. Hart, *Human Brain and Human Learning* (Village of Oak Creek, Ariz.: Books for Educators, 1992), pp. 36–40. Paul D. MacLean himself, however, has very little to say about the classroom implications of his theory; see Paul D. MacLean, "A Mind of Three Minds: Educating the Triune Brain," in *Education and the Brain: The Seventy-seventh Yearbook of the National Society for the Study of Education*, eds. Jeanne S. Chall and Alan F. Mirsky (Chicago: University of Chicago Press, 1978), pp. 308–342.

31. Hart, *Human Brain and Human Learning*, pp. 51–52, 6, emphases in original. Leslie A. Hart, "Brain, Language, and New Concepts of Learning," *Educational Leadership*, March 1981, p. 443.

32. Hart, *Human Brain and Human Learning*, pp. 132, 158.

33. Ibid., pp. 81, 139–140. Leslie A. Hart, "The New 'Brain' Concept of Learning," *Phi Delta Kappan*, February 1978, p. 396. Robert Sylwester, *A Celebration of Neurons*, p. viii.

34. Jensen, *Brain-Based Learning*, pp. xiii, 190.

35. Ibid., pp. 230, 233. See also Robert Sylwester, *A Biological Brain in a Cultural Classroom* (Thousand Oaks, Calif.: Corwin Press, 2000), p. 39. The evidence Jensen cites, however, is irrelevant for conditions in the normal classroom: the studies proving damage to the hippocampus involved Vietnam war veterans suffering from posttraumatic stress disorder, adults who had been sexually abused as children, laboratory rats exposed to severe stress, infants born to mothers suffering from major depression, and monkeys living in terror of the dominant male in the pack. See Ronald Kotulak, *Inside the Brain: Revolutionary Discoveries of How the Mind Works* (Kansas City: Andrews McMeel, 1997), pp. 46–47.

36. Jensen, *Brain-Based Learning*, pp. 239, 116, 300. Eric Jensen, *Teaching with the Brain in Mind* (Alexandria, Va.: Association for Supervision and Curriculum Development, 1998), p. 30.

37. Gardner, *Multiple Intelligences*, p. 8. Armstrong, *Multiple Intelligences in the Classroom*, p. 107.

38. Howard Gardner, "The Theory of Multiple Intelligences," in Fogarty and Bellanca, eds., *Multiple Intelligences: A Collection*, pp. 88–89, 94.

39. Sylwester, *A Celebration of Neurons*, p. 56. See also Jensen, *Brain-Based Learning*, p. 344.

40. Sylwester, *A Biological Brain in a Cultural Classroom*, pp. 59, 68–69, 78, 91, 93.

41. Sylwester, *A Celebration of Neurons*, p. 121. Sylwester, *A Biological Brain in a Cultural Classroom*, p. 88, emphasis added.

42. Gardner, *Frames of Mind*, p. 385, and for assessment in general, Gardner with Walters and Gardner with Krechevsky, *Multiple Intelligences*, pp. 31ff and 86ff.

43. Gardner, *Multiple Intelligences*, pp. 78, 181, 228, 229. Jacqueline Anglin, "Reflections on 'The Unschooled Mind': An Interview with Howard Gardner," in Fogarty and Bellanca, eds., *Multiple Intelligences: A Collection*, p. 46. Kirschenbaum, "An Interview with Howard Gardner," p. 14.

44. Rita Dunn and Kenneth Dunn, "Learning Styles, Teaching Styles," *NASSP Bulletin*, October 1975, pp. 38, 44, 48.

45. Thomas Armstrong, "Learning Differences — Not Disabilities," in Fogarty and Bellanca, eds., *Multiple Intelligences: A Collection*, p. 224. Gardner as quoted in Kathy Checkley, "The First Seven . . . ," *Educational Leadership*, September 1997, p. 10. Carolyn S. Hughes, foreword to Guild and Garger, *Marching to Different Drummers*, p. v.

46. Sylwester, *A Biological Brain in a Cultural Classroom*, p. 26, emphasis added. Jensen, *Brain-Based Learning*, pp. 70, 342, 4, 353.

47. Tina Blythe and Howard Gardner, "A School for All Intelligences," in Fogarty and Bellanca, eds., *Multiple Intelligences: A Collection*, pp. 172, 175, as well as Gardner with Blythe, *Multiple Intelligences*, p. 75. Kornhaber and Gardner, "Varieties of Excellence," in Fogarty and Bellanca, eds., *Multiple Intelligences: A Collection*, pp. 115–118. Gardner, *Multiple Intelligences*, p. 118. Gardner with Joseph Walters, *Multiple Intelligences*, p. 30.

48. Renate Nummela Caine and Geoffrey Caine, *Making Connections: Teaching and the Human Brain* (Alexandria, Va.: Association for Supervision and Curriculum Development, 1991), pp. 112–113. A similar multi-disciplinary project on boats may be found in Rugg and Shumaker, *The Child-Centered School*, p. 98.

49. Caine and Caine, *Making Connections*, pp. 128, 15.

50. Jensen, *Brain-Based Learning*, pp. 167, 223.

51. Ibid., p. 309.

52. Armstrong, *Multiple Intelligences in the Classroom*, pp. 121ff, or Jensen, *Brain-Based Learning*, p. 220.

53. Armstrong, *Multiple Intelligences in the Classroom*, pp. 122–124. Guild and Garger, *Marching to Different Drummers*, pp. 60–61. Dunn and Griggs, *Learning Styles*, pp. 14ff.

54. Dunn and Griggs, *Learning Styles*, p. 45.

55. Barbe and Milone, "What We Know About Modality Strengths," p. 378. Dunn and Griggs report similar numbers (*Learning Styles*, p. 43).

56. Dunn, Beaudry, and Klavas, "Are Schools Responsible for Students' Fail-

ure?" p. 16. Dunn and Dunn, "Learning Styles/Teaching Styles: Should They . . . Can They . . . Be Matched?" pp. 239ff.

57. Dunn and Griggs, *Learning Styles*, pp. 21, 62.

58. Ibid., p. 14. Harper Lee, *To Kill A Mockingbird*, Chapter 2. The students' reactions when I tell them of Progressive education are noteworthy. Unanimously the students think Miss Caroline is crazy for discouraging Scout or any student from reading. When I tell the class about the Project Method, and the idea that students should decide what they want to learn, a few students—usually the ones most prone to goofing off—love the idea, whereas all other students, including the best and the worst, convince them they are wrong. "We wouldn't learn anything if we didn't have to!" they say, incredulous that anyone would suggest so silly an idea.

59. Armstrong, "Learning Differences—Not Disabilities," in Fogarty and Bellanca, eds., *Multiple Intelligences: A Collection*, pp. 227–228. Gardner later rejected that idea: "But there is no point in assuming that every topic can be effectively approached in at least seven ways, and it is a waste of effort and time to attempt to do this." Howard Gardner, "Reflections on Multiple Intelligences," *Phi Delta Kappan*, November 1995, p. 206.

Chapter 6: Pedagogue-Centric Education

1. One exception is the excellent book *Beyond the Classroom*. Steinberg et al. call the viewpoint that schools determine student achievement "myopic" and argue that we should instead focus on the lives that students lead (p. 194). One finds similar statements in books on education in other countries; see Chapter 7 on Japanese and other schools.

2. "Cannot justify pay hike," *Houston Chronicle*, May 2, 1995, p. 19A. The other reason given by the author is that teachers supposedly work only nine months of the year; yet if the salary is figured by the hour, I earn $23.45, from which money is deducted for insurance premiums, retirement, social security, and, of course, federal income tax. Financially it's not a bad living, but it isn't great. Since American teachers teach more hours per day than teachers in other countries do, they are paid less per teaching hour than their foreign counterparts. See *Education at a Glance*, OECD Indicators 2001, Table D3.1.

3. Jim Barlow, "Plan for schools: evaluate and pay," *Houston Chronicle*, August 29, 2000, p. 1C.

4. Jesse Jackson, as quoted by Clarence Page, "There's a cost to overselling vouchers," *Houston Chronicle*, September 9, 2000, p. 38A.

5. James Glassman, "Let's try competition to fix public education," *Houston Chronicle*, December 25, 2000, p. 47A. Glassman is a fellow at the American Enterprise Institute.

6. Arthur K. Smith and Linda Clarke, "Start by preparing our teachers for new century," *Houston Chronicle*, October 9, 2000, p. 25A. He is the chancellor of the University of Houston system, she the executive director of the Houston Annenberg Challenge.

7. Tyce Palmaffy, "Measuring the Teacher Quality Problem," in *Better Teachers, Better Schools* (Washington, D.C.: Thomas B. Fordham Foundation, July 1999), p. 27. Note, of course, the non sequitur of the title of the collection.

8. Ibid., p. 29.

9. Recruiting New Teachers, *The Essential Profession* (1998), p. 1.

10. Rita Kramer, "Impact of High School Preparation," *Partisan Review* (3) 1998, p. 370.

11. Jim Nelson, Commissioner of the Texas Education Agency quoted by Chris Roberts, "Teachers are wary of changes in TAAS," *Houston Chronicle*, August 13, 2000, p. 6E. See also John W. Gonzalez, "TAAS Scores Bloom Again Across State," *Houston Chronicle*, May 18, 2000, p. 1A.

12. National Commission on Teaching and America's Future, *What Matters Most*, p. 6, emphasis in original.

13. Bill Harshbarger, "Looking for Inspiration?" review of *The Courage to Teach* by Parker J. Palmer, *The NEA Today*, September 1998, p. 61.

14. Professional Development and Appraisal System, Texas Education Agency, T6, p. 16, emphasis in original.

15. John Biggs, "Western Misperceptions of the Confucian-Heritage Learning Culture," in *The Chinese Learner: Cultural, Psychological, and Contextual Influences*, ed. David A. Watkins and John B. Biggs (Hong Kong: Comparative Education Research Centre, and Melbourne: Australian Council for Educational Research, 1996), p. 50. Terence Marton, Gloria Dall'Alba, and Tse Lai Kun, "Memorizing and Understanding: The Keys to the Paradox?" in Watkins and Biggs, eds., *The Chinese Learner*, pp. 69–83.

16. National Commission on Excellence in Education, *A Nation at Risk* (1983), p. 1. See also Ravitch, *Left Back*, pp. 408–415.

17. Carnegie Forum on Education and the Economy, *A Nation Prepared: Teachers for the 21st Century* (1986), pp. 14, 15, 26, 87, emphasis added.

18. National Commission on Excellence in Education, *A Nation at Risk*, pp. 1, 2, 5, emphasis added.

19. Carnegie Forum on Education and the Economy, *A Nation Prepared*, pp. 39, 87, 107.

20. Ibid., p. 25.

21. Ibid., p. 25.

22. Ibid., pp. 45, 49. Note the preposterous wording. Cf. also their recommendation: "Restructure schools to provide a professional environment for teachers, freeing them to decide how best to meet state and local goals for children while holding them accountable for student progress" (p. 55).

23. Ibid., p. 47.

24. Ibid., pp. 48, 50, 51.

25. Holmes Group, *Tomorrow's Teachers: A Report of the Holmes Group* (1986), p. 3.

26. Ibid., p. 15. It is ironic that a document that so roundly attacks teachers for their incompetence, and that was read by the nine deans of colleges of education who were contributors and signatories to the report, should contain grammatical errors and even a misspelling. There is the mysterious word "riffing" (probably a typo for "firing," p. 9). There are a few problems with subject-verb agreement: "But candidates' performance on such tests are very poor predictors . . ." (p. 12); ". . . since such competence and dedication in teaching is unfortunately not as common . . ." (p. 29); "Scholarship and empirical research in education has matured . . ." (p. 50); "The successful transmission of these attitudes and values are more a function . . ." (p. 54). Is it too much to ask the leaders of the teachers—deans in the colleges of education—to know what a student is supposed to learn in ninth-grade English?

27. Ibid., pp. 29, 16.

28. Ibid., pp. 27, 28.

29. Nobuo K. Shimahara, "Overview of Japanese Education: Policy, Structure, and Current Issues," in *Japanese Educational Productivity*, ed. Robert Leestma and Herbert J. Walberg (Ann Arbor: Center for Japanese Studies, 1992), p. 10. James S. Coleman and Thomas Hoffer, *Public and Private Schools: The Impact of Communities* (New York: Basic Books, 1987), pp. 64ff, 99, 127, 129, 192–195, 207–210. See also Coleman et al., *High School Achievement*, pp. 140, 144, 168. See Hirsch, *The Schools We Need*, pp. 41–42, 96; and Richard P. McAdams, *Lessons from Abroad: How Other Countries Educate Their Children* (Lancaster, Pa.: Technomic Publishing Co., 1993), p. 165.

30. Holmes Group, *Tomorrow's Teachers*, p. 39, emphasis added. Tyce Palmaffy, "Measuring the Teacher Quality Problem," p. 20, emphasis added.

31. Holmes Group, *Tomorrow's Teachers*, p. 5.

32. Ibid., p. 23.

33. In 1999 I was teaching at a school where the student population had shifted, within the space of ten years, from middle-class white and Asian to lower-class black and Hispanic, and during that time the overall quality of the students' work had declined, though there were still many good students of all races. The faculty remained much the same, and many refused to lower their standards for the new types of students. Consequently the failure rate escalated, and the administration pressured teachers to lower standards so that fewer students would fail. Here is a message we received from one principal a few days before grades were due: "Please take a careful look at your grades and remember that grades are very subjective. Many times we let the computer do our averaging and we forget that the kids are humans and not robots and that they do have feelings. For many of our kids, you might be one of the few adult models they have in their lives. What you say and do can truly

affect them. We appreciate all of your efforts to ensure the success of our students."
In a meeting with that principal, I was informed that the high failure rate of the students in one class proved that I was not a good teacher, because I wasn't meeting
their needs.

34. See Chapter 7 and references therein. Hirsch reports that in France the
écoles maternelles (the French version of Head Start) and the public schools with
their national curriculum are much more effective in closing the achievement gap
between the advantaged and disadvantaged (*The Schools We Need*, pp. 80, 41–42).
Coleman and Hoffer, *Public and Private High Schools*, p. 120.

35. Steinberg et al., *Beyond the Classroom*, p. 92.

36. The National Commission on Teaching and America's Future, *What Matters Most: Teaching for America's Future*, pp. vi, 2.

37. Ibid., pp. 6, 8, 105, emphases added. Other examples: "Students and teachers
[in a large, bad school] experience the anonymity of the factory model school, which
produces far less learning for them both" (p. 107); and "to produce much higher
achievement for pupils" (p. 117). One principal is quoted as saying, "Now, good
teaching is judged by how much learning occurs" (p. 85). The authors recommend
"renewing the national promise to bring every American child up to world-class
standards in core academic areas" (p. 64).

38. Ibid., pp. 75, 19, and Chapter 7.

39. Ibid., pp. 25, 129.

40. John I. Goodlad, *Educational Renewal: Better Teachers, Better Schools* (San
Francisco: Jossey-Bass, 1994), pp. 9–29, 76. John I. Goodlad, *Teachers for Our Nation's Schools* (San Francisco: Jossey-Bass, 1990), pp. 63, 347, 365.

41. Goodlad, *Teachers for Our Nation's Schools*, p. 372. Goodlad, *Educational
Renewal*, p. 4.

42. Goodlad, *Teachers for Our Nation's Schools*, p. 46. Goodlad, *Educational Renewal*, p. 7.

43. National Center for Education Statistics, *The Condition of Education 1999*,
Tables 10 and 252. Goodlad, *Teachers for Our Nation's Schools*, p. 226.

44. Goodlad, *Educational Renewal*, pp. 181, 46. Real teachers of the arts, physical education, and vocational education would be very amused at the assumption
that all, or even most, of the students in their classes are necessarily interested in the
course.

45. Ibid., pp. 183–184, 38.

46. Ibid., p. 19. Goodlad, *Teachers for Our Nation's Schools*, p. 17.

47. R. Bruce Raup, "The New Conception of the Profession of Education," in
Kilpatrick, ed., *The Educational Frontier*, p. 102. Holmes Group, *Tomorrow's Teachers*, p. 39.

48. Goodlad, *Educational Renewal*, pp. 136, 229–230. The statement itself is
ironic, for the tenets of educational ideology certainly were not questioned or exam-
ined when I was working on my teacher's certificate in 1987 and 1988, even though

the recent publication of Allan Bloom's *The Closing of the American Mind*, E. D. Hirsch Jr.'s *Cultural Literacy*, and Diane Ravitch's *The Troubled Crusade*, not to mention *The Graves of Academe* by Richard Mitchell and the classics of educational criticism (*Educational Wastelands* by Arthur Bestor; *Quackery in the Public Schools* by Albert Lynd; and *And Madly Teach* and *The Diminished Mind* by Mortimer Smith, among others), provided ample material for discussions and examination of education ideology. Colleagues, friends, and former students who either have recently completed or are now working on their teacher's certificate inform me that in their education classes there is *no* discussion of alternative views. Teachers in training are still told that the ideal is to allow students to learn what they feel like learning, at their own pace, and that education before Dewey is portrayed as a benighted era.

49. Goodlad, *Educational Renewal*, p. 208. William Heard Kilpatrick, "The Theories Underlying the Experiment," p. 99.

50. Goodlad, *Teachers for Our Nation's Schools*, pp. 267, 360. See also *Educational Renewal*, pp. 19–20.

51. Holmes Group, *Tomorrow's Teachers*, p. 52.

Chapter 7: Where Education Succeeds

1. For statistics on the Third International Mathematics and Science Study, see U.S. Department of Education, National Center for Education Statistics, *The Condition of Education 1999*, Figure 31, p. 449, or Harold W. Stevenson, *A TIMSS Primer: Lessons and Implications for U.S. Education* (Washington, D.C.: Thomas B. Fordham Foundation, July 1998). One can download the report at *http://www.edexcellence.net/fordham/foreports.html*. Stevenson and Stigler, *The Learning Gap*, p. 35. Thomas P. Rohlen, *Japan's High Schools* (Berkeley: University of California Press, 1983), pp. 160, 267.

2. For Monbusho and the curriculum as a whole, see Robert Leestma, William J. Bennett, et al., *Japanese Education Today* (Office of Educational Research and Improvement, ED 275, 620, 1987), pp. 5–10, 26; Douglas Trelfa, "The Development and Implementation of Education Standards in Japan," in *The Educational System in Japan: Case Study Findings* (Office of Educational Research and Improvement, 1998), pp. 24ff; and Harry Wray, *Japanese and American Education*, pp. 76–77. Merry White, *The Japanese Educational Challenge* (New York: Free Press, 1987), p. 70; Stevenson and Stigler, *The Learning Gap*, pp. 55–56.

3. Leestma, Bennett, et al., *Japanese Education Today*, pp. 41, 43; Rohlen, *Japan's High Schools*, p. 117. Stevenson and Stigler, *The Learning Gap*, pp. 98, 103. Wray, *Japanese and American Education*, p. 85. Gail R. Benjamin, *Japanese Lessons*, pp. 215–216.

4. Leestma, Bennett, et al. *Japanese Education Today*, pp. vii, 41; Gerald Le-Tendre puts the percentages of 75 percent to academic and 25 percent to vocational (Introduction to *The Educational System in Japan*, p. 8). U.S. Department of Education, National Center for Education Statistics, *The Condition of Education, 1999*, p. 44. Note that the number not earning a diploma does not include those who later complete night school or who earn a GED. Trelfa, "The Development and Implementation of Education Standards in Japan," p. 58, and Wray, *Japanese and American Education*, p. 263.

5. Benjamin, *Japanese Lessons*, pp. 209, 208. See also Rohlen: "In Japan, how one does during two days of answering questions makes all the difference. It is the sole and final measure of academic accomplishment" (*Japan's High Schools*, p. 94).

6. Benjamin, *Japanese Lessons*, p. 208, and Benjamin Duke, *The Japanese School: Lessons for Industrial America* (New York: Praeger, 1986), pp. 164–165.

7. Rohlen, *Japan's High Schools*, pp. 106, 81, 77. Wray, *Japanese and American Education*, p. 48. Duke, *The Japanese School*, pp. 149, 163–165; White, *Japanese Educational Challenge*, p. 12. Benjamin, *Japanese Lessons*, p. 210.

8. Anne E. Imamura, "Interdependence of Family and Education: Reactions of Foreign Wives of Japanese to the School System," in Shields, ed., *Japanese Schooling*, p. 21. See also Tony Dickensheets, "The Role of the Education Mama," *Japan Quarterly* (July–September 1996) pp. 73ff. White, *Japanese Educational Challenge*, pp. 97, 14.

9. White, *Japanese Educational Challenge*, pp. 89, 66; Trelfa, "The Development and Implementation of Education Standards in Japan," pp. 49, 77–78; John Singleton, "*Gambaru*: A Japanese Cultural Theory of Learning," in Shields, ed., *Japanese Schooling*, p. 13.

10. Benjamin, *Japanese Lessons*, p. 10. See also Wray, *Japanese and American Education*, pp. 11, 12. Duke, *The Japanese School*, p. 185. Leestma, Bennett, et al., *Japanese Education Today*, p. 34.

11. White, *Japanese Educational Challenge*, p. 31.

12. Stevenson and Stigler, *The Learning Gap*, p. 95.

13. Hidetada Shimizu, "Individual Differences and the Japanese Education System," in *The Educational System in Japan*, p. 88.

14. Wray, *Japanese and American Education*, p. 56.

15. Benjamin, *Japanese Lessons*, p. 208.

16. Duke, *The Japanese School*, p. 87.

17. Harold W. Stevenson, "The Asian Advantage: The Case of Mathematics," in Shields, ed., *Japanese Schooling*, p. 93.

18. McAdams, *Lessons from Abroad*, p. 269.

19. Duke, *The Japanese School*, pp. 122, 126, 145. See also Singleton, "*Gambaru*," pp 8–15. Gerald LeTendre, introduction to *The Educational System in Japan*, p. 19.

20. Wray, *Japanese and American Education*, p. 54. LeTendre, "The Role of

School in Japanese Adolescents' Lives," in *The Educational System in Japan*, p. 148. Steinberg et al., *Beyond the Classroom*, p. 97.

21. Leestma, Bennett, et al., *Japanese Education Today*, pp. 3, 26. Benjamin, *Japanese Lessons*, p. 154. Shimizu, "Individual Differences and the Japanese Education System," p. 115.

22. Stevenson and Stigler, *The Learning Gap*, p. 105.

23. Biggs, "Western Misperceptions of the Confucian-Heritage Learning Culture," p. 63. White, *Japanese Educational Challenge*, p. 13, as well as Duke, *The Japanese School*, p. 124. Wray, *Japanese and American Education*, p. 133.

24. Steinberg et al., *Beyond the Classroom*, p. 19; Stevenson and Stigler, *The Learning Gap*, p. 55. See also McAdams, *Lessons from Abroad*, p. 79 (Danish Gymnasium students—more than two hours a night), 100, 115 (two hours for fourth-, fifth-, and sixth-grade German students), and 203 (Japanese students do three to four hours a day); White, *Japanese Educational Challenge*, p. 70. Rohlen: "Our top 5 percent does less homework than the average Japanese!" (*Japan's High Schools*, pp. 276–277) Benjamin tells that the homework required of children over summer vacation, while not as demanding as during the regular school year, still calls for attention to detail and persistence (*Japanese Lessons*, pp. 89–92). In contrast, one notes that the parents in Prince William County schools so strenuously objected to their children being assigned to read *two to five* books over summer vacation that the school rescinded the requirement and made it only a recommendation. Christina A. Samuels, "Rethinking a Reading Requirement," *Washington Post*, April 4, 2000. See Wray, *Japanese and American Education*, p. 268. Dickensheets, "The Role of the Education Mama," p. 74.

25. Benjamin, *Japanese Lessons*, pp. 43, 48, 157.

26. Leestma, Bennett, et al., *Japanese Education Today*, p. 36. LeTendre, "The Role of School in Japanese Adolescents' Lives," pp. 152–153; Carol Kinney, "Teachers and the Teaching Profession in Japan," in *The Educational System in Japan*, pp. 224, 229; Rohlen, *Japan's High Schools*, p. 180.

27. Wray, *Japanese and American Education*, pp. 136–141. Duke, *The Japanese School*, p. 72. In contrast, one notes the many misspellings and grammatical errors on the signs and documents that students and even administrators shamelessly post in public schools in the United States. A French class near my classroom one year, for example, made and posted in the hall cute little drawings of things the students like and do not like to do, with the French phrase "*J'aime . . .*" (I love, I like) or "*Je n'aime pas . . .*" (I don't love, I don't like). Many of the phrases, however, were grammatically wrong, one example being, "*Je n'aime pas et etudier*" ("I don't like and to study"). While visiting another high school for an academic competition, I saw in one French class the poster, "*Laissez les bons temps roulez!*" in which the last word should be the infinitive, *rouler*. A sign, posted in the teacher's lounge by the PTO, read, "You [teachers] Are Top Bananna." John Dewey, *Interest and Effort in Educa-*

tion, p. 36; Leigh Burstein and John Hawkins, "An Analysis of Cognitive, Noncognitive, and Behavioral Characteristics of Students in Japan," in *Japanese Educational Productivity*, ed. Robert J. Leestma and Herbert J. Walberg (Ann Arbor: Center for Japanese Studies, University of Michigan, 1992), pp. 209–210; see also White, Japanese Education Challenge, p. 100.

28. White, *Japanese Educational Challenge*, p. 121, emphasis in original. Singleton, "*Gambaru*," p. 10. Stevenson and Stigler, *The Learning Gap*, p. 191.

29. Yvonne Fournier, "What a Problem—A Child Who Makes Straight A's," in *"Yo!" Magazine, Houston Chronicle*, October 2, 1992, p. 2. Fournier writes for the Scripps Howard News Service.

30. In-service on dyslexia given at Elsik High School, October 26, 1998.

31. A comment by an official at a high-performing private school shows why the students there generally succeed. She told me that when students first enter her school from public schools they struggle to meet the higher standards. "The students come here, read a book, take the test on it, and then are shocked to see that they got a D on the test. 'But I read the book!' they complain. We tell them, 'Well, next time read it twice or even three times.'" While those of a more sentimental outlook would condemn this seeming harshness, another way of looking at it defines it as tough love, for such teachers respect their students and their abilities so much that they do not become enablers of submediocre achievement and wasted potential.

32. Wray, *Japanese and American Education*, pp. 91, 96; he states that in one poll no Japanese student chose school as the worst thing about life (p. 59). Benjamin, *Japanese Lessons*, pp. 142, 217, 19–20. LeTendre: "School [for students in junior high] is an intense but often enjoyable experience," in "The Role of School in Japanese Adolescents' Lives," pp. 151, 180. Burstein and Hawkins, "An Analysis," p. 200; Steinberg et al., *Beyond the Classroom*, p. 68, passim. Stevenson and Stigler, *The Learning Gap*, p. 57.

33. Stevenson and Stigler, *The Learning Gap*, p. 128. Burstein and Hawkins, "An Analysis," p. 197. Steinberg et al., *Beyond the Classroom*, pp. 186, 94–100. See also James S. Coleman, "Equality of Educational Opportunity," in *Equality and Achievement in Education* (Boulder, Colo.: Westview Press, 1990), p. 114. White, *Japanese Educational Challenge*, p. 137.

34. Shimizu, "Individual Differences and the Japanese Education System," p. 118. Kilpatrick, "Dewey's Influence on Education," p. 455; Goodlad, *Educational Renewal*, pp. 229–230. Rohlen, *Japan's High Schools*, p. 151.

35. Duke, *The Japanese School*, p. 64.

36. Ibid., p. 84.

37. Stevenson and Stigler, *The Learning Gap*, p. 194.

38. Ibid., pp. 179, 166.

39. Ibid., p. 162; Duke, *The Japanese School*, pp. 183, 86. Leestma, Bennett, et al., *Japanese Education Today*, pp. 19–20. McAdams, *Lessons from Abroad*, p. 243. Rohlen, *Japan's High Schools*, p. 218.

40. Rohlen, *Japan's High Schools*, p. 172; Leestma, Bennett, et al., *Japanese Education Today*, p. 42. Stevenson and Stigler, *The Learning Gap*, pp. 163–164. The class sizes are much larger, however, and the teachers bear heavier administrative tasks. McAdams, *Lessons from Abroad*, pp. 239, xi. *Education at a Glance, 2001 OECD Indicators*, Table D3.1.

41. McAdams, *Lessons from Abroad*, p. 266. Stevenson, "The Asian Advantage: The Case of Mathematics," in Shields, ed., *Japanese Schooling*, p. 95.

42. Benjamin, *Japanese Lessons*, p. 43. McAdams, *Lessons from Abroad*, pp. 240, 310.

43. Leestma, Bennett, et al. *Japanese Education Today*, p. 15. Kinney, "Teachers and the Teaching Profession in Japan," p. 202. U.S. Department of Education, National Center for Education Statistics, *The Condition of Education 1999*, Table 73.

44. Wray, *Japanese and American Education*, p. 141.

45. Stevenson and Stigler, *The Learning Gap*, pp. 24–25, 61, 148, 155, 166–173, 198, 211; Duke, *The Japanese School*, pp. 230, 201.

Chapter 8: What Is to Be Done?

1. Kurt Scholz, as quoted in "Impact of High School Preparation," *Partisan Review* 3 (1998), p. 368.

2. For authors who have discussed a national curriculum, see Hirsch, *The Schools We Need*, pp. 17ff; Stevenson and Stigler, *The Learning Gap*, p. 202; White, *Japanese Educational Challenge*, p. 189.

3. McAdams, *Lessons from Abroad*, pp. 50, 268; Wray, *Japanese and American Education*, pp. 28, 232; Singleton, "*Gambaru*," pp. 11, 14.

4. U.S. Department of Education, National Center for Educational Statistics, *The Condition of Education 1999*, Table 73.

5. *Education at a Glance, OECD Indicators 2001* Section D3. For Stevenson and Stigler, decreasing the number of hours elementary teachers teach per day is their first recommendation for changing the schools.

6. Shields, introduction to *Japanese Schooling*, p. 3; Stevenson and Stigler, *The Learning Gap*, p. 223; Duke, *The Japanese School*, p. 146; Steinberg et al., *Beyond the Classroom*, pp. 93–94.

INDEX

A NOTE ON THE AUTHOR

Paul A. Zoch was born in Houston, Texas, and studied classics at the University of Texas at Austin and at Indiana University at Bloomington, where he received an M.A. degree. Since earning a teacher's certificate at the University of Houston, he has taught high school in Texas for fifteen years; he now teaches Latin at St. Agnes Academy in Houston. Mr. Zoch has also written *Ancient Rome: An Introductory History*. He is married with a daughter, and lives in Missouri City, Texas.